1 MONTH OF
FREE
READING

at

www.ForgottenBooks.com

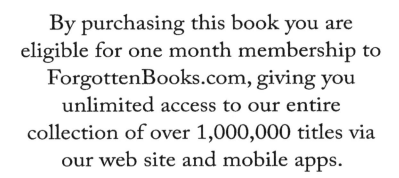

By purchasing this book you are eligible for one month membership to ForgottenBooks.com, giving you unlimited access to our entire collection of over 1,000,000 titles via our web site and mobile apps.

To claim your free month visit:
www.forgottenbooks.com/free918518

ISBN 978-0-266-97794-0
PIBN 10918518

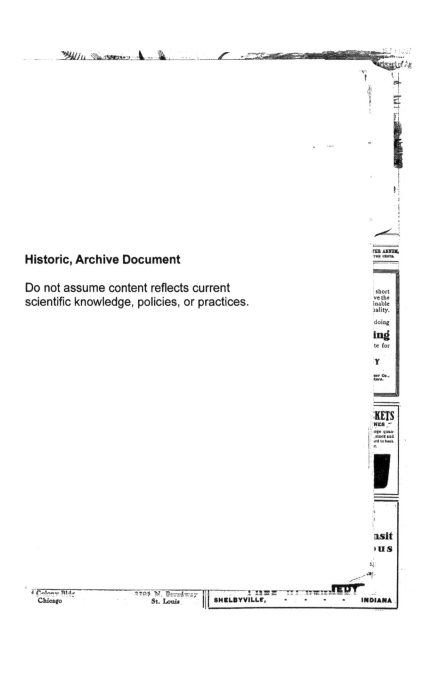

Historic, Archive Document

Do not assume content reflects current
scientific knowledge, policies, or practices.

THE AMERICAN ELEVATOR AND GRAIN TRADE.

Entered at the Post Office at Chicago, Ill., for transmission through the mails at second-class rates.

A MONTHLY JOURNAL DEVOTED TO THE ELEVATOR AND GRAIN INTERESTS.

PUBLISHED BY MITCHELL BROS. COMPANY (INCORPORATED) | VOL. XXV. | CHICAGO, ILLINOIS, FEBRUARY 15, 1907. | No. 8. | ONE DOLLAR PER ANNUM, SINGLE COPY, TEN CENTS.

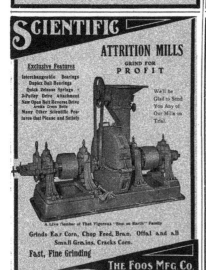

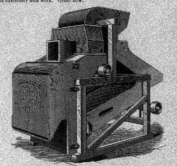

THE AMERICAN ELEVATOR AND GRAIN TRADE.

A MONTHLY JOURNAL DEVOTED TO THE ELEVATOR AND GRAIN INTERESTS.

PUBLISHED BY
MITCHELL BROS. COMPANY
(INCORPORATED).
Vol. XXV.   CHICAGO, ILLINOIS, FEBRUARY 15, 1907.   No. 8.   ONE DOLLAR PER ANNUM, SINGLE COPY, TEN CENTS.

NATIONAL GRAIN INSPECTION.

In addition to the bills to the same effect by Senator McCumber of North Dakota and Mr. Watson of Indiana, Mr. Pearre, a member of the House from Maryland, has introduced a bill to create a system of Government grain inspection.

The bill seems to be constructed on more practical and common sense lines than any of the bills to this purport previously offered to Congress. It provides among other things—

Section 6. That the Secretary of Agriculture be, and he is hereby, authorized and required, as soon as may be after the enactment hereof, to determine and fix, according to such standards as he may prescribe, such classification and grading of wheat, flax, corn, rye, oats, barley and other grains as in his judgment the usages of trade warrant and permit, having reference to the standard classification and grades now recognized by the several chambers of commerce, boards of trade of the United States; provided, however, that the reference to such classifications and grades shall serve only as a guide and suggestion in the matter of determining and fixing by the Secretary the United States standard herein provided for, but he shall not be controlled thereby, but shall determine and fix such standard and such classification and grades as will, in his judgment, best subserve the interests of the public in the conduct of interstate trade and commerce in grain.

Sec. 7. That when such standard is fixed and the classification and grades determined upon, the same shall be made matter of permanent record in the Department of Agriculture, and public notice thereof shall be given in such manner as the Secretary shall direct, and thereafter such classification and grades shall be known as the United States standard. All persons interested shall have access to said record at such convenient times and under such reasonable regulations as the Secretary may prescribe, and on the payment of such proper charge as the Secretary may fix a certified copy of the classification and grades shall be supplied to those who may apply for the same.

In respect to the inspection service, it is proposed to create under the department a bureau of grain inspection and a force of inspectors, to be stationed at the leading centers of trade in grain, such inspectors to be appointed under the rules of the civil service. The rules for the inspection of grain are to be provided by the Secretary of Agriculture, and from a charge to be made for such inspection it is proposed to obtain sufficient revenue to meet the expenses of the inspection service and no more.

A Chicago firm is said to have gained practical control of the Illinois River grain carrying by recent purchases of canal barges owned at the river towns between Peru and Peoria.

Iowa farms eat up 70 per cent of the oat crop of the state and the cereal mills of Cedar Rapids buy all the good white milling oats they can find. At present 40 per cent of Iowa's oats are of the Russian green and yellow varieties, which are not in favor with either the manufacturers or the consumers, and consequently are subject to more or less discount in value. It is suggested to county institutes by the grain dealers that they secure on their programs addresses by Professors Curtiss, Holden and others, members of the agricultural college faculty, to tell them how to improve their oats both in quality and in quantity, the average yield being only 31 bushels.

RE-ENFORCED CONCRETE SEED WAREHOUSE.

A seed warehouse of more than ordinary interest, owned by W. H. Small & Co., at Evansville, Ind., has just been completed by the MacDonald Engineering Co. of Chicago, engineers and contractors. So many new things in re-enforced concrete construction have been developed recently that it is hardly safe to claim originality in any of its many applications, but this building is probably the first building that has ever been erected with poured re-enforced concrete, using a single movable form from foundation to the roof.

The building is 195 feet long by 95 feet wide, having five stories, one of which is a basement story; and all walls, floors, columns and roof are constructed of re-enforced concrete with fireproof windows and doors. When the foundation footings were completed, a mould was built over the entire area of the building, which provided for the pilasters, columns and walls of the building and which formed also a complete deck, or platform, covering the entire property. The mould openings for pouring the different parts of the building were only three feet deep, and the concrete and re-enforcing steel were deposited in the various portions of the mould, and at the same time the mould was slowly raised by a system of jacks operated from the top of the platform and which in turn rested on metal supports buried in the concrete in short sections.

This is a patent system of concrete construction used by the contractors in building grain elevators and it worked very successfully in the building of this warehouse. When the forms and walls were finished to the level of a story, the girder boxes were inserted and the girders poured monolithic with the walls and columns.

W. H. SMALL & CO.'S RE-ENFORCED CONCRETE SEED WAREHOUSE, EVANSVILLE, IND.
The MacDonald Engineering Co., Chicago, Engineers and Contractors.

The sides of the girder boxes, being loose, moved upwards without interruption during 'the bottom of the box shored from below, so as to support the green concrete of the girders while setting. The forms were then raised to the next story and the same process repeated for each story until the roof level was obtained. At this point the platform of the mould became the support for the roof slab, which was also made of concrete. Our illustration shows the mould at the last stage of the operation, with the cornice and roof in position. In the meantime, the concrete floors were under progress with the building entirely enclosed and under cover. This enabled work to proceed without interruption during the exceedingly rainy month of January in Evansville, and became a valuable feature of the scheme of construction.

The problem of fireproof construction for buildings of all kinds will undoubtedly be solved by the use of re-enforced concrete, and whatever contributes to the simplification and cheapness of its production will advance the date when combustibles will be entirely displaced in building constructions. The method above described of moulding the building is a decided step in this direction, and already places this class of constructions in active competition with wooden mill construction buildings.

The building has become necessary for the owners, owing to the rapidly increasing volume of their business for the storage and treatment of seeds, which are distributed East and West and to all parts of the South.

TESTING CORN FOR MOISTURE.

Expert John D. Shanahan has been making moisture tests on corn throughout the West during the past thirty days, and has awakened a lively interest in the trade in that important problem, hitherto a mere matter of guesswork with most dealers, to whom indeed the subject had little more than an academic interest. Wichita, St. Louis, Kansas City, Omaha, St. Joseph, Des Moines, Decatur, Peoria and other places have been given the benefit of the tests with good results.

The amounts of moisture found in corn at these various places did not materially vary, but everywhere there was more moisture than corn that is contain that is expected to grade well or to be sent to store. At Wichita the results of the tests were as follows, the figures indicating the percentage of moisture found:

N. E. G. Corn	20.7
No. 3 Yellow Corn	19.0
N. E. G. Wheat	20.2
No. 3 White Corn	17.1
No. 4 White Corn	21.0
No. 4 Yellow Corn	19.8

At St. Louis the tests showed the following percentages:

No. 4 Mixed Corn	18.9 to 19.9
No. 4 White	19.8
No. 4 Corn	14.7
No. 2 and No. 3 White	17.5

It is said that the immediate result of Mr. Shanahan's visit to St. Louis will be the establishment of a testing apparatus in the grain inspector's office.

At St. Joseph, the tests showed the following percentages:

No Grade Corn	21.0 to 21.5
No. 4 Corn	18.6
No. 3 White	16.5
No. 3 Mixed	17.5 to 17.6

"Different grain men have used different methods of testing corn and grading it," said one St. Joe spectator of the tests. "We judge by the feel, by the appearance, by the way a small quantity runs through the hand, by all sorts of ways, but a test like this would be very valuable to us."

"I wish that I had had an apparatus like this in Kansas City a few years ago," said John Winn, now state grain inspector in St. Joseph. "For instance, an elevator man would put 200,000 bushels of corn into his elevator, but it might shrink 30,000 bushels before he took it out again. It sold, though, as 200,000 bushels. I experimented by taking a quantity of grain and drying it for a month in my office, and after I had made several experiments and struck off an average, I showed the grain men how I had discovered that a large percentage was lost by shrinkage. After that they were compelled to bring in receipts for certain percentages of their grain. and we canceled them, thus maintaining a more accurate record of the grain in elevators, and protecting the buyers."

W. A. BENNETT.

The new president of the Cincinnati Chamber of Commerce, W. A. Bennett, of the firm of Bennett & Witte, is a lumber merchant and not a grain dealer; but he is a lumberman of the big class who do things and give power and commercial importance to the trade they are interested in.

Born on January 8, 1854, in Dover, Mason

W. A. BENNETT,
President Cincinnati Chamber of Commerce.

County, Ky., Mr. Bennett was educated at Kentucky University, Lexington, and at eighteen went to Cincinnati as an employe of C. W. & S. G. Boyd in the lumber trade. He was with that firm for twelve years, and then the firm of Bennett & Witte was organized. Mr. Witte (C. H.) died in 1896, but the business has been continued under the same name. George C. Ehemann is now, however, a partner.

Mr. Bennett has occupied many important positions as representative of the associated lumber interests, having been the first president of the National Hardwood Lumber Association; chairman of the advisory committee of the Lumbermen's Exhibit at the Paris Exposition of 1900, having been elected by a mail ballot of the various lumbermen's organizations of the United States. The exhibit was housed in a building erected by the lumbermen, and was a great success in every way. It resulted in a large increase in the export lumber trade of the United States, in which the firm of Bennett & Witte are among the leaders.

Mr. Bennett is a militant citizen of Cincinnati, which he holds is the true gateway to the South across the Ohio River. As the Chamber of Commerce membership week a large per cent of their trade from that section, and as the city of Cincinnati owns the Cincinnati Southern Railway, he insists that the city should have something to say about the Southern trade and rates of freight. Cincinnati, too, through her industrial bureau, as well as all other allied organizations, is interested in new enterprises and welcomes the capitalist, the manufacturer, dealer, artisan, mechanic and laborer. "We have," says President Bennett, "a good citizenship and we offer a warm welcome to all."

[For the "American Elevator and Grain Trade."]

NEW DOCTRINE AS TO LIABILITY OF BANKS BUYING DRAFTS REVIEWED AND REPUDIATED.

BY J. L. ROSENBERGER.
(A Member of the Bar of Chicago and Cook County, Ill.)

The Supreme Court of Tennessee says in the case of Lewis Leonhardt & Co. vs. W. H. Small & Co. and others (96 Southwestern Reporter, 1051), involving the liability of certain banks for a breach of contract for hay after purchasing drafts attached to bills of lading therefor, that the theory of the complainants, which was adopted by the lower courts, was that when the defendant banks purchased said drafts they became the owners of the hay and responsible for the performance of the shippers' contract for its sale as to quality, quantity and delivery, and were liable for damages to the purchaser for the shippers' breach of the contract in any of said respects, although the drafts were negotiable and said banks were innocent purchasers thereof, and on presentation to the drawee they unconditionally accepted and paid the drafts. The complainants' contention was supported by the cases of Landa vs. Lattin Bros., 19 Tex. Civ. App. 246, 46 S. W. 48; Finch vs. Gregg, 126 N. C. 176, 35 S. E. 251, 49 L. R. A. 679; and J. C. Haas & Co. vs. Citizens' National Bank, Supreme Court of Alabama, reported in 39 South. 129, 1 L. R. A. (N. S.), 242; Searles vs. Smith Grain Co. (Miss.), 32 South. 287.

The case of Finch vs. Gregg, when reported in 49 L. R. A. 679, the court goes on to say, did not meet the approval of the annotator in that valuable set of reports; and many cases are cited to show that the rule laid down in the case is unsound and out of line with the great weight of authority; and he concludes his notes and criticism as follows:

"From these cases, all of which hold that after a draft attached to a bill of lading is accepted the consignee becomes absolutely liable on the acceptance, and that after payment thereon is made he cannot recover it back, notwithstanding any failure of consideration between him and the drawer, it would seem that the decision in the main case and in Landa vs. Lattin Bros., 19 Tex. Civ. App. 246, 46 S. W. 48, were based on a wrong principle, and that, if the right principle had been considered, the decisions must have been different."

The latest case upon the subject is that of Tolerton & Stetson Co. vs. Anglo-California Bank, by the Supreme Court of Iowa. This case repudiates the doctrine laid down in the cases of Landa vs. Lattin Bros. and Finch vs. Gregg, relied upon by the complainants in the case at bar, and reaffirms the long-established doctrine insisted upon by the defendants.

In the cases relied upon by the complainants and followed by the Court of Chancery Appeals, the courts of the states of Texas, North Carolina and Alabama erroneously assumed that the purchase of a draft with a bill of lading attached was a purchase of the goods represented by the bill of lading, and that a presentation of the draft for payment was a contract by the bank to sell the goods to the drawee, when, as a matter of fact, the goods had already been sold by the drawer to the drawee, and, as a matter of law, the bill of lading and goods only passed as collateral security for the draft, which was the only thing the bank bought.

Furthermore, if the sale of the drafts was in fact a sale outright of the bills of lading and in legal effect a sale of the hay to the defendant banks, as held in the case of Landa vs. Lattin

Bros., then the entire transaction was ultra vires, beyond the corporate powers of the banks, and no obligation arising therefrom could be enforced against the banks. National banks may take personal property as security for loans, or as security for bills of exchange purchased by them, but national banks have no power whatever to deal in merchandise of any kind or in stocks or bonds.

It is a fact of common knowledge that a large part of the commercial business of the country is carried on through the medium of drafts and that the immense crops of the South and West are marketed under contracts to draw for the purchase price with bills of lading attached. If the courts shall adopt the rule insisted upon by the complainants and enforced by the decree of the Court of Chancery Appeals, it will result in destroying this convenient method of handling, moving and paying for the crops of the country; for the banks will necessarily be compelled to refuse to buy drafts with bills of lading attached or to handle them as collateral security or otherwise. Banks have neither the time nor the facilities to investigate the genuineness of bills of lading or the contracts made between their customers with parties residing in other states, and to hold them responsible for the frauds and mistakes of shippers would utterly destroy the negotiability of drafts with bills of lading attached.

The case of Haas vs. Citizens' Bank, above cited, has also been adversely commented on by the annotators of the L. R. A. reports, in an exhaustive note, citing many authorities.

With all due deference to the ability and standing of the courts of Alabama, Texas and North Carolina, which have been cited and relied upon, this court is of opinion that the rule which they announce is unsound and contrary to the otherwise unbroken weight of authority.

They proceed upon the incorrect theory that the bill of lading so vests the property in the indorsing banks that they are substituted to all the liabilities of the original drawer and are the absolute owners of the property, while the true rule is that the indorsing banks hold the bills of lading simply as collateral to secure the drafts drawn against them, but they are not the guarantors of the quantity or quality of the goods shipped under the bill of lading. That is a matter between the drawer and the drawee.

Again, all but three of the drafts in this case were stamped by the bank which cashed them first and took the bills of lading, with this indorsement: "This bank hereby notifies all concerned that it is not responsible, either as principal or agent, for the quantity, quality or delivery of the goods covered by the bills of lading attached to this draft. (Signed) Citizens' National Bank." The argument was made that, because these three of the drafts were not thus indorsed, it was the intention of the parties that, as to these three drafts, a different rule should apply; that the holders or purchasers of these drafts would be guarantors of quality, quantity and delivery; and that, inferentially, at least, the bank omitting to thus indorse the three drafts impliedly said: "We will be responsible for defects in the hay covered by these three drafts, but not that covered by the other drafts."

The court thinks this contention not sound. The indorsement was surplusage; and under it the bank was in no. better condition than if it had not been made.

The court cannot infer that the bank intended to render itself liable for the three drafts by failing to stamp the restrictive indorsement on them. For all the court knows, they were overlooked. But, however that may be, they were put into circulation without any agreement or contract that a purchaser would be liable for the goods; and the court must give them the same status as any other draft of like character.

The Santa Fe at Chicago has restored the reconsignment charge of $2, in order, as explained,

to keep its own cars on its own tracks. It is the only line in Chicago making this charge, which was abolished about a year ago.

HARRY H. BINGHAM.

Harry H. Bingham, who represented the Louisville market at the Uniform Grade Congress, is head of the Bingham-Hewett Grain Company of that city, successors to the Strater Brothers Grain Co. and one of the leading firms in the Southern and Southwestern trade.

Mr. Bingham is a Tennesseean, having been born at McLemonsville in 1863. He lived on his father's cotton plantation until he was seventeen years of age, when he left school to go to Danville, Va., to go into the mercantile business under the patronage of his uncle. He remained there for five years, when, believing he could do better for himself further West, he went to Louisville and entered the wholesale drug house of J. B. Wilder & Co. When this firm went into liquidation soon after, he went to the mill supply house of W. T. Pyne Mill and Supply Co., where he remained from 1886 to 1892.

HARRY H. BINGHAM.

In the latter year he entered the grain business as bookkeeper for the firm of Strater Bros., grain merchants, retaining his connection with that firm until 1903. When the former partners of this company, having large interests elsewhere that claimed their entire attention, incorporated their partnership as the Strater Brothers Grain Company, Mr. Bingham and Leonard A. Hewett became stockholders and the active managers of the business, Mr. Bingham taking the office of treasurer of the company. In July, 1906, in connection with Leonard A. Hewett, he acquired the interests of the Strater Brothers Grain Co. and changed the name of that corporation to the Bingham-Hewett Grain Co., which was incorporated under the laws of the state of Kentucky, Mr. Bingham becoming president and treasurer of same.

Mr. Bingham, December, 1886, married Miss Nina Harlan of Louisville, and they have one son, who is attending the University of Virginia, and three daughters in the Louisville schools.

SWITCHING BY CONVEYOR.

There are more ways than one for skinning the cat; and more ways than one for "switching" grain are available to the ingenious. For example, adjoining the tracks of the C. G. W. Ry. at Minneapolis is a grain elevator of some 4,000,000 bushels' capacity, with ample sidetracks and unloading machinery, which receives and stores all the grain consumed by a flouring mill with a

capacity of 3,500 bushels a day, a very large linseed oil mill, and a large brewers' malt mill. These three mills were provided only with sidetracks for shipping out their products.

Instead of following the method usual in Minneapolis of transferring grain from elevators to railroad cars and switching it to the several mills, the owners of this elevator have installed a system of belt conveyors from the elevator to the mills, carried in elevated galleries. Each belt has a capacity of transferring 15,000 bushels an hour. This system of belts does away with the constant employment at that point of about 200 cars and one locomotive, which are left free for the general use of the railroad.

[For the "American Elevator and Grain Trade."]

THE PUBLIC ELEVATORS AT ST. LOUIS.

BY L. C. BREED.

As defined by the laws of the state of Missouri, all buildings, elevators or warehouses of not less than 50,000 bushels' capacity, for the purpose of storing grain of different owners for a compensation, the owners of said buildings having complied with the laws regulating such houses, are public elevators within the meaning of the statute.

The owners of these houses must receive for storage any grain offered them, if they have room; and discrimination between different persons is forbidden. Grain shall be stored with similar grades, unless by arrangement a special bin is provided for the applicant. Warehousemen are not allowed to mix grain, but this provision is not intended to apply to grain belonging to the owners of the elevator. Permission is also given to dry, clean, or otherwise change the condition and value of grain stored in special bins on the request of the owner. Grain cannot be mixed until it has been inspected.

It was not until within recent years that grain inspection was considered necessary except for the purpose of grading grain going into storage, which disposition of it made this separation as to quality absolutely necessary.

In the state of Missouri, prior to some ten years ago, the mixing of grain was not allowed at public elevators. The change in the law was brought about through the influence of parties interested in the elevator business. It is doubtful if the average legislator realized that he was not merely taking down the bars of the fence, but actually tearing it away altogether when voting in favor of allowing this privilege. It is, however, fair to suppose that these lawmakers assumed that, as it was provided that no grain could be mixed before it was inspected, and that, of course, the inspection department, whose business it was to see that grain was rigidly inspected, would efficiently attend to the duty they had been sworn to perform, there could no harm arise to innocent parties through obliging the elevator proprietor in the way he had petitioned.

The characterization given the elevators known as "public" by a prominent grain man here is "Legalized Mixing Houses"; and it is through the abuse of the privilege above mentioned that a man as well qualified as any member of the Merchants' Exchange to pass on the matter is, or feels, warranted in giving them this definition. It is a fact that, in the original meaning or construction of the law, there is no public elevator at St. Louis or East St. Louis; that is, no house run solely for the storage and transfer of grain belonging to various parties. The case is pretty nearly reversed; that is to say, as to the grain in store, the elevator interests probably are the actual owners of four-fifths of the stock, on the average, which is contained in the public elevators. Technically, they may not be interested so largely, as a considerable portion may be sold for future delivery, but, for the purposes of this article, as they are holding this grain for the purpose of applying it on such sales, the point the writer is making is clear.

It is claimed that an elevator conducted solely for storage and transfer purposes will not pay; and in support of this contention, if anything is said to the elevator proprietors, they will very promptly offer to sell one or more of their elevators, after earnestly assuring you that you could not possibly make both ends meet. But when one observes that the elevator men are the healthiest men on 'change, whose faces are placid and indicate, in addition to their being well fed, that they evidently sleep soundly, it is good proof that, under present conditions at any rate, it is a paying business.

It is claimed that changed conditions are responsible for the necessity of warehousemen being in the grain business; that the narrow margin in recent years in carrying charges forces them into merchandising. This doubtless, to a certain extent, is true; but an important matter is that some of the old elevators in St. Louis are unfavorably situated, necessitating switching charges, and some of them are at a disadvantage as compared with elevators operating on the east side of the river, with regard to Eastern business, since if grain is properly billed, the bridge toll is absorbed in the Western freight. A cent per hundred extra cost is quite an item in the grain trade as now handled. An additional reason is found in the gradual decline in the volume of wheat received at this center.

One of the older members of the Exchange, a level-headed man of experience in grain, stated to the writer that if a company should build a modern elevator, it would be possible to make it pay without engaging in merchandising. This result would be secured by two things—correct inspection and reliable weights. If absolute confidence were felt by parties using the elevator, that a "square deal" was the motto, at the time and all the time, the trade would be willing to pay the usual charges, and this would enable the company, through getting the preference, to do a paying business. There is no excess of storage room at St. Louis; in fact, the head of the Traffic Bureau (Mr. Lincoln, the well-known railroad expert) states there is crying need of more and better elevators to relieve the congestion of loaded cars in the yards.

The insurance question is a serious one. It is now too high; and besides this, it is not possible, at times, to cover all grain because the limit of insurance is reached, this being a matter fixed by the underwriters. However, this is exceptional and is experienced only when there is more than the usual quantity of grain in store. If there were new and modern steel or concrete elevators in St. Louis, a lower rate of insurance could be obtained. The present storage capacity of the ten public elevators of St. Louis is about seven and one-half million bushels. The private houses and mill elevators, twenty-five in number, carry about 2½ million bushels additional. Very few of the houses are equipped with modern sacking arrangements, which necessitates sacking on the tracks, a slow and expensive method.

The Exchange and the elevators are at loggerheads on the matter of establishing what should be regarded as the contract grade of grain. The directors sought to allow the grain committee of the Exchange to pass on the quality of grain offered by them in satisfaction of the warehouse receipts held by buyers, but this they refused, and stood for their rights, which they claim do not require them to recognize any control over the grain tended to or by them, beyond that of the state inspection department, subject to an appeal to the State Committee on Arbitration. The moment any pressure on the matter is brought to bear on them, they immediately threaten to become private houses; and this, of course, would mean the destruction of the speculative business of the Exchange.

A MICHIGAN ELEVATOR.

Commend us to Michigan when you are sending us on a hunt for an elevator that has "fetching" quality. In these columns several houses of that type have been illustrated from time to time; but none that now comes to mind strikes one as more truly of the right sort than the premises of Fred Welch at Fenton, shown in the accompanying picture.

The house is 93x23 feet on the ground, and has 17 bins with a total storage capacity of 20,000 bushels. Needless to say the house is a "good looker."

And it is just as attractive on the inside as on the outside. The bean department has the best of light, and is equipped with a bean cleaner, two machine bean pickers, a bean polisher and 32 hand-picking machines. In the grain and seeds department there are cleaners for all grain and seeds handled, two hopper scales, two Hall Distributors and a corn sheller. There is also a three-pair-high 9x24-inch Noye

FRED WELCH'S GRAIN AND BEAN ELEVATOR, FENTON, MICH.

Feed Mill. The power is furnished by a 25-horsepower engine.

Mr. Welch was a farmer previous to eight years ago, when he went to Fenton and entered the grain business. The elevator in question he erected five years ago, and it is rightly considered one of the best in every respect in the state of Michigan. Besides grain, beans and seeds Mr. Welch handles building materials, coal, wood and all kinds of feed; and to the successful business here he has recently added to his holdings and is operating an elevator at Linden.

GRAIN BAG SCARCITY.

As there seems to be no prospect of a decrease in the prices of jute grain bags, Calcuttas now selling at 10 cents in Walla Walla, many wheat growers in Washington are becoming uneasy at the probable expense of bagging their growing crop. The demand for jute in Europe and in the United States will have something to do with keeping up prices, and there seems to be a genuine demand for raw jute in these countries. The demand in the United States for gunnies is heavy and is likely to increase rather than diminish. The consumption of jute per annum in the United States is figured at 600,000 bales, with a probability of large increase; the consumption on the continent is 2,100,000 bales per annum; the consumption in Great Britain per annum is 1,250,000 bales; the mills in Calcutta consume 3,750,000 bales; and the mills in upper India consume 500,000 bales.

The India mills consumed 4,250,000 bales out of the total consumption throughout the world, which is estimated at 8,200,000 bales, or a little more than half of the raw products," says Consul-General Michael of Calcutta.

Washington state prison bags will probably be higher than last year, the warden has announced. The works are now shut down for repairs and to put in machinery to effect some economies made necessary by a 50 per cent advance in the price of jute. The system of distribution from the institution will be the same as last year—those getting in orders first will be supplied first until the output is exhausted."

MUST STAND TRIAL.

As might have been expected, in view of Judge Landis's decision on the immunity question, in the Standard Oil cases, Judge Morris, at Minneapolis, on January 26, overruled the demurrers in the cases against certain railroads and grain dealers who are charged with giving and receiving rebates. The decision was a written one and very lengthy, but would hardly interest the non-legal mind. As to the first point of the demurrers, the court says:

The contention, if I understand it, is this, that if the full amount of the legal schedule rate was in form paid and received as a cover or fraudulent device pursuant to a prearrangement or understanding that less than the legal tariff rate should be in fact paid and accepted for the services rendered, it should have been so charged in the indictment.

The argument proceeds upon the assumption that the indictment was based upon sections 2, 3 and 6, particularly section 6, of "An Act to Regulate Commerce," approved February 4, 1887, and the acts amendatory thereof prior to the passage of the act of June 29, 1906, commonly known as "The Hepburn Act." It is sufficient to say, in answer to this, that the indictment is not based upon said sections, but is based upon the first section of the "Elkins Act," and that under said section of the latter act no such allegation is necessary.

The argument further proceeds, as I understand it, upon the theory that if it were conceded that the defendant, without any prearrangement or understanding, express or implied, at some time after the service was performed and paid for, refunded to a shipper a sum equal to a given per cent of the tariff before paid, that would not necessarily be a violation of any federal statute; because if the defendant railway company, on account of certain conditions or circumstances, found it necessary, in order to compete with a rival railroad and to build up a through business over its line and the Great Lakes to the East, to pay the cost of transferring such grain, after it had been transported over its line, through an elevator to the vessels, or what would be on principle the same, having an elevator of its own, to pass the grain through it without charge, by first receiving the rates and charges set forth in the published tariffs and schedules and afterwards refunding to the shipper the cost of such transfer; or if, in order to compete with a rival company, it offered and gave to the shipper of such grain storage free in its elevator while awaiting shipment, or for such grain it furnished side-tracks and the use of its cars, without charging demurrage, while awaiting shipment, by first receiving the published rates and charges and afterwards refunding to the shipper the cost of such storage or demurrage, hoping thus to build up such a traffic over its line, that would not be illegal.

It is sufficient to say, in answer to this contention, that even if such conditions or circumstances, if they actually existed, might be shown in defense (which I extremely doubt, but which I do not think it necessary now to decide), it was not necessary under the Elkins act in addition to the allegation that the defendant did on the 15th day of February, 1906, wilfully and unlawfully grant and pay certain rebates and concessions in respect to the transportation of the grain whereby the said grain was transported in interstate commerce from the city of Minneapolis to the city of Duluth at a less compensation and rate than that named therefor in the published tariffs and schedules, to make any allegations negativing the existence of such conditions or circumstances.

It seems to me, therefore, that this ground of demurrer is not well taken.

The second point is, of course, the more important one, being the claim of immunity. The ruling here is substantially the same as that of Judge Landis, referred to above, the court holding, in reply to the defendants' plea, that they were immune from prosecution under the Hepburn act, on the ground that there can be no prosecutions under the Elkins act except against those who were indicted before the passage of the Hepburn act. The court holds that it was not the intention of Congress to allow any guilty persons to escape, and bases his opinion upon section 4 of an act entitled "An Act prescribing the form of the enacting and resolving clauses of acts and resolutions of the Congress and rules for the construction thereof." "All that is left to the courts," says the decision, "is to say whether or not they find in the repealing act an express provision releasing offenders, or any class of offenders, from prosecution under the repealed act. There is no such provision in the repealing act now under consideration."

The grain companies under indictment are the Ames-Brooks Company, Duluth-Superior Milling Company, McCaull-Dinsmoor Company, W. P. Devereaux Company.

PUBLIC OWNERSHIP OF ELEVATORS.

The public ownership craze has taken the form in the Canadian West of a demand for the public ownership of terminal elevators; and Mr. Mac-Pherson, M. P., of Vancouver, will father a resolution of Parliament declaring it advisable for the government to take active steps toward the establishment of terminal elevators at Vancouver for the better handling of grain and other crops of Alberta, whose natural outlet, the resolution declares, is the Pacific coast.

Messrs. Sifton, Greenway, Burrows, Crawford, Jackson and Cyr, members of the House for Manitoba, and Senators Young and Watson, with the same idea in mind, recently waited upon the Prime Minister to bring to his attention the question of the terminal elevators at Port Arthur. It was represented to him that it is feared that these elevators may pass out of the hands of the railway company into the control of grain buying or grain operating concerns; and that it is believed this would result in great dissatisfaction to the farming population, "who would suspect manipulation of the grain buyers and operators in having an interest in it."

A memorial also was presented to the Prime Minister asking him to have the terminal elevator question submitted to the Grain Commission for immediate investigation and report, without waiting for the completion of the general report.

Edward Brown, Liberal leader in Manitoba, is said to favor public ownership of grain elevators, and will do his best to bring about the acquirement of the elevators throughout the province by the government under the Liberals should that party be returned at the next elections, during the coming spring or summer.

"BUSTED."

If the shipper of the grain in the car shown in the illustration had reversed the Pike's Peak story and tagged the car "Chicago or Bust," the sequel to the episode would be "busted." Just where the accident occurred that resulted in the spilling of the shipper's grain is probably known only to the skilled artisans, who evidently had hammer, tongs and a shotgun to do the work of mending. The repairing had been done on the

HOW IT ARRIVED AT CHICAGO.

road and the car had been leaking continuously until its arrival at destination.

The car contained wheat and was unloaded at Calumet Elevator A, South Chicago, on January 25, 1907. Judging from the appearance of the car, the shipper had both faith and hope when he trusted his grain to it. A little good work, however, would probably have saved him some money, along the lines of getting a good car that would have stood the strain of somewhat heavy bunting. The wreck was caused by the railroad company, however, and it should be held responsible for all loss from leakage.

ILLINOIS WAREHOUSE COMMISSION.

Gov. Deneen has reorganized the Railroad and Warehouse Commission by the appointment of B. A. Eckhart of Chicago and Jas. A. Willoughby of Belleville to the Commission, to which some weeks ago he appointed W. H. Boys of Streator.

Mr. Eckhart is senior member of the Eckhart & Swan Milling Co., and one of the most prominent of Chicago's business men, a heavy shipper and a member of the Chicago Commercial Association. He is a big man, who will bring the Commission up to his level.

Mr. Willoughby is a publisher at Belleville.

Cold, dry weather is good time to run over the grain in elevators. It freezes the weevils, which are more numerous than usual this season. Most oats need some care.—King & Co.

NEW ENGLAND GRAIN DEALERS.

The fourth annual meeting of the New England Grain Dealers' Association was held at Boston on January 25 at the Chamber of Commerce.

Several matters of importance came up for consideration, among them the question of reciprocal demurrage, for which a bill is pending in Congress. The grain men are for it. Another question on which they are agreed is the necessity for a uniform grading of grain, as there is at present no standard governing all the markets of the country.

The directors of some of the experiment stations in New England read papers dealing with their experiments of the past year, some of them proving of great value.

The following officers were elected: H. L. Buss of Boston, president; Abner Hendee of New Haven, vice-president; J. W. Cox of Boston, secretary; Henry J. Wood of Boston, treasurer; E. B. Ham of Lewiston, Me.; E. P. Knight of Boston; W. E. Hardy of Boston; H. J. Crossman of Wenham; C. R. Crosby of Brattleboro, Vt.; D. K. Webster of Lawrence; J. Peterson of Derby, Conn.; E. A. Garland of Worcester; Frank E. Potts of Riverpoint, R. L; Frank Cressy of Concord, N. H., directors.

It was also decided to form a mutual insurance company to insure grain elevator property and grain in New England. For the purposes of examination into the facts and prospects the following committee had been appointed: Frank A. Noyes, vice-president Boston Chamber of Commerce; Charles M. Cox, president St. Albans Grain Company, St. Albans, Vt.; Dean K. Webster, treasurer H. K. Webster Company, Lawrence; George W. Kent, president Narragansett Milling Company, Providence; Abner Hendee, New Haven; Eben Ham, J. B. Ham & Co., Lewiston, Me.; O. B. Tilton, Nashua, N. H.; Prentiss Brooks & Co., Holyoke; R. G. Davis, New Haven. In their report this committee said:

As nearly as one can judge by results obtained elsewhere, we can split our insurance bills just about in halves. Your committee wishes to impress on the minds of all, however, that in order to accomplish anything we must all work together. Grain dealers all over New England must pull together for the common good. This simply means taking out a policy in the new company as soon as it is possible. At the start no policy will be written for more than $4,000 on any fire risk, and no policy smaller than $500. In order to get under way the same rate will be charged for the first year as is now being paid to the line companies. The saving is to come in renewals in the shape of dividends. For the very first thought in this matter must be safety. First: Safe insurance. Second: Low cost insurance.

The meeting was addressed by J. P. Gray, president of the Boston Manufacturers' Mutual Fire Insurance Company; Charles M. Cox of the Boston Chamber of Commerce, and D. K. Webster, treasurer of the H. K. Webster Company of Lawrence, who have been the chief promoters of the plan. It was announced that applications amounting to $500,000 for fire insurance have already been sent in by the grain dealers.

The first meeting of the corporation was announced for February 6.

At the banquet at the American House in the evening speeches were made by Lieut.-Gov. Draper, Henry L. Goemann, president, and John F. Courcier, secretary, of the National Association; Prof. H. J. Wheeler of Rhode Island Experiment Station, and Frank Cressy of Concord, N. H., president during 1906.

TELEGRAPH RATES ADVANCED.

The Western Union and Postal Telegraph Companies have advanced rates on telegrams to members of the grain exchanges to the regular rates paid by the general public. Various reasons for the advance are given, the only one having a shadow of justification being one that the Hepburn law forbids discriminations of any kind by the common carriers.

Peoria and the Illinois River corn markets have been buying heavily since the cold weather set in.

PRAIRIE STATE ELEVATOR.

We hear much, every autumn, of the harvest problem and the men, money and cars required to "move the crops." Little is said or realized, however, of the important part which the grain elevator plays in the great work of handling, grading, storing and marketing the cereal products of our vast farming areas. Scattered thickly throughout the country are small elevators, simply shipping houses which receive the grain of the farmer and load it into cars for shipment, often with little or no attempt at cleaning or grading. At important transportation centers are located transfer elevators, these being houses of comparatively small storage capacity but well equipped for handling, cleaning, grading and shipping the grain brought in from the country houses naturally tributary to them. Graded to recognized standards of quality in the transfer elevator, the grain is shipped on directly to market or to storage in some of the terminal elevators at the principal grain handling centers of rail and water transportation.

The Prairie State Elevator at Kankakee, Ill., is a transfer house erected in 1905 by the White & Rumsey Grain Co. of Chicago, an Illinois corporation under the management of I. P. Rumsey, president; F. M. Bunch, vice-president; H. A. Rumsey, treasurer; C. A. White, secretary. Operation of the elevator is in charge of Selsor Orr, superintendent.

The house was e₁e₂e₃e₄ for the purpose of taking care of the grain purchased by the White & Rumsey Grain Co. at its own country elevators in Illinois, and also for handling other grain purchased in the West and passing eastward via Kankakee. A thorough system of grading and weighing is in effect, inspection being under the supervision of the Illinois state authorities. Kankakee is an excellent point for a transfer elevator, for the reason that railroad facilities provide means of economical shipment into a wide territory, large quantities of

in and out, were handled in 7½ hours. The house was designed and erected by E. Lee Heidenreich, C. E., of Chicago, and the working equipment throughout was furnished by the Dodge Manufacturing Co.

An exterior view of the elevator is presented

Fig. 1.—PRAIRIE STATE ELEVATOR.

in Fig. 1. Above a 6-foot basement the house is 75 feet high to the distributing floor at the top of the main building, where the lower line of windows appears. Above this floor in the cupola are the scale floor, the garner floor and the head floor, the latter nearly 150 feet above the foundation.

The power house, as usual in elevator practice, is a separate and detached structure. The boilers are two in number, 72 in. x 18 ft. in size, of the horizontal tubular type, worked at 100-pound steam pressure and fired with coal. To each furnace may be connected one of the swinging spouts, through which the waste from the grain cleaners

Co. The engine is rated at 300 horsepower, runs at 84 revolutions per minute and delivers its power from a 16-foot grooved flywheel by the American System Rope Drive to a receiving sheave on the headshaft section of the main lineshaft, which is carried on bridgework across the intervening space directly into the elevator building. The engine drive consists of 12 wraps of rope. The tension carriage travels on a horizontal track overhead.

Entering the elevator building, the main shaft extends full length of the working floor, carried in self-oiling ball-and-socket pillow blocks on bridge-trees overhead. At intervals along the main lineshaft power is taken off for driving the several stands of elevators, the car puller, the car unloading shovels, the belt conveyors, the cleaning machinery, etc.

Fig. 6 shows the method of unloading grain from the cars in which it is received, large wooden shovels being operated alternately and automatically by the Dodge-Clark Shovel Machines on the shovel lineshaft overhead. Scooped out of the car door, grain falls through iron gratings into a hopper feeding a belt conveyor running through a trench and discharging into the boot of a receiving elevator leg, which carries the grain to the top floor of the cupola, Fig. 4. There are two pairs of shovel machines, so that two cars may be unloaded at one time. Two tracks are laid through the carshed, so that cars may be set on one track while others are being unloaded on the opposite track.

Overhead in Fig. 2 may be seen the three-wrap rope drive by means of which the shovel lineshaft is driven from the main line. This drive, as also practically all others throughout the house, is arranged for independent control by means of a split friction clutch. Fig. 3 shows the receiving sheave of the shovel lineshaft drive, including also the second unloading station.

Fig. 2 shows the heavy car puller by means of which cars and shifted and set for unload-

Fig. 2.—HEAVY DODGE CAR PULLER.

Fig. 3.—CAR PULLER SHEAVES, GRAIN UNLOADING.

grain going to Michigan, New England and Canada, as well as to seaboard cities and the Southeast.

Bin capacity in a transfer house is made only sufficient to provide for storage of the grain actually passing through. Thus, while the aggregate of bin capacity in the house is only 100,000 bushels, the movement of grain in and out is about 50 cars per working day of 10 hours. The house was built for a rated capacity of 40 cars per day, but has proved itself so fast that 50 cars are regularly handled. As a record, 66 cars of grain,

in the elevator house may be fed to the fires. A spring, found on the site of the elevator when excavations for the foundation were made, supplies all necessary water for boiler feeding, fire protection, etc. As an auxiliary source of water supply, however, a 5-inch drilled well, 100 feet deep, is available, water being drawn by a deep well pump. In the engine room is also an underwriters' fire pump.

The engine is a 20x48-inch Twin City Corliss, built by the Minneapolis Steel & Machinery

ing in the carshed and for loading outside, as per Fig. 1. The illustration shows plainly the three drums carrying wire cable for serving these three separate tracks independently. The car puller is driven directly from the main lineshaft by a drive of seven wraps, with a vertical tension carriage. Operation of the car puller as a whole is controlled by a large and powerful split friction clutch, and each individual drum is thrown in or out by engagement or release of a jaw clutch.

While slippage in a friction clutch is not usually

a desirable characteristic, it is found in operation of this car puller, and in similar service, that the ability to slip the clutch under perfect control by partial release of the operating mechanism is a feature of great value in the accurate setting and slight movement of cars.

Fig. 4.—ELEVATOR HEAD FLOOR IN CUPOLA.

The head floor lineshaft is driven by a seven-wrap vertical rope drive from the sheave on the main lineshaft just inside the elevator building, as shown in the upper left-hand corner of Fig. 2. Carried clear to the top of the elevator cupola, past a guiding idler on the distributing floor, Fig. 5, the ropes of this drive reach the main receiving sheave on the head lineshaft, as seen in the distance of Fig. 7. This line is carried in self-oiling ball-and-socket pillow blocks on low, adjustable floor stands. Each drive for the three elevator stands is fitted with a split friction clutch. Two of these elevator stands are receiving legs, while the third one, the middle one of the three, is the shipping leg by which grain is elevated from beneath the storage

basement, the grain may be transferred, mixed, turned over, cleaned, shipped or disposed of in any other desired way. Such is the absolute facility of working and handling provided in a well-equipped elevator. That the Prairie State Elevator is a very fast and economical working house is due not only to Mr. Heidenreich, the designer, and to the Dodge Manufacturing Co., which furnished the working machinery, but also to Mr. Orr, under whose direction the house is operated.

For the illustrations and facts above, the editor is indebted to "Power and Transmission," Chicago.

Owing to the shortness of fuel farmers in the vicinity of Washtucna, Wash., have burned a large quantity of fodder corn on the cob.

At a conference of representatives of continental grain buyers, held at Berlin in December, it was voted to reject American corn certificates altogether

Fig. 5.—DISTRIBUTING FLOOR.

bins below for weighing out and spouting to cars as per Fig. 1.

Grain brought to the top of the elevator by the by the receiving legs is spouted into "garner" bins on the floor below, whence it is dropped into scale hoppers on the next floor for weighing. Then it is spouted on the distributing floor, Fig. 5, into any desired ones of the 21 bins beneath.

On the distributing floor also are the heads of two small elevator stands, the one for receiving grain brought by wagon and the other for handling grain in connection with the cleaning machinery on the main or working floor below.

Spouted from any bin to a belt conveyor in the

Fig. 6.—AUTOMATIC SHOVELS.

and demanded the introduction of a new grain contract, the form of which was discussed and agreed upon.

A furious storm at Buffalo played havoc among the twenty grain boats tied up in the harbor. Some went ashore and others were jammed in collision.

Russian newspapers announced on January 29 that the Volga mill owners have begun ordering American wheat, owing to the short Russian supply. The first consignment from the United States will arrive shortly at Riga. It will be delivered at Rybinsk, where the chief Volga corn exchange is located, at 71 cents per thirty-six pounds. Local wheat costs there 79 cents.

MYSTERIOUS AFFAIR.

On the evening of January 24 H. E. Agar, secretary-treasurer and principal stockholder of the Princeton Elevator Company of Princeton, Ind., fell off a barge of the steamer Lafayette into Wabash River near Mt. Carmel, Ill., and has not since been seen alive nor has his body been recovered. The story told by Mt. Carmel papers is that, "The Lafayette had gone up the river after a load of corn, and at about nine o'clock Wednesday night had reached the little dam in safety on the return trip. Mr. Agar at this point went up into the pilot house and talked with Captain Harrington. He then went down and said to the engineer that he would go out on the barge and see how it was getting along, as it had been leaking. While on the barge he accidentally lost his footing and fell overboard, Captain Harrington seeing him fall. Every effort was made to locate him, but the body did not rise to the surface after going down. He was weighted down with a heavy overcoat, leggings and other clothing."

After his disappearance, an examination into his affairs uncovered the fact that Mr. Agar was heavily involved. Creditors began to put in an appearance from Indiana, Kentucky and Missouri, necessitating the appointment of John P. Miller as receiver. It now stated that the shortage in the company's accounts will reach $150,000, including $30,000 in cash which disappeared with Mr. Agar. Worse than that, there are charges of forgery of notes amounting to $100,000. It is supposed that Mr. Agar committed suicide rather than face the world, and on that supposition funeral services, without the body, were conducted at his home in Princeton on January 30; but there are those who believe Mr. Agar is still alive.

Agar, in addition to his holdings in the Princeton Elevator Company, was connected with the Telephone Company and with two banks in Princeton; was manager of the Agar department store in Princeton, and local secretary and treasurer of the Central Trust and Savings Company of Evansville, besides being connected with various other minor business affairs in and around Princeton. He was a member of the last legisla-

Fig. 7.—HEAD FLOOR LINE SHAFT.

ture of Indiana, being elected on the Republican ticket, and prominent in politics of southern Indiana.

The Princeton Elevator Co. had a capital stock of $50,000 and operated grain elevators in Princeton, Mount Carmel, Evansville and six or eight other towns in southern Indiana and southern Illinois. The company did a big business, being reputed to be the biggest shipper between St. Louis and Louisville on the Southern road. The assets are placed at $30,000, and counting the sureties on the notes as good, creditors are expected to realize about 75 per cent of their claims.

ANNUAL MEETING INDIANA GRAIN DEALERS.

An unusually large gathering of Indiana grain dealers attended the fifth annual convention at Claypool Hotel, January 17 and 18. Following the call to order President E. M. Wasmuth of Roanoke read his annual address as follows:

PRESIDENT'S ADDRESS.

Another year has gone and stock taking has developed the measure of profit or loss. With bountiful crops which have given all a fair volume of business, and with markets that have not been attended by violent or rapid fluctuations, there have been opportunities for profitable business operations, which I hope have been taken advantage of by all.

During the year much work has been accomplished by the Association, your secretary having been active in looking after your interests at all times. There were three meetings of the board of managers, two of which were called for the purpose of considering the routine business and one to take up the demurrage question.

Demurrage.—At this meeting, which was held early in the year, it was decided that the Association should join with the Indiana Shippers' Association and others in petitioning the state Railroad Commission to formulate rules to govern the Indiana Car Service Association in the collection of demurrage charges, and if within its power make rules to govern the movement of loaded cars and the furnishing of empty equipment, and to assess a like or reciprocal demurrage charge in the event of their failure to observe them, against the transportation companies. A committee consisting of John McCardle, Clayd Loughrey and A. F. Files was appointed, which met with like committees from other associations, and the case was heard by the Commission in August. Much evidence was furnished demonstrating the injustice of the rules in force and favoring reciprocal rules.

Rules recently announced by the Commission and becoming effective January 1, last, are the outcome of this case. They apply only to the collection of demurrage from the shipper and receiver, and by their failure to act, the Commission acknowledges its lack of authority to assess penalties against the railroads as demurrage charges. It is hoped and expected that the legislature at its present session will enact a law granting the Commission the power to make and provide for the enforcement of such rules as will exact from railroad companies penalties for the failure to move loaded cars a reasonable distance per diem, and also for the failure to furnish empty equipment when needed.

The one real impediment in the way of the grain dealer's successful prosecution of his business during the year has been the absolute failure of the railroads to furnish equipment for the prompt movement of the grain. Many elevators have been closed, and at others corn has been thrown upon the ground without protection of any kind, and has been greatly damaged by the recent heavy rains. These deplorable conditions are not confined to the grain business nor to Indiana, but extend to every other commodity, and all over the country. In one place there is congestion, and in another famine, and it is apparent that some drastic measure must be taken to secure relief. Recent developments indicate that the time is not far distant when there will be enacted a national reciprocal demurrage law, framed on as conservative lines as possible to bring the desired result, and it is hoped that our state legislature will act in such a manner as to make this legislation cover intrastate as well as interstate commerce. The effect of their failure to do so in the event of national legislation, is easy to foresee. Other states are falling in line, and before the legislatures have all adjourned it is probable that a dozen states will have enacted reciprocal demurrage laws.

Following these enactments, the shippers of this state will be in worse condition than now if relief does not come speedily, as the empty equipment and motive power will be used where failure to furnish it would be followed by a penalty. This Association should authorize a committee to act in this matter and give all possible assistance to the Indiana Shippers' Association in its efforts to secure this and other legislation increasing the power of the state Railroad Commission.

The Hepburn Bill for the regulation of railroad rates has been enacted by Congress. This legislation goes a step farther in the interests of shippers and in the prevention of discrimination. It should not be forgotten that the Indiana railroad commission law, of which this Association was the principal instigator and champion, was the stepping-stone to this very important and far-reaching reform. Many, if not all, of the grain shippers of Indiana have been greatly benefited by this law already. A notable instance of the benefits received is the removal of the so-called "plus-rates" enforced by several railroads within the state before this law went into effect. Dealers who had never been upon an equality with their competitors on other roads have been made so by this legislation.

Legislation.—At the last meeting of your board of directors it was decided that the committee on legislation, which acted for the Association during the last session of the general assembly, should be reappointed, and they were instructed to seek such modifications of the landlord's lien law as will result in the elimination of the responsibility now attaching to the grain dealer by reason of the provisions of the present law without destroying the reasonable interests of the landlords. A bill for this purpose is being framed by this committee, which consists of Charles S. Bash, P. E. Goodrich, T. A. Morrison, James W. Sale and W. W. Alder. Our members should make themselves acquainted with its provisions and secure the support of their representatives for it.

Uniform Grades.—Recently, through the efforts of our National Association, a conference of delegates from the different receiving markets and associations was held in Chicago, and uniform rules for the grading of grain were formulated. These rules have been adopted by a number of the exchanges and such action will be taken by others. It now seems probable that the much-desired adoption of Uniform Grading Rules will soon be an accomplished fact. It should not be forgotten, however, by those in control, that uniform rules will not be taken as a panacea for all ills by shippers, but that in addition to this there must be as nearly uniformity of inspection as is possible. Inspectors should hold frequent meetings and confer with each other as to the application of these rules, and act in such a manner that their integrity and honesty of purpose cannot be questioned.

Government Inspection.—A year ago this Association endorsed the McCumber Bill for government inspection. I do not wish to be understood as favoring such legislation. On the contrary, it would be a question whether it would not be undesirable; but it seems apparent that the time must come when the inspection departments of all receiving markets shall be managed by entirely disinterested parties or by those responsible equally to both parties to the contract.

Arbitration.—Experiences of the year show plainly that we should carry with more dignity and urge upon our members more strenuously the use of our arbitration committee. To my mind, this is one of the important works of the Association. It affords an opportunity for the settlement of difficulties and disagreements without resort to the courts. The work of the committee should be done with painstaking care, and should command the greatest respect, but the use of this court should be insisted upon. In the event that a member continues to refuse to arbitrate, the board of managers should have and use the power to suspend or expel him. There should be no laxity.

I desire to urge upon all that while we associate together to devise means of correcting the abuses of markets and in bettering the trade conditions that affect us in all our transactions, that we do not forget that the care with which we keep our contracts and the clean and fair manner in which we prosecute our business will largely determine the measure of our success.

Contributions to Corn Show.—In a circular letter to our members in December, I urged a contribution to the Indiana Corn Growers' Association for the purpose of increasing the fund for the payment of premiums at their annual corn show, which is being held at the experiment station at Lafayette this week. I wish to take this opportunity to thank those who responded. The benefits derived by the grain dealer from the improvement of the corn crop are large, and as the means for securing funds for the purpose are very limited, our members should help willingly.

Corn Contest.—For your entertainment and profit the board of directors arranged for a corn contest at this meeting. These contests, which are encouraged by the Indiana Corn Growers' Association, are being held in numerous counties of the state as well as at the experiment station at Lafayette. They prove to be an effective way of interesting the farmer in the improvement of his crop, and if it is the wish of the officers of the Corn Growers' Association, I trust that the dealers in every county in the state will take the initiative in holding these contests. A few years of this work would result in cutting down to a minimum our receipts of immature, cobby and unmerchantable corn, and would result in much profit to us. Dealers who had contests last year, report that they could plainly see the effect in the corn that came to their elevators this fall.

Support Association.—I want again to urge the support of the Association upon the dealers of the state. While the secretary's report will show the Association to be in healthy condition, we only avoid debt by the strictest economy. While the membership holds up and slowly increases, still less than half of the dealers of the state are doing this work and bearing the expense, while all reap the benefits. There should be more loyalty among the dealers and more unanimity of action. If you are not a member, be manly enough to join to-day, and if your neighbor is a non-member shame him into joining.

Secretary J. M. Brafford then read his annual report as follows:

SECRETARY'S REPORT.

Your secretary begs leave to submit the following report: Our membership at present is 287, which is the largest it has ever been in the history of the organization, and consists of 243 country grain dealers, 40 receivers and four special members; and we are receiving dues on 119 additional stations. We have gone through the last year, as you will see by the detailed financial report herewith submitted, with everything paid; and I am glad to say, with a balance in the treasury of $166.56. Total receipts for the year were $3,842.09; total expenditures, $3,675.53; balance, $166.56, which is gratifying. The response to the statements of dues sent out the first of the year has been extremely liberal and our collections to date are about $1,000, for which I am under great obligations to the members, and I cannot help but feel that they appreciate what we have been trying to do for them, and show it in their prompt payments.

Your secretary has attended about 100 meetings of local associations in the different parts of the state in the past year, besides the annual convention of the Grain Dealers' National Association and the Uniform Grades Congress in Chicago.

State of Trade.—The general state of the trade over Indiana during the year has been extremely good. There are some rough places but not very many. The phenomenal yield of wheat gave the dealers an excellent crop to handle and it was taken care of and marketed in splendid condition. The oats crop, while not large, was handled fairly well and to the satisfaction of most of the dealers. The corn so far has been a disappointment. Two things have militated against the handling of it. The one which has bothered the majority of the dealers the most has been the extreme shortage of cars; the other has been the extraordinary rainy, soft, mushy weather, which has caused a large proportion of all the corn in the different markets to grade No. 4 and quite a bit of it "no-grade." There is one thing, however, we can congratulate ourselves on, and that is that the corn does not heat this year like it did last. With the same kind of corn as last year and this weather, the losses entailed would have been a great deal larger than last year.

Farmers' Care of Corn.—There is one thing that will probably be touched on by a number of speakers, and that is the carelessness of the farmers in keeping their corn uncovered and permitting all the rains and snows of the winter to soak down through the crib. There will have to be a difference made in this kind of corn. It is unfair to the careful farmer who buys lumber and covers his cribs, and it is impossible for the dealer to handle this kind of grain and get out even on it. He cannot tell how many pounds it will take to make a bushel, and even if he discounts it three or five cents a bushel, he is not sure that he has bought a bushel of corn. The strange thing is, why they will take such care of the wheat and oats and be so careless with the corn. There is only one explanation for it and that is, that they are able to sell the wet, damp corn at the same price that their neighbors do the dry.

Prizes for Corn.—Your board of managers have seen fit to instruct your secretary to offer six prizes for the best five ears of corn raised in Indiana, barring professional seed growers and those who have heretofore taken premiums at Purdue University. They have offered a larger premium for the yellow because at all times of the year it usually sells for from one-half to two cents more than mixed corn. However, there are some portions of the state that raise pure white corn and are able to sell it to industries at a premium over mixed, equal to the premium on yellow. Still, it is not general, and it is not to the interest of the grain dealers to encourage the raising of white corn. But we felt that white corn, being a pure corn, was entitled to a premium as an encouragement for those sections that raise exclusively white corn. The Corn Growers' Association of Indiana has consented to have two of their members, in company with their president, who will address us to-morrow, score this corn, and we hope the interest taken in it will encourage the raising of better corn.

Uniform Grades Congress.—The general sentiment of the Uniform Grades Congress in Chicago was that unless all of the boards of trades in the United States speedily adopted uniform grades, the national government would pass a law giving over to the Secretary of Agriculture inspection of all interstate grain. Some of the boards of trades have adopted it and some have not; and from appearances, the old-time jealousies and bickerings between the different boards will prevent it; and in the opinion of your secretary the ultimate result will and should be government inspection or supervision.

Thanks for Assistance.—The secretary desires to thank each one personally for the assistance you have all been to him during the year. I have never asked a single dealer to do anything in the interest of the trade which has not been cheerfully and willingly done. Your secretary has been able to settle a number of cases by personal intercession and it has only been necessary to resort to arbitration in two cases, and it is surely less expensive than the old-time lawsuits, and I am sure that whoever may be your secretary, that they will be perfectly willing to take up differences at any time between receivers and dealers and help them arrive at a settlement without the expensive lawsuit.

Claim Attorneys.—Your secretary would recommend that a good firm of attorneys be selected in Indianapolis, to whom all claims against the railroads should be referred by dealers throughout the state, either before or after they had exhausted their efforts in making the collection. I have in mind a number of honest and meritorious claims that have been rejected by the different railroads, simply because the roads feel that the individuals would not sue them, as an individual. I believe we could make arrangements with a firm of attorneys to handle them on a commission, and I am sure that all of them centralized and given to men who would familiarize themselves with the different railroad usages and laws, pertaining to the same, would be a great deal more able to collect them than individual attorneys throughout the state, and that it would have a great deal more weight than if presented by the grain dealers themselves. I would suggest that your president appoint a committee to take this into consideration.

Landlord's Lien Law.—The legislature is now in session, and your secretary would very much like to see the landlord's lien law amended in such a manner as to protect the grain dealers. We are willing to pay for grain once, but do not care to pay for it twice. There has already been a bill introduced known as Senate Bill No. 10 by Senator Cavins from the southern part of the state and we would very much like to see a committee appointed, to whom this bill could be referred. We have already interviewed the senator, and he has promised to assist us in any way that we deem advisable, or to accept any amendments that will not weaken the landlord's lien law as it now exists, but that will protect the grain dealers from dishonest tenants or dishonest landlords, because there can be a collusion between landlords and tenants, as the law exists now, from which the grain dealer would be the sufferer.

Conversion of Grain.—There is another paragraph in the grain laws of Indiana that none of you probably have ever noticed, but which is very dangerous to any grain man who takes grain on store and ships it out and sells or stores it elsewhere without the written consent of the depositor. The latter has plenty of power under the law to go into court and have you indicted and subjected to a very heavy fine or a penitentiary sentence, and unless it can be amended I would advise you all to have written or stamped across your deposit tickets a contract, giving you the authority to ship the grain out of store or sell it at some terminal market for the account of the depositor, and thereby only be liable for the grain alone and not under the criminal code. The statute I refer to is 8726 R. S. on page 1221, Vol. No. 3.

Reinspection of Grain.—We would also like to see Statute No. 8718, page 1219, Vol. No. 3, on the subject of reinspection of grain changed to give the Railroad Commission authority to appoint the inspectors in Indiana, supervise the inspection of grain by making all the necessary rules therefor, and take the authority away from the commercial organizations, boards of trades and county judges to appoint the inspectors. As it is now, we have a dual inspection in Indiana, half state and half board of trade and commercial organizations. At Indianapolis the inspectors are appointed by the Board of Trade; at Lafayette they were at one time appointed, one by the county judge and the other by the Commercial Club. At South Bend, Wellsboro and La Crosse they are appointed by the county judge, and in that way are state inspectors. The country grain shipper pays all this expense anyway, and it does not cost the organizations or the state one cent; and, therefore, I think it just as well be all lodged under the control of the state.

We congratulate the general assembly on having an up-to-date grain man for Speaker of the House, and there are three or four other members who are country grain dealers, so that our interests under the circumstances should be reasonably well taken care of, although we are not asking any favors whatever.

I again thank you, one and all, for the assistance you have been to the secretary during the past year, and if I have served you in any way to your betterment, I feel duly paid for all the trouble incident thereto.

The report of Treasurer Bert A. Boyd showed total receipts for the year ending January 1, $3,842.09; total expenditures, $3,675.53, leaving cash in the treasury, $166.56.

On motion by John W. McCardle the reports of the president and secretary were accepted and the recommendations contained therein were referred to a special committee.

The report of the treasurer, on motion by Geo. C. Wood, was referred to the auditing committee.

President Wasmuth appointed the following committees:

Nominations—Chas. Mollett, Robt. Alexander, Thos. Ryan, J. W. Sale, Walter Aiman, Fred Kennedy, C. M. Barlow.

Railroad Claims—O. J. Thompson, Bert A. Boyd, A. F. Files, John W. McCardle, Clarence Valentine.

On Laws—P. E. Goodrich, Jas. Sale, E. W. Ball, T. A. Morrison, Cloyd Loughry.

Resolutions—Geo. C. Wood, A. E. Reynolds, N. H. Robinson, J. S. Hazlerigg, E. K. Sowash.

Auditing Committee—T. B. Wilkerson, A. E. Betts, A. B. Cohee.

Secretary Brafford read a letter from Fred Mayer of Toledo, who, as president of the Produce Exchange, asked that the Association take steps to secure the publication of the Toledo market reports throughout the state in all such papers using the Associated Press service. The matter was referred to the committee on resolutions.

John W. McCardle read the following resolution, which was referred to the committee on resolutions:

Whereas, The Hon. James E. Watson, member of Congress from the sixth district, this state, has recently presented a bill to Congress seeking to secure the enactment of a law providing for the government inspection of all grain and seed that enter into and become a part of interstate and international commerce; and

Whereas, The different markets in this country have so far failed to maintain a system of uniform grades and uniform inspection of grain and seed, therefore, be it

Resolved, That we, the grain dealers of Indiana, in annual session, endorse the measure proposed by Mr. Watson and earnestly urge upon Congress the importance of the enactment thereof; and we further urge upon the senators and members of Congress from this state the importance of this legislation and the desire that they will render all the assistance possible in securing the enactment of this or a similar measure that will insure government inspection of all grain and seed that may become a part of the interstate or international commerce, and the secretary is directed to transmit a copy hereof to each of the honorable senators and congressmen from this state, and to the honorable secretary of agriculture, with such further statement as may seem proper.

THURSDAY AFTERNOON.

The afternoon session opened with an address by U. B. Hunt, chairman of the Indiana Railway Commission. Mr. Hunt congratulated the Indiana dealers on the interest they had shown in securing a Railway Commission and said that now the Commission would ask the legislature of the state to give it more power. They wanted to be able to bring about reciprocal demurrage and have broader powers, as the Commission had been hampered the last two years because of the inability of the law that created it to give it power. They wanted larger equipment of railroad rolling stock, better physical condition and safety devices that should preserve the life and limbs of the public. In closing he asked the support of the dealers for these measures and their influence in securing such legislation that would serve all the people of the state alike.

E. W. Bassett of Indianapolis read the following paper on Reinspection in Terminal Markets:

REINSPECTION AT TERMINALS.

The necessity for rules for reinspection in terminal markets, as well as some of the unfair results, seem to arise from the lesson taught in the illustration of the mote and the beam. It is as true to-day in the grain business, and in other lines, as it has been in all ages, that we hypocrites can all unerringly discern the mote in our brother's eye, but the large beam in our own eye lies quite unobserved. If we can assist in removing both mote and beam, the object of this little address shall have been attained. Please bear in mind that the trade rules as spread upon the pages of our commercial exchanges and of our grain dealers' associations, like the laws on our statute books, are very largely the result of some actual experience which was duly tabulated by one of the affected parties or by an observer.

We will admit frankly that at first blush it would seem that there should be no rule for reinspection at terminal markets. Why should there be? Why should not the initial inspection be final? Let us see. Do you recall the almanac story of the Irish lady who said to her son, "Mike, quit scratching yer head, bye?" And he replied, "I won't, marm. They began on me first."

Shippers to Blame.—We are compelled to declare, much as we regret to do it, that the primary cause for reinspection rules did and does lie with the country shippers, in the proof of which we append two experiences which can doubtless be duplicated by any receiver.

In a certain November not many years ago, Mr. A, who is located on a railroad running west from Indianapolis, shipped us car No. 23 loaded with something over 60,000 pounds of corn. We will say for Mr. A that he is a large and honorable shipper as the term usually applies. That is, he seldom if ever overdraws. He fills his contracts to the letter, or pays the penalty willingly. If he fails to get cars or if for any reason he fails to fill his November contracts, he pays the market difference for extension into December. His word is always good. His contracts for new corn often run to two and even three hundred thousand bushels before shipments commence.

In the ordinary course of business, we received car No. 23 on a certain day in November which was passed by the inspector as No. 3 corn. We should say that we bought from this party, as has been our custom for years past, on Indianapolis inspection and export weights final. And so car No. 23 was duly reported as No. 3 corn and forwarded to Newport News for export. But something happened. Car No. 23 reached Newport News in a muck, scarcely fit for first-class fertilizer. It was so badly grown, so caked and matted that it required pick and shovel to remove it to the floor of the elevator; and as for elevation it would not run through the spouts at any time. Well, that car brought barely freight and the firm that pays our salary was put back about four hundred dollars financially.

There seemed to be something wrong, but the contract was plain—Indianapolis inspection and export weights final—and Mr. A received his credit accordingly. Several weeks later Mr. A came into the office to make a friendly call. He seemed to be in a good humor. Finally he said, "Well, I see car 23 got through all right."

We replied, "Yes, at least it got through; but what was the matter with that car? It seemed to go to pieces so."

"Well, now that it's all over, I'll tell you. My men were loading that car and had it two-thirds loaded when there came up suddenly a very heavy rain. The men ran for shelter and left the car doors open and a ton of water entered the corn. After the rain the men, being in great haste, completed the loading with dry corn and shipped it over here. I really didn't expect it to grade."

We looked at him in blank amazement, whistled a tune and said, "What's the use?"

Another car was received in Indianapolis by a commission man, inspected and sold for No. 3. Later inspection East developed the fact that the car had been systematically plugged. The eastern inspection so stated and the shipper practically admitted this fact, yet on account of technical Board rule, refused to pay one cent toward the loss which his sharp practice brought to an innocent buyer. There is but one word to characterize such conduct and that word is, fraud. But so long as that word remains in the dictionary, reinspection rules will be necessary.

But there is also the other side. You will recall that the noble judge ruled that Shylock was entitled to his pound of flesh; but not in the estimation of a hair was the scale to go beyond. Some of us are charged with the duty of making and enforcing these rules. We are not less guilty than Shylock, who really wanted the merchant's life, if we abuse this privilege and make our demands more exorbitant than necessity requires. If we go farther, we are no better than the shipper who deliberately plugs his car. Our avarice is as criminal as his fraud.

The rules of the Indianapolis Board of Trade provide, Sec. 29, that the seller of a No. 3 or better grade shall guarantee the grade sold for a period of six days and the buyer may at any time within that period demand reinspection and grade difference if found to be of lower grade. Sec. 24 also specifically declares that where a car is conclusively shown to have been plugged, the buyer may demand the grade difference, thus carrying out the old common law principle of clean hands.

In addition to the common cases here cited as wilful, many cars are plugged by accident; corn loading for a straight color becomes mixed in bin or car; many cars are loaded to roof, making thorough inspection not only difficult but often impossible.

We trust that we have all been fully able to see the mote in the eye of the country shipper, his unfair loading, likewise the beam in our own, the receiver's eye, in that if we have done as some of our exchanges undoubtedly have, in the making of unjust rules for reinspection.

Another important point: We have given the exceptions and not the rule. By far the most of the country shippers are honest and would not deign to deceive inspector or buyer in the matter of loading. Our rules must be framed to protect both shipper and receiver, both seller and buyer, while punishing fraud at every step.

Let us look for a moment at the commercial standard. If standard granulated sugar is worth five cents per pound and you buy of your grocer twenty pounds and lay down your dollar and accept your purchase wrapped in heavy brown paper and find on arriving home that it is heavily water-soaked, would you call an arbitration committee? No, you would demand a reinspection by the grocer and demand the standard bought or your dollar back, and if he should refuse you, you would fight or quit his shop forever, or both.

The simile is not different. The No. 3 corn is the accepted standard at practically all markets west of the Alleghanies. Now the buyer who lays down forty cents for 56 pounds of No. 3 corn is entitled to receive what he bought and paid for. But what do we mean by No. 3 corn? Most grade rules say reasonably sound, reasonably dry and reasonably clean. We contend that the seller should guarantee this grade for a period of twelve days. Why? Because very much of our corn is exported via Atlantic seaboard ports and the buyer has a right to expect that he is buying a grain suited to go aboard ship as a sailgrade and the average haul to seaboard from our state or Illinois is about twelve days. In fact, the price which the buyer pays contemplates this very thing. We, therefore, deduce that the Indianapolis rules referred to are very liberal. We have heard of markets that permit a reinspection after thirty days, but this is manifestly unfair to shipper, as this places all the risk of possible deterioration due to natural causes on the shippers.

In considering this question fairly and on its merits, please bear in mind that we as grain or commission merchants have a merchant's interest only, or a broker's interest, or a commission man's interest only at heart. The only people really affected are the producer and consumer. We in a sense are their guardians during the transactions of buying, selling and shipping. To illustrate, John Smith raised last year forty acres of corn which produced thirty bushels per acre and the entire 1,200 bushels was for sale. But John Smith is lazy. The crop was planted late and weeds throttled it. It did not mature and was, therefore, soft.

Sam Jones also planted forty acres which produced fifty bushels per acre. Sam is industrious. It was planted early, plowed five times, cribbed early and when shelled was plump, clean, dry and fit to keep in store until consumed, if that should be years. On a certain day a wagonload of corn comes both from Mr. Smith's and Mr. Jones' farm. There is a difference of at least ten cents in value per bushel of the two loads. You are that dealer. Do you pay both farmers the same price? Do you keep the two grades separated? Do you ship the two grades separate? Or do you take the chance of mixing as much poor corn as the good will stand, hoping to make a skin grade of No. 3 and taking a long chance at losing both?

Another Point.—Most grade rules state and all imply that a No. 3 grade of corn must be fit for warehousing. If your No. 3 will not retain its grade for twelve days in a car, think you it is fit for warehousing? And again, bear in mind that as grain merchants, purchasing from farmers, that whenever a load of corn is bought it must average at least thirty days, counting delay in elevator, average delay in shipment, etc., before your final risk is done and another three months before the corn is actually consumed. Think you, then, it is business sense, even if strictly fair, to endeavor to ship the skin grade? Or is it not the wiser course to ship the average or top of the grade, paying the farmer respectively the full price for the top and the proper discount for the lower grades?

We, therefore, declare this principle: That the interests of the grain trade demand rules for reinspection, and that in our opinion seller should guarantee a three or better grade for a period of twelve days, after which the buyer should assume all risk and that shippers from country points should buy at such price, and clean in such manner, as will fulfil these requirements.

If the country shipper will remove the mote by shipping a good grade, the city receiver will be glad to remove the beam by his full measure of assistance, in the full respect and obeyance of all trade rules made for shippers' and receivers' mutual benefit.

James W. Sale of Bluffton, Ind., read a paper on "Uniform Bill of Lading."

John W. McCardle introduced the following resolution on "Discounts for Off Grades," which was adopted:

Whereas, It is the practice in some markets for track buyers to apply off grades on sales at what they consider a fair discount; and

Whereas, Said discounts may or may not be as satisfactory to the shipper as when said off grades are submitted to all the buyers in said markets, therefore, be it

Resolved, That the Indiana Grain Dealers' Association requests dealers in the markets where this plan is used to submit to all buyers samples of cars that inspect below the grade sold, thereby giving the shipper the benefit of competition for such cars.

Geo. C. Wood then made the following report for the committee on resolutions

FEDERAL SUPERVISION OF INSPECTION.

We, the majority of your committee, to whom was referred the resolution indorsing the bill introduced in Congress by the Hon. James E. Watson for the federal inspection of grain beg leave to report as follows: In lieu of the provisions in said measure calling for federal inspection we recommend the substitution of provisions calling for uniform grading of all grain and seed under a standard fixed by the bureau of agriculture and under its direct supervision, leaving the different boards of trade of the country free to make their own appointments as to inspectors, grain commissioners, etc. Signed by Geo. C. Wood, J. G. Hazelrigg and A. E. Reynolds.

E. K. Sowash, the minority member of your committee to whom was referred the resolution indorsing the bill introduced in Congress by the Hon. James E. Watson for the federal inspection of grain, recommends the adoption of said resolution.

A very animated discussion took place over the resolution. Both the majority and minority reports had friends, the adherents for each being pretty evenly divided. The most radical supporters of government inspection thought that Uncle Sam would be able to do things about right and that shippers throughout the country were in a frame of mind favoring this action.

Others thought it was too great a step for government to take up the inspection at the present time and that it should come, if it did come, not hastily but gradually. Present methods in Eastern terminal markets were defended, and it was shown that the shippers' interests were safeguarded as well as possible under existing conditions. A motion to adopt the minority report was lost by a vote of 35 to 37, and following this action a motion prevailed that the resolution be referred back to the committee. The committee subsequently brought in a resolution as follows, which was adopted:

Your committee, to whom was recommitted the resolution providing for the endorsement of the Watson bill, beg leave to submit instead of said resolution the following:

Resolved, That we, the members of the Indiana Grain Dealers' Association, in annual convention assembled, do hereby endorse the action of the Uniform Grades Congress, recently assembled in Chicago, and recommend the adoption of this or a similar uniform classification of grains and seeds throughout the United States. Further,

Resolved, That we recommend to the United States Congress the enactment of such laws as will put into effect these classifications of grading, under the supervision and control of the federal government. Further,

Resolved, That we recommend to Congress the consideration of the bill recently introduced by the Hon. James E. Watson of Indiana, and that we hereby tender Mr. Watson our thanks for his kindly interest in our behalf. We further recommend such legislation as will put under federal supervision and control the public weighing, as well as the inspection, of all grain and seeds.

FRIDAY'S SESSIONS.

Friday's sessions were taken up principally with the election of officers, reading of reports and papers and unfinished business. The election of officers resulted as follows: President, T. A. Morrison, Kokomo; vice-president, P. E. Goodrich, Winchester; board of directors, M. C. Burt of Morristown, Robt. Alexander of Lafayette; director of the National Association, A. E. Reynolds, Crawfordsville.

Following the call to order at 11 a. m. by the president, J. V. Zartman, secretary of the Indiana Manufacturers' and Shippers' Association, made a short address, urging the support of dealers in securing further legislation to add to the power of the Railroad Commission.

A motion carried that a committee of three be appointed to confer with the Indiana Shippers' Association on this question.

A committee composed of J. W. McCardle, E. A. Reynolds, C. B. Riley, Jas. W. Sale, P. E. Goodrich, Geo. C. Wood, Cloyd Loughry and T. A. Morrison was appointed to go to Washington, at their own expense, to appear before the agricultural committee in support of the resolution on federal grades and inspection.

An address was made by D. F. Maish, president of the Indiana Corn Growers' Association. Mr. Maish's subject was: "The relation of the corn growers to the grain shippers and how they can best co-operate to conserve each other's interests."

John F. Courcier, secretary of the Grain Dealers' National Association, read a paper on uniform grades, substantially as follows:

UNIFORM GRADES CONGRESS.

It has been with some reluctance that I have prepared a paper on the information compiled during my official connection with the preparation for, and holding of, the Uniform Grade Congress, which was held in the directors' room of the Chicago Board of Trade, December 11, 12, 13. Not reluctant because of any doubt as to the right of every individual grain dealer to the information, but because of the fear that our action in doing so might be construed as a desire merely to exhibit our work, rather than as an endeavor to instruct and prove in my humble way the necessity of concentrating our individual and collective strength and energies upon the completion of a work so well begun.

At the outset I wish most earnestly to assure the individuals and committees who drafted the twenty-five sets of rules from which we drew our conclusions, and upon which we based our comparisons, that whatever references we may make to words and other usages embodied in the phraseology now in vogue will not be made in a spirit of humorous criticism, but, on the contrary, with a profound sense of the important bearing their elimination has upon the final institution of uniformity, and in full appreciation of the difficulties under which they have labored from year to year, endeavoring to conserve the interests of their respective markets and their markets' patrons.

At the time the resolution creating the Uniform Grade Congress was recorded in the minutes of the tenth annual convention of the Grain Dealers' National Association, it would have been hard to find more than a handful of influential grain dealers willing to assume the responsibility of openly advocating and championing uniformity, but when the proof of the necessity for prompt and decisive action was laid before the Congress and when, after adjournment, the splendid results attained became known, it is to the credit of the grain trade that able and consistent champions of uniformity stepped to the front and can now be found throughout the length and breadth of the land.

In preparing what is to follow, I was forced to cut out a great deal of interesting matter, because of the time at my disposal for the work. You will find that I have not gone beyond the grades of Nos. 1, 2, 3 and 4, and that I have not taken up the many indefinite phrases, clauses, transpositions, negative and affirmative uses of quality words, etc., such as abound in plenty.

My list of comparisons consists of 277 sheets 12 inches wide and 36 inches long; 104 for wheat; 59 for corn; 57 for oats; 45 for barley; 10 for rye; 1 for no grade general rule, and 1 for no established grade. In these 277 sheets, we find 336 different names or grade titles; 133 for wheat; 63 for corn; 77 for oats; 53 for barley, 10 for rye and 1 each for no grade general rule and no established grade.

In the phraseology describing these 338 grade titles, we find the following words used in an absolutely indefinite sense: Very, provided, well, inferior, greater, limited, suitable, fair, some, enough, fit, unfit, much, allowed, merchantable, judgment, otherwise, choice, prime, somewhat, moderate, considerable, customary, fairly, slightly, strictly, exceedingly, excessively, badly, practically, warehousable, largely, mainly, thoroughly, principally, occasionally, sufficiently and reasonably—the last but by no means the least in evidence. By actual count, the word "reasonably" occurs 96 times in the stock heading.

[Mr. Courcier then follows with a summary of the variations found in the percentage of color, pounds and words used in describing and defining the various old grades, which we omit for want of space. In addition to giving the words used in defining the old grades, I have recorded the number of words used in the new phraseology, so as to give a better idea of what the Congress has done for the grain trade, provided its recommendations shall be adopted and put into practical operation.]

Total number of old words used in grades just given, 4,691; words used in new grades, 1,532; total number of words eliminated 3,159.

Is it any wonder that the delegates who composed the Uniform Grade Congress, with this evidence before them, saw the wisdom of promptly putting their knowledge and experience into an effort to bring order, simplicity and precision out of chaos, complexity and doubtful meaning?

It would be inconsistent to claim that these rules could not be improved upon, but it is generally conceded that a long stride forward has been taken, and a good, firm foundation laid for ultimate uniformity, in the full meaning of the term.

A question has been raised concerning the possible attitude of some buyers of grain to take an unfair advantage of the difference between the minimum of one grade and the maximum of the next lower, and we have given it as our belief that if the grades promulgated by the Uniform Grade Congress shall prove practical, the range and compass of the standard grades will ultimately be narrowed down and rules provided to take care of the intermediate weights and qualities. Until that can be done, it was agreed by the Congress that local rules might be made to take care of local conditions; but it is to be hoped that no undue advantage will be taken of this prerogative and that no local rules will be made to interfere with the application of the phraseology of the standard grades as recommended by the Congress.

We believe that while certain commercial relations exist between the grades of grain and the range of prices, yet, as a general proposition, the grading of grain and the price that is to be paid for it should be as absolutely separate as oil and water. As I understand it, rules of grade were instituted to describe and define the properties of grain and to establish standards upon which the buyer and the seller might base their offers to buy and sell.

It has been held that the percentage system of grading would require so much time in its execution that congestion would result, thus rendering it impracticable. We give it as our conviction that the number of cars of grain that would have to be submitted to the percentage test would not exceeed the present number of appeals, and we further think that the present number of appeals would lessen in the same proportion as our inspectors and dealers would gain experience in determining percentages.

I would especially recommend that each and every grain dealer carefully study these new grades, and I do not think any form of endeavor could bring better results than for you to teach your farmers to know the meaning of the different grades, and thereby start a movement that would eventually result in your being able to buy their grain on grade. The outcome of such a practice would be, that you would either have the same protection at the hands of the farmer that now is guaranteed to him who buys of you, or, the producers would decline to sell until they could make delivery; both alternatives being designed to relieve you of the responsibility of carrying both ends, as you must now do if you wish to sell against purchasers from producers for future delivery.

The activity and earnestness of the delegates since the adjournment of the Uniform Grade Congress has been a source of special gratification to us. We are also grateful for the friendly attitude of the grain exchanges of the country. As we have stated in communications recently sent from our office, we do not consider this work to be more than half done, and upon each and every individual grain dealer shall the outcome depend.

The attitude of some of the smaller grain exchanges has been to wait to see what some of the larger markets would do. When such cases have come to our notice, we have respectfully urged immediate action. We know that many of the exchanges are prepared to reach conclusions more quickly than others and it seems to us that simple expedience would dictate that it were better for them to act promptly than to run the chance of having their waiting attitude construed as disapproval.

I have no doubt the future will develop strenuous opposition in some quarters (what great reform was ever accomplished without it?) and while we have not outlined any plans for coping with such a condition, it is likely that you will be called upon to use your influence, and when the time comes, if come it must, and we sincerely hope it may not, unanimity of action will be the only means by which we can hope to attain the coveted end.

Above all things we should not affect a spirit of indifference. If we do not feel that the recommendations of the Uniform Grade Congress are what we would have them, it is our plain duty to investigate; to weigh the advisability of laying a foundation before trying to build the house; to clear our minds of all doubt, and then to roll up our sleeves and go to work.

Geo. C. Wood, chairman of the committee on resolutions, made the following report, which was adopted as read:

REPORT OF COMMITTEE ON RESOLUTIONS.

Resolved, That we heartily endorse the recommendation of the president: That we favor and encourage the holding of corn shows for the improvement of seed corn in each county, and we recommend that our members assist to the best of their ability.

Resolved, That we recommend that that part of the president's address which recommends the appointment of a committee to act with the Shippers' Association be adopted and that a committee of three be immediately appointed by the president.

RECIPROCAL DEMURRAGE.

Whereas, The grain shippers of many sections of the country have been compelled to shut up their elevators and suspend business, because of houses being full of grain and the refusal of the railroads to furnish cars needed: and,

Whereas, Grain shippers have been put to unusual expense for insurance and interest on borrowed money and compelled to stand heavy losses by reason of deterioration of grain stored out of doors, and by declining markets, therefore be it.

Resolved, That the Indiana Grain Dealers' Association, in convention assembled at Indianapolis this 17th day of January, 1907, do hereby instruct our secretary to send a copy of these resolutions to the Indiana representatives in both houses of Congress and petition them to give their earnest support to House Bill

No. 28,558 and assist in securing its enactment into law, and that a member of our Association be appointed by the president to act for us with the National Reciprocal Demurrage Association recently organized in Chicago.

GRAIN STANDARDIZATION.

Whereas, The United States Department of Agriculture, Bureau of Plant Industry, through John D. Shanahan, expert in charge, has invited the co-operation of this Association in the work of the project of grain standardization, therefore, be it

Resolved, That we, the Indiana Grain Dealers' Association in convention assembled, accept the invitation, and the officers of the Association are hereby instructed to keep in touch with the work of said project and to assist it in every way consistent with the customs and usages of the grain trade.

REINSPECTION AFTER FORTY-EIGHT HOURS.

Resolved, That it is the sense of the Indiana Grain Dealers, in annual convention assembled, that we protest against any market allowing a reinspection of grain after forty-eight (48) hours unless the car on being unloaded shows plainly that it was plugged with intent to deceive.

TOLEDO MARKET REPORTS.

Whereas, Toledo is the natural market for a large part of our membership; and

Whereas, It is absolutely necessary in using this market that we be fully posted on prices of the various grains prevailing there; and

Whereas, The Associated Press does not, at the present time, quote Toledo market, therefore, be it

Resolved, That we, the Indiana Grain Dealers' Association, in convention assembled, hereby request the Associated Press to make the necessary arrangements and see that the closing Toledo grain market is quoted in all the newspapers in Indiana connected with said Associated Press and a copy of these resolutions sent to the main office of the Associated Press as well as to the Indianapolis papers.

THANKS.

Resolved, That we extend to our president and secretary and in fact to all the officials of this Association our sincere thanks for the faithful discharge of the duties entrusted to their care, and we wish further to congratulate this Association upon the unselfish attitude that has characterized at all times its entire membership.

O. J. Thompson, chairman of the committee on railroad claims, read the following resolution, which was adopted:

REORT. OF RAILROAD CLAIMS COMMITTEE.

Whereas, Experience of elevator owners and grain shippers has demonstrated that in many cases the railroad claim agents have adopted the motto, "Might makes right," and applied it in the non-adjustment of claims coming before them; and

Whereas, We realize that, individually, the collection of these claims by law would be burdensome, therefore, be it

Resolved, That the board of managers of the Indiana Grain Dealers' Association be hereby instructed to make investigation as to the advisability of an arrangement with a competent attorney or firm of attorneys for the collection of any claims that, after consideration by the board of managers or state secretary, may be deemed of sufficient merit to warrant legal action, if necessary; and be it

Resolved, That the board of managers be authorized to enter into such arrangement as may be deemed advisable by a two-thirds vote of the entire board of managers, with this proviso, that no such contract shall in any way implicate or bind the Indiana Grain Dealers' Association in all or any part of any expense involved in such collection of claims.

John D. Shanahan, expert in charge of Grain Standardization Bureau of Plant Industry at Washington, read a paper on grain standardization.

A motion made by Mr. Brafford carried that the Association tender a vote of thanks to Secretary Wilson for sending Mr. Shanahan to address them.

Each of the newly elected officers made short addresses, after which the meeting adjourned.

CONVENTION NOTES.

Baltimore was represented by H. M. Hammond, P. W. Pitt, E. H. Beer, H. S. Carroll, D. Y. Huyett.

The Buffalo market was represented by A. T. Ward, of Townsend & Ward, S. W. Yantis and B. Burns.

E. W. Seeds, of Seeds Grain & Hay Co., and J. W. McCord, of McCord & Kelley, were in attendance from Columbus, Ohio.

There came from Toledo W. W. Cummings, of J. J. Coon Grain Co.; F. W. Jaeger, of J. F. Zahm Co.; Chief Grain Inspector Edward W. Culver.

W. E. Smith, Chicago, representing the Richardson Automatic Grain Scale, interested the dealers in a working model of the scale in a room adjoining the convention hall.

At the opening of Friday's session a wire was read from Fred Mayer, president of the Ohio Grain Dealers' Association. It read: "The Ohio Grain Dealers' Association sends greetings and best

wishes. While you are the youngest, you are making all the others sit up and take notice. Success to Indiana."

A little pamphlet on financial gossip was distributed by Fred W. Kennedy of Shelbyville. The "meat in the cocoanut" was: "To prevent losses by leakage in transit use Kennedy Car Liner."

One of the souvenirs worth taking home was a celluloid ruler, the gift of the Grain Dealers' Fire Insurance Co. of Indianapolis. The watchword was: If you are with us stay with us. If you are not with us, get with us, if you can.

Two popular grain cleaning machinery men renewed acquaintance with old friends, A. C. Garman, representative of Huntley Mfg. Co., Silver Creek, N. Y., and C. M. Hogle, representing the Invincible Grain Cleaner Co. of Silver Creek, N. Y.

Illinois was more neighborly than usual, being represented by H. N. Knight of Monticello, Secretary S. W. Strong of Pontiac, H. L. Baldwin, Decatur; Tom Abrams, Tuscola; J. B. Collins, Garrett; F. D. Vorhis, Neoga; Oscar Jones, Chrisman.

Unusual interest was shown by dealers in inspecting the moisture tests in special apparatus, by John D. Shanahan, expert in charge of Grain Standardization Bureau of Plant Industry of the Department of Agriculture, Washington, D. C. Mr. Shanahan made several tests to accommodate the large number that wished to see them.

The delegation from Cincinnati included A. C. Gale and P. M. Gale, of Gale Bros. Co.; H. W. Brown, of Henry W. Brown & Co.; H. H. Hill, of Southern Grain Co.; W. R. McQuillan, of Queen City Grain Co.; F. E. Fleming, of Ellis & Fleming; D. B. Granger and J. F. Costello, of Union Grain & Hay Co.; Chief Grain Inspector Homer Chisman.

THE CORN CONTEST.

A special feature of the meeting was the corn exhibit and the competition for prizes for the best ears of yellow and white corn. The corn was arranged on tables in the assembly room, and winners in the contest were as follows:

Yellow Corn—First prize, $18.00, to Chester De Veare of Franklin, average $7.5; second prize, $7.00, L. H. Houser of Roanoke, average .88; third prize, $5.00, A. H. Swain of Arlington, average $7.5.

White Corn—First prize, $12.00, Thomas Owens of Franklin, average $7.5; second prize, $5.00, R. Clore of Franklin, average 84.5; third prize, $3.00, Carrie Boonhiser of Franklin, average 84. The judges were Scott Melks of Shelbyville, F. H. Collins of Carmel, members of the Indiana Corn Growers' Association, associated with the Purdue University.

GRAIN CONSPIRACY CASE.

The suit brought at Winnipeg by the Manitoba Grain Growers' Association against J. C. Gage and other members of the Winnipeg Grain Exchange, charging them with conspiracy to control and fix the price of grain, and with other acts in restraint of trade, heard recently by a local police magistrate, has been sent to a higher court. The complaint was based on evidence taken by the Royal Grain Commission.

Hon. T. Mayne Daly, stipendiary magistrate for the city of Winnipeg, who heard the charge, has delivered a careful summing up and finding in the case. Under section 601 of the criminal code, Mr. Daly announced that he did not find the defendants either guilty or innocent of conspiracy to restrain or injure trade and commerce, but referred the case to a higher court for further reference, and admitted them to bail in their own recognizances of $1,000 each and two securities of $500 each.

The magistrate made this decision on account of the high standing in the community of both the informant and the accused, realizing also the important interests each had at stake in the matter, namely, the grain producers of the West on the one side, and the most important grain market in Canada on the other.

MR. GOEMANN RESIGNS.

Mr. Henry L. Goemann, president of the Grain Dealers' National Association, sends us the following communication, under date February 11:

Editor American Elevator and Grain Trade:—
I am in receipt of your telegram of this date.

My reason for resigning the presidency of the Grain Dealers' National Association is that it takes up considerable time, and owing to the increased amount of work required by the Goemann Grain Company, on account of the increased elevator facilities that they have put up within the past six months, I simply must pay more attention to the affairs of my firm, and, therefore, thought it best to resign.

As Mr. Charles England of Baltimore, Md., succeeds me for the balance of the term, being first vice-president—I feel that the Association will be in good hands and will not suffer in any way because of my resignation.

Yours very truly, HENRY L. GOEMANN.
Toledo, Ohio.

CHARLES ENGLAND.

Charles England, who succeeds Mr. Goemann, as both the grain and hay trades of the country know, has been a prominent receiver in Baltimore for

CHARLES ENGLAND.

many years. He has also been a conspicuous member of the Chamber of Commerce, of which he was vice-president in 1903 and president in 1894 and 1895, besides for a number of years at different periods having served on the board of directors and the executive committee of that organization. In 1904 he was elected president of the National Hay Association. Furthermore he has been a director and a member of the executive committees of both the National Hay and the Grain Dealers' National Associations.

As a representative grain man, Mr. England was a member of Baltimore's committee appointed to maintain the railroad differential freight rate, and was one of its most active members. He was also a member of the committee having in charge the movement to prevent any abnormal diversion of grain to the Gulf ports, and his wide acquaintance in the West has been very beneficial to Baltimore, while putting him in touch with Western men who so largely compose the National Association. During the negotiations for the sale of the Western Maryland Railroad, Mr. England was a member of the joint committee of trade bodies which recommended that the city's holdings be sold to interests friendly to George Gould (the Wabash), who were the ultimate purchasers.

The Corn Trade News of Liverpool reports an increase of grain and flour imports to the port of Manchester, in 1906, of $80,000 hundredweight, while a falling off is recorded in both London and Liverpool over the previous year.

COMMUNICATED

[We invite correspondence from everyone in any way interested in the grain trade on all topics connected therewith. We wish to see a general exchange of opinion on all subjects which pertain to the interest of the trade at large, or any branch of it.]

MORE UNIFORM GRADE ACCEPTANCES.

Editor American Elevator and Grain Trade:—
The roll of honor continues to grow. It is my privilege to advise you of the receipt of official notice that the Pittsburg Grain & Flour Exchange has adopted the grades of grain recommended by the Uniform Grade Congress, effective August the first next, without further procedure, provided similar action shall have been taken by three-fourths of the leading markets.

I am just in receipt of some important information concerning the grain inspection situation abroad, which I shall take pleasure in reporting to you within a day or two.

Yours very respectfully,
Toledo.   J. F. COURCIER, Secy.

WILL BUY ON TRACK.

Editor American Elevator and Grain Trade:—
I beg to advise that on and after the first of February I will be a track buyer of hay and country produce and would be pleased to represent any reputable house in soliciting consignments for them on reasonable basis.

The car shortage has everything almost tied up; in fact, I have not had a car this month so far; and have orders for fourteen carloads of Arkansas prairie hay, with facilities for loading a car a day. This shows how the railroads do.

Oats in good condition so far and pastures are green as springtime. Weather warm and fair generally; a mild winter, in fact, for here.

Wishing you a prosperous year, I remain,
Yours very truly,   MIKE McCUING.
Gillett, Ark.

PHILADELPHIA ACCEPTS THE UNIFORM GRADES.

Editor American Elevator and Grain Trade:—
Replying to yours of recent date, I have delayed answering in order to do so more fully.

I am pleased to say that I have heard practically no unfavorable comments on the uniform grain-grading rules adopted at the Uniform Grades Congress. The general opinion of our members appears to be that, if generally adopted, they will be of great benefit to all classes dealing in grain, both at home and abroad.

Our grain committee has unanimously recommended them favorably, and I confidently expect that they will be finally adopted by our Commercial Exchange, at the meeting to be held for the purpose on the 18th inst.

Yours very truly,
Philadelphia.   JAS. L. KING, President.

MORE ABOUT UNIFORM GRADES.

Editor American Elevator and Grain Trade:—
I am just in receipt of an official notice that the Joint State Inspection Board of Minnesota has voted to accept the grades of grain recommended by the Uniform Grades Congress, to be adopted by the next annual meeting of the Board, which, according to the statutes of Minnesota, must be held on or before September 15 next, for the purpose of fixing the grades of grain for the ensuing year.

Because of the importance of the state of Minnesota as a surplus grain state, and the enormous amount of grain inspected by this department, we feel that the delegates of the Uniform Grades Congress may justly congratulate themselves upon this important addition to the roll of honor.

I also take pleasure in informing you that at a meeting on the 25th inst., the board of directors of the Commercial Exchange of Philadelphia adopted the grades of grain recommended by the Uniform Grades Congress, with the reservation that they were not to go into effect until all of the other Atlantic seaboard markets had taken similar action.

Since my last advices the recommendations of the Uniform Grades Congress were endorsed by the Indiana Grain Dealers' Association at their annual meeting, held in Indianapolis on the 17th and 18th inst., also by the New England Grain Dealers' Association at their annual dinner held in Boston on the 25th inst.

We have other very favorable information, but it is not yet in shape to be announced officially.

Yours very sincerely,
J. F. COURCIER, Secretary G. D. N. A.
Toledo.

UNIFORM RULES AT LITTLE ROCK.

Editor American Elevator and Grain Trade:—
In reply to your favor of 4th I desire to say that up to the present time our Board of Trade has taken no action in regard to adopting the uniform grain rules and the rules of the National Hay Association. As state vice-president of the National Hay Association here, I am using my best efforts to get our body together, and feel quite confident of the result, as the rules we have here now are almost same as the rules of the National Hay Association. I would be glad to advise you as soon as any action is taken.

I have recently joined the Grain Dealers' Association and National Hay Association, and expect to join the Chicago Board of Trade at an early date.   Yours truly,
Little Rock, Ark.   A. L. DEIBEL.

CINCINNATI ADOPTS UNIFORM GRADES.

Editor American Elevator and Grain Trade:—
Referring to your favor of recent date to hand, I deferred answering, pending the action of our committee on grain inspection with reference to uniform grades as promulgated by the recent Congress in your city.

It is with great pleasure and gratification that I inform you the committee on grain inspection have unanimously recommended the adoption of the rules for uniform grading, effective July 1, 1907. Our board of directors, as you are no doubt aware, represents many other interests besides the grain business in our Chamber of Commerce, and final action on this subject will not be taken until the first Tuesday in February, when the Board holds its regular meeting. The trade generally here are well pleased with the rules as promulgated by the Congress; the percentage basis is the feature that appeals to them as quite a progressive step in the proper grading of all kinds of grain.

With kind regards I am, believe me,
Very sincerely yours,   F. F. COLLINS.
Cincinnati.

ON THE COLLECTION OF CLAIMS.

Editor American Elevator and Grain Trade:—
It seems that the freight claim agents of the country held a convention last summer, at which they agreed among themselves to make an attempt to reduce each proper claim of grain dealers an insignificant amount, saving, first, a few cents for their companies, and, second, the delay of many weeks or months in the payment of just claims, their demand being to deduct from each proper claim either 1 per cent or ½ of 1 per cent before paying.

It is apparent that while in some cases, where claims are of a doubtful character and loss is not disclosed, as due to accident to car, claim agents might properly make the proposition to divide the claim or to take off a certain percentage which might be mutually acceptable to both shipper and railroad company, yet we refer to claims where, on account of wreck or accident, the loss is known.

For instance, and to make the matter plain, we will give you one illustration only which applies to a number of roads and with each road to a number of cases. A given car which was in transit to us at Indianapolis was in a train which parted on a grade. The two parts of the train came together, and this particular car was damaged and a considerable quantity of the corn in the car was thrown out of the end doors by the force of the contact. The records of the transportation department show that the car was wrecked in this manner and the railroad company so acknowledges it. We secured an affidavit of the loading weight from the shipper and an affidavit of outturn weight in this city, and the difference estimated at contract price at point of shipment amounted to $48.65.

Now the claim agent of this road, while acknowledging all these facts, demands one per cent reduction for possible variation of scales. The amount, of course, is trivial and not worth either the correspondence, or delay in the payment of claim which this demand entails, but, from the standpoint of principle, and although we are making the collection for the shipper, we have declined to reduce the claim one penny, claiming that scales as constructed nowadays are accurate and our claim represents our loss to a penny and must not be abridged nor declined.

We have made the proposition to try one case in court of this nature unless payment is made promptly and have had two claim agents acknowledge that we are right and promise payment in full, but the other claim agents have not done so as yet. We feel that the grain dealers of the country should know of these actions and, for reasons of precedence, should not reduce a claim one penny, under circumstances where the facts are so clearly known and proven.

BASSETT GRAIN CO.
Indianapolis, Ind.

MORE MISERY AT KANSAS CITY.

Commerce Commissioner Clark resumed hearing complaints against the railroads at Kansas City. It appears that the C. G. W. Ry. is giving free storage for 10 days and free handling, and other roads have to come to these terms.

E. O. Moffatt, president of the Moffatt Commission Company, testified that 75 million bushels of grain pass through the Kansas City market each year. This is 75,000 cars. More than 50 per cent of this is transferred through local elevators; 15 per cent is consumed by mills, and the rest is shipped through without handling. This free handling and ten days' free storage gives the Kansas City grain men an advantage over competitive points.

It was shown, also, that the Murray Elevator, operated by the Chicago, Burlington & Quincy Road, and some of the other elevators, handle grain free. Since last October the Atchison, Topeka & Santa Fe has charged for transferring grain at the Argentine Elevator, but has given ten days' free storage.

"A most peculiar condition exists in this whole elevator situation," said Mr. Clark. "They have charges, no two of which are alike. There is such a muddle that the conditions and charges at one elevators cannot be compared with conditions and charges at another."

On the following day, Geo. H. Crosby of the Burlington was under fire, when Commissioner Clark said: "I wish a law might be enacted that would enable us to put all railways out of the elevator business." "We are not in it from choice," replied Mr. Crosby, "and we would welcome a chance to get out." The colloquy then continued:

"This hearing has revealed a hopeless muddle of conditions existing in the grain traffic," said the Commissioner. "A decision of the Interstate Commerce Commission [in the allowances case] is responsible for the present conditions," said Crosby.

The reply further irritated Commissioner Clark, who said: "Explain to me or anyone who is neither a shipper nor a carrier, how the railways and the Kansas City Board of Trade can levy a tribute upon every bushel of grain that enters the city." He referred to the rule of the Board of Trade that all grain received here shall be weighed at an elevator. "The railways are not responsible for that condition," said Crosby. "No, but you help and are a party to the scheme." "It is forced upon us," said Crosby.

Counsel for the Atchison grain men are protesting against railway discrimination in the matter of elevator charges. Mr. Crosby said: "Other railways, that do not enter Atchison or compete for business there, have forced us to meet conditions here. They furnish free elevator service in Kansas City, and if the Burlington expects to get its share of the business it must meet the competition."

It developed that the railways at Kansas City undertake to pay all charges the elevator companies designate under the traffic rule, "transfer of grain from car to car, and to ascertain weight." It was shown that this rule is elastic. It may enable the railways to give facilities there which might be denied at other points. Inasmuch as the railways really own or control the elevator companies that handle the grain, these charges, Mr. Crosby said, really amount to nothing.

POPULARITY OF HUMPHREY'S EMPLOYE'S ELEVATOR.

Although the Humphrey Employe's Elevator, illustrated herewith, has been familiar for many years to grain men and millers, it may surprise

HUMPHREY EMPLOYE'S ELEVATOR.

some to know into what general use this labor-saving device has come during the past fifteen years. A circular which we have just received from S. K. Humphrey, 640 Exchange Building, Boston, shows the present distribution of the elevator, by states; a good proportion of them are in grain elevators, and the others are in flour mills.

Twenty-eight states are represented on the list. Minnesota leads with thirty-five elevators, thirteen of which are in Minneapolis. Kansas, Iowa and Missouri are even for second place, with an aggregate of forty-two elevators; in short, wherever the grain and milling business thrives this elevator is found in like proportion, from Canada to South Africa, South America and China.

Mr. Humphrey is making a special effort this year with terminal grain elevators. His list certainly shows a good start with the grain men, and there is no reason why it should not be as generally adopted in grain elevators as in flour mills.

[For the "American Elevator and Grain Trade."]

CAR SHORTAGE—NO RELIEF IN SIGHT.

BY HARRY W. KRESS.

While this subject is getting to be a chestnut and farce from a humorous standpoint, we should stop and ponder over the situation in order that we may discover a means for bettering conditions. The country elevators, with very few exceptions, are all crying for cars in vain. There are hundreds of elevators closed down to-day, and as a consequence are losing thousands of dollars. The seriousness of this condition is far-reaching in its effects. I was speaking to one of the largest shippers in the state over the 'phone last night, and he informed me that he had to stop the farmers hauling, for the first time since they have been in business, having over 70,000 bushels of grain in one house alone, which is a large storage capacity for any country elevator. This party took a train for Columbus, Ohio, to-day, to meet the head officials of his road, and he is going to have the satisfaction of giving them a piece of his mind if nothing more.

Now, this shipper happened to be located near two good-sized towns; and, as his neighboring towns receive merchandise, etc., they have a better chance to obtain cars, and as a consequence we have the following conditions: This shipper's trade is the backbone of his prosperity, and when he sees his farmers hauling past his door to these neighboring towns, one can readily imagine his thoughts. Help must be paid, and besides that the tax assessor will give him a dose, long to be remembered, for all the grain he is forced to carry. (It's a case of where it's all going out and nothing coming in.)

The car shortage question presents a serious aspect in its present form; and with all this grain still to be hauled to the markets, and with no immediate relief in sight, but instead the coming of another new crop five months hence, it behooves us to sit up and take notice. The railroads have handed us a dose of medicine, the effects of which cannot be counteracted, with no prospect of a cure in sight. Their promises have proven so utterly false, as to the fulfillment of the same, that shippers are fast becoming discouraged. As a consequence, a little germ known as public sentiment is spreading rapidly among our shippers. This sentiment is beginning to wonder how conditions could be any worse with Government control or ownership of railroads. And while this would be trampling down our American pride and liberty, which every American citizen prizes, we must remember that it would be to benefit the masses instead of the few, if such changes were brought about.

There are not any of us but dislike the idea of a guardian appointed over us, but, then, when necessity demands it, we should put our pride out of the question. It is beginning to look now as though our state associations will have to take up the car question before many days, and make a hard fight through our National Association, demanding relief.

UNIFORM GRADING.

Since the January issue of this paper, the Philadelphia Commercial Exchange has voted to adopt the uniform grades recommended by the Uniform Grades Congress and will put the same into effect as soon as other Atlantic seaports do the same.

Cincinnati, also, through the Chamber of Commerce, has accepted the recommendation of the board of directors of that body to adopt the uniform grades, and will make them effective on July 1, 1907. This opens uniformity to the Southeast and the Carolinas.

H. F. PROBST.

No one is quite so welcome to any collective body of men as the man who carries his good nature about with him as an asset to be drawn at all times and under all circumstances, by checks payable to bearer. Most of us take life too seriously. It is the part of the good-natured man to show us how to get the fun also as we go along.

The Kansas grain dealers have troubles of their own; and the more welcome then to their late convention at Wichita was H. F. Probst of Arkansas City, who brought his wit with him and enlivened a really serious protest at the continued existence of the bucket-shop by a genial sarcasm that was more telling than any philippic.

Mr. Probst was born in Berlin, Germany, in 1860. During the war of '70 and '71, known as the Franco-Prussian War, his parents lost what little property they had and then emigrated to North America in 1872. They landed poor enough

H. F. PROBST.

in a financial sense, but not otherwise; and it was a question of work. The son of the family, being a stout boy, went to work in Newark, N. J., at twelve years of age. He lived until he was eighteen years old in Newark, N. J., where he mastered the white leather tanner's trade, and then like most German journeymen artisans he drifted from one large town to another for two and a half years, landing finally in southern Kansas, where he farmed for twelve years, proving up on a piece of land. He married Sallie B. Sassmen of Kokomo, Ind., in 1886; and in 1893 went into the coal, feed and grain business in Bluff City, Kan., which business he still continues. In 1900 he entered the New Era Milling Company by buying $13,200 of the company's stock, but after eighteen months of non-success in this line, he stepped out of the company and embarked in the grain business, with headquarters at Arkansas City, Kan., in which line he is making a name for himself.

Mr. Probst's paper on the escape of the bucket-shop and his banquet speech on "Babylon Compared with Wichita" were the "hits" of the meeting; and at the future meetings when Mr. Probst fails to show up business will be suspended until a deputation brings him in.

There are more than 223,000 farmers' leagues in Italy. In Servia there are 508, with a total of 17,858 members.

[For the "American Elevator and Grain Trade."]

ANNUAL MEETING OF THE KANSAS GRAIN DEALERS' ASSOCIATION.

About 200 delegates were in attendance at the ninth annual convention of the Kansas Grain Dealers' Association at Wichita on January 22 and 23. The program was carried out practically as previously announced, except that the address of John D. Shanahan, set for Tuesday afternoon, was postponed until the next morning, and the address of C. A. Smith, set for Wednesday morning, was heard Wednesday afternoon. Senator Noftzger was unable to be present and his address was read by Secretary Smiley.

On Wednesday night, January 23, the visiting delegates were entertained at a banquet held in the Carey Hotel dining-room by the members of the Wichita Board of Trade. Plates were laid for 160 people.

Besides the banquet, there was an informal toast program.

TUESDAY MORNING, JANUARY 22.

The meeting was called to order by President L. Cortelyou at 9:30, and after the usual formality he continued with his annual address, as follows:

Gentlemen, the time has come to call the ninth annual meeting of the Kansas Grain Dealers' Association to order. In fact, it is past time, but it is a hard matter to get a meeting of this kind called to order on time.

It is an honor as well as a great pleasure to call this meeting to order as the president of your Association. We were honored at the last meeting in Kansas City, which was held last January, by the mayor and the clerk of this city inviting the Kansas Grain Dealers' Association to hold its next annual meeting in Wichita. This invitation was extended so cordially that the board of directors decided it best to call this annual meeting in Wichita.

It seems proper, and it really is proper, that an association of the state of Kansas should meet in a city in Kansas instead of in Missouri; and in the state of Kansas, where is there a more appropriate city than this, your city of Wichita, a live, energetic place with its young Board of Trade—a city proud of its enterprises, and justly entitled to the distinction of the name "The Peerless Princess of the Plains?" It is a great pleasure to meet the members of the Association here year by year, and I am very glad to extend a very hearty greeting to them.

We realize that a great many of the trade evils have been eradicated and are a thing of the past; yet there are very grave questions coming up before the Association year by year, and as the influence of our Association broadens we meet these broader questions which are before us and which will be discussed, I hope, fully by this meeeting.

We have gotten up a program which I think you will all find interesting. The subjects to be discussed will be treated in a thorough manner and will, I hope, meet with discussion afterwards. The subjects to which we are obliged to give our attention are very important to us as grain dealers; and I hope the members will all take an interest in them and give their views and discuss the subjects thoroughly.

The most important subject is car shortage. We know this is very important, as we feel it especially in our pocket. We feel that we are unjustly treated by this car shortage, and as grain dealers we realize that the returns of our business are very seriously hampered by that condition. I assume you have all read in the papers lately of the two great railroad kings, Hill and Harriman, both of whom say, or, at least, are reported to have said, that it will take one hundred million dollars a year for the next five years to put the railroads in a position to handle the traffic of the country; to get increased trackage, motive power and equipment to take care of the immense increase of business that has resulted from the great wave of prosperity that has swept over the United States. This sounds like a very large expenditure but it may very well be true. It is a question of legislation which faces our Association and which the grain dealers of Kansas, at least, are interested in. Part of the legislature at least is doubtful on this question of a demurrage law, which comes up in various forms; and it is questionable whether anything can be done. I think the Association should pass some resolutions, as it seems only fair that if the railroads may charge a shipper for delaying a car for twenty-four or forty-eight hours, the shipper should have just as much right to demand that it shall pay a like amount to him; and it would be a very great boon to the shipper if some such resolutions should be passed.

We have come to a time again when it seems necessary to the membership and the board of directors that we should amend our Constitution and By-Laws. As our Association has grown it has been necessary to change a document that seemed originally to be sufficient; and we would recommend that a committee be appointed for that purpose.

We also would recommend a resolution to provide a different method of electing the board of directors. Our present board was elected promiscuously, each person voting for three directors, the three having the highest number of votes being declared elected. This has resulted in putting the whole membership of the board of directors in the northeastern part of the state. The board of directors by resolutions did what they could to rectify this matter and added a fourth director, electing W. A. Miller of Anthony, Kan., as our fourth director; and I would recommend that a resolution be introduced to change the manner of electing the board of directors so that one director be chosen from each part of the state—from the northeast, the southeast, the southwest and the northwest, so that each part of the state will be represented on the board.

Our relations to the railroads, gentlemen, are, of course, very close, as we are more or less dependent on the railroads. We are aware of that; but it seems to me the railroad people of the United States, and of Kansas especially, should give more interest to the questions which are of such vital interest to shippers, and thereby avoid what may prove to be very drastic legislation. Of course, we know that railroads dominate the houses of Congress, the Senate especially. This brings up a question of politics in which I don't like to involve our Association, yet I feel that the Association should take cognizance of this matter, and it looks to me that we ought to go on record in some way to express ourselves as wishing that the Senate be elected by a direct vote of the people.

The meeting will be in your hands, gentlemen, and it will be up to you to make it interesting. I hope that you will discuss the questions that are up before you. It is usual that in a meeting of this kind that the affirmative will vote and no one seems to have the courage to vote in the negative. I hope everyone will express his opinion freely, and each one express fully by voting according to his conscience. Gentlemen, I thank you.

The minutes of previous meetings having been

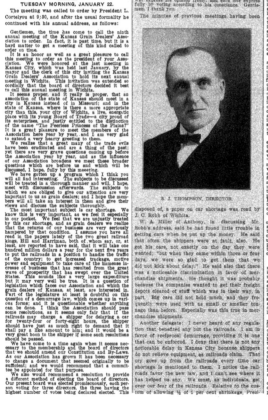

S. J. THOMPSON, DIRECTOR.

disposed of, a paper on car shortage was read by J. C. Robb of Wichita.

W. A. Miller of Anthony, in discussing Mr. Robb's address, said he had found little trouble in getting cars when he put up the money. He said that often the shippers were at fault, also. He got his cars, not exactly on the day they were wanted; "but when they came within three or four days, we were so glad to get them that we did not kick about delay." He said also that there was a noticeable discrimination in favor of merchandise shipments. He thought it was probably because the companies wanted to get their freight depots cleared of stuff which was in their way, in part. Big cars did not hold much, and they frequently were used with as small or smaller tonnage than before. Especially was this true in merchandise shipments.

Another delegate: I never heard of any regulation that benefited any but the railroads. I am in favor of reciprocal demurrage, providing it is one that can be enforced. I deny that there is not any noticeable delay in Kansas City because shippers do not relieve equipment, as railroads claim. That cry goes up from the railroads every time car shortage is mentioned to them. I notice the railroads favor the new law, and I can't see where it has helped us any. We must, as individuals, get over our fear of the railroads. Relative to the custom of allowing ½ of 1 per cent shrinkage, President Cortelyou said, in answer to a question, that it was an arbitrary ruling by the railroads, not necessarily a legal one.

A delegate from Kansas City said he never had allowed it—he stood out for his rights and got them.

Weighmaster Goodwin of Kansas City had found that there is an average shrinkage of about ¼ of 1 per cent in reality. Their shipments to Minneapolis showed a shrinkage amounting to 1-16 of 1 per cent. The railroads claim ½ of 1 per cent. Out of 500 cars received in Kansas City within a given time, 341 were or had been leaking.

C. S. Wilson of Ottawa read the following paper on collecting claims:

PROPER METHODS FOR THE COLLECTION OF CLAIMS.

This subject is given space in almost every issue of the various grain journals. There is very little left to be said in regard to it. I will first read you a circular issued by one of the railroads relative to this matter:

"To All Concerned:—A claim for loss of or damage to freight proceeds upon the proposition that property received for transportation in good order reaches destination in bad order or fails to arrive in whole or in part. To accomplish the prompt adjustment of any such valid claim there are required: (1) The bill of lading, because, among other reasons, it gives evidence of the apparent quantity and condition of the goods, the terms of the contract of transportation, and the interest of the claimant in the transaction; (2) the expense bill, if issued, because among other reasons, it likewise is evidence of the interest of the claimant and gives billing reference; (3) the original invoice, or a properly attested copy, to establish the amount claimed, or if there is no invoice, then reasonable evidence to support the account.

"A claim for overcharge, which is based upon the assumption that too much has been assessed for transportation, should always be supported by (1) the original expense bill, or by the prepaid bill of lading, if transportation charges have been prepaid, these furnishing evidence of the amount collected; (2) copies of invoices or other substantial evidence if the matter is one of weight; (3) reference to tariff numbers or other authority upon which the claim for overcharge is based. A bill of lading, while frequently of less importance in an overcharge than in a claim for loss or damage, is often necessary, as setting forth the condition upon which the claim rate applies. It is always of importance on any claim as an evidence of interest of the claimant in a transaction. Every claim should have attached a bill setting forth clearly the name of the claimant, with a definite statement of the account.

"Judging from the frequent absence of supporting evidence, the opinion seems to prevail that any of these documents may be waived at pleasure. For example, requests for bills of lading are usually met with the declaration 'never received the bill of lading,' 'the shipper has the bill of lading,' 'will sign an agreement in place of the bill of lading,' and the like. To waive this instrument may mean that although the agent at Kansas City, for instance, has already certified on the bill of lading to the apparent condition and quantity of property to be transported, the claim must be sent to that agency for another certificate to take the place of the one already issued. This multiplied many times over at St. Louis, Memphis, Little Rock and Wichita or other shipping centers, means that claims are delayed, local offices crowded with correspondence, much of which should be avoided, and other important work is retarded.

"Agents and others interested are requested to co-operate so that claims reaching this office will be suitably supported and the time and labor needed for their adjustment minimized. It is seldom that a claimant who 'never received a bill of lading' will be unable to produce this document or any other needed proof, if reasonable effort is made, and it is seldom that an agent will fail to get it if he states to the claimant the reason for its requirement.

"Signed, etc. ————————"

This circular of course covers claims for all commodities as freight and should be strictly followed in preparing claims, except for claims covering shipments of grain and grain products. These commodities are always billed "shippers' order," and generally the expense bill is used for reconsignment or transit privilege. These two most important documents are in the railroads' possession at the time the claim is presented and cannot be furnished, which is unnecessary, as the railroads have a form when properly filled out and signed by claimant releases them from further liability after claim is settled.

It is important that you have a just claim, supported by all necessary documents, bearing on the loss in weight or damage. We advise keeping a copy of all the papers relative to the claim, for sometimes in their haste to make settlement, claim departments have been known to lose all the correspondence relative to the claim, and your duplicates will be appreciated by the railroad. File these duplicates with card received from the claim department acknowledging receipt of your claim, giving same a certain number. In the course of a few months, generally in about a year's time, you will receive the claim back from the claim department with a letter attached, about as follows:

"After prompt and careful investigation of your claim, which shows no loss or damage while in our care, same is respectfully declined. Kindly return all papers for record."

Now, don't drop the matter here, but look over carefully all the correspondence covering investigation of the claim. You will find some place where the seal record is not clear, or at some division point the car was reported lacking. Tell them you know their clerical force is the best and receive large salaries, nevertheless they have overlooked the above facts, and if, upon further investigation they do not care to adjust the loss, to return all papers to you, and you will try in another way to obtain settlement.

We had a similar case—shipment of corn for export, about 150 bushels short at destination. Investigation by the railroad showed statement made by agent at a division point that car was received in bad order—one end busted out, leaking badly, and shipment transferred to another car. The claim department had the nerve to attach a letter to this correspondence, respectfully declining payment upon the grounds that loss did not occur while in their possession. We respectfully called their attention to the statement made by the agent at the division, and the fact that the car was in bad order or it would not have been transferred. They promptly made settlement, less one-half of one per cent "natural shrinkage." (We cannot figure out where they got any natural shrinkage in this case. This natural shrinkage, ½ of 1 per cent, is too much, and shippers should not stand for it. A shortage is a shortage, and we should be paid for our losses. There are many cases where shortage amounts to from $2 to $4 per car, but after deducting ½ of 1 per cent natural shrinkage from net weight, it leaves too small an amount to bother making a claim.) Make out your claim for actual loss with all the evidence you possibly can obtain supporting it. Then stand pat on the amount first claimed until you get a settlement. A follow-up or tracer system we would recommend. Make it a point every so often to write to the claim department to know what has become of a certain claim. This will keep your claim moving and hurry settlement.

We have collected all our claims so far except several presented for loss caused by delay in transit. The railroads claim they give the shipments the best attention that circumstances admit and that they do not agree to deliver in time for any particular market. We understand the law allows a penalty of $5 per day during time shipment is in transit after allowing fifty miles per day, the statutory time, in which to transport and deliver shipments at destination. There is now a case against the Rock Island in the courts at Topeka in which $300 is involved. If this case is decided in favor of claimant, we will dig up our claims of like nature and try again.

It would greatly help the adjusting of claims if all shippers would bill out their grain at actual weight, and if there is any shortage at destination, the receiver would insist upon the railroad's making notation on the expense bill of amount short before receipting for the shipment. This would give the railroad a record of the shortage—something to work on when claim was presented. Would suggest that shippers keep a seal record of all cars loaded. Better still, a private seal of your own, as cars are sometimes pilfered before leaving your own station.

Claim bureaus have been established by several grain dealers' associations with a view to help the dealers collect amounts due them.

Mr. Wilson was followed by H. F. Probst of Arkansas City, Kan., with a paper on bucket shop methods, as follows:

PERSONAL OBSERVATIONS OF THE SINCE DEFUNCT A. C. BUCKET SHOP.

If the gentlemen will look upon the program, they will find it reads, "H. F. Probst, address." I think there ought to be a question mark at the right side of that line; then I could answer in my manly voice, "Arkansas City, Kan." But this would not satisfy my friends. I call many "my friends" because I am so easy. But in this case I would say that we are both easy, because you have given me the two hemispheres from which to choose my subjects, and, therefore, it ought not to be hard to find a subject. Yet, when a person has so much latitude, he talks on things close to home. Therefore I will talk on the great discovery I made at Arkansas City some time ago; and it is fortunate that we hold the meeting behind bolted doors and barred windows, so that the four winds will not spread it broadcast with a toot.

The members of this Association from Arkansas City will bear me out in the following statement as regards the absent-mindedness of the late lamented grain, stock and pork broker, Neoman, from everywhere, but when last heard from he was "from" Arkansas City.

When I stepped out of the New Era Milling Company, which is famous for its "Polar Bear," I was induced by said Neoman to share the office in which he "kept his futures," as he told me to add dignity to his "board of trade." As he promised me free rent, use of his private wire and other privileges, I thought it a fair exchange, so I moved in with my dignity. I found him a pleasant, absent-minded fellow, often talking in a strange tongue; yet he was considered by all the investors who came to avail themselves of the bargains he had in futures at ruinous prices as a thorough and revised encyclopedia on anything from the tariff on straw to the altitude of the market ten days hence. Yet when he went to the postoffice he would probably mail his pocketbook and carefully bring his letters back to his office because he worried so much about his customers not wanting to get "right."

One day he received a 'phone message from Oklahoma to buy 500 barrels of pork. This customer is still alive, therefore I will call him Stephenson, though that was not his name. Neoman, in his dreamy way, 'phoned his customer that he was in at $18 per barrel, because the last quotation was $12.45. This deal was very flourishing to the board of trade. Stephenson sent $750 margin. Neoman credited Stephenson with 500 barrels of pork of his own make, thinking that Stephenson, being a grain dealer, the pork business was new to him, and he would not care so much for the brand as the quality, and both were happy. Yet as the days went by to make up the irredeemable past, pork climbed toward the $20 mark, and Stephenson signaled Neoman over the 'phone to sell his swine product and he would be over the next day for the money. Neoman told him that this was not proper, as the market would go higher, and he did not see why a good customer wanted to close his deal on an advancing market, but, of course, if he insisted upon going against the better judgment of an experienced commission broker and ruin himself, all right. Stephenson said he had recently embarked in the ruining business, and needed the cash to close up the deal. So Neoman said: "All right, but you will regret it."

Neoman went and took the pork Stephenson had to his credit and tried to dispose of it; but to his horror he found by opening the first imaginary barrel that it only contained a very robust squeal from the pork, which packers have so long tried to turn into money, having made this ludicrous mistake when be filled the order. This threw Neoman into his half-comatose, brown study, from which he did not awaken until several days after. During this dreamy state he arose from his bed during the night, dressed himself, took the Santa Fe to Chicago, and the next day drifted across the lake into Canada. He must have been in the same dreamy way when he put his wife on the train, for when he came to in Montreal he found that he had made a most egregious mistake and had taken somebody else's wife and had left his own at home with two children.

Stephenson, the next day, came through the sultry morning with his sack and his banker for the money, but when I broke the news to him and showed them the state of affairs and their property, they turned loose some of the biggest squeals that split the air asunder, smashed all the buckets in the bucket-shop, but leaving enough of the squeals to go round to Neoman's other and various customers—which came handy during the chaotic state of affairs. I could not help them, as I had a strange yearning for home, myself. When all had cleared out I found myself heir apparent to all of the board of trade and fixtures, consisting of a long-legged stool, two earthen cuspidors, some chalk, that part of the private wire that projected through the wall of the office and a bill for unpaid rent, which I repudiated.

Parties who have met Neoman lately assert that his absent-mindedness has increased since he left, as the mere sudden mentioning of his name gives him a nervous shock.

The president then appointed the following committees:

On resolutions—W. A. Miller, Anthony, chairman; A. Aiken, St. John; P. M. Kelly, Hiawatha.

On Trade Rules—W. S. Washer, Atchison, chairman; H. Work, Ellsworth; F. B. Bonebrake, Osage City.

On Constitution and By Laws—R. E. Cox, Elsmore, chairman; C. B. Guant, Wichita; I. J. Thompson, Holton.

On Arbitration—A. H. Bennett, Wichita and Topeka; Perry N. Allen, Coffeyville; L. Noel, Glasgow.

Adjourned.

AFTERNOON SESSION.

After the announcement of an invitation to a banquet given by the Wichita Board of Trade, the secretary read his annual report as follows:

SECRETARY'S REPORT.

Gentlemen and Members of the Kansas Grain Dealers' Association:—In submitting my ninth annual report I have endeavored to make same as brief as possible, not wishing to tire you with a long report.

The past year has been a prosperous one for the Association, it having increased in membership from 240 to 290 members, making a net gain in membership of fifty for the year, and representing 380 country elevators in the state. When you take into consideration the fact that none of the line elevator companies, members of the Kansas City Board of Trade, are included in this list, nor the large milling concerns operating lines of elevators, you will admit that this is a creditable showing. We have found by experience that in order to interest an elevator owner in association work it is necessary to call on him at his place of business and fully explain to him the objects of the Association, the work accomplished by it and the benefits to be derived by becoming a member. I spent the greater portion of my time during the months of August, September, October and November traveling through the state, with the result that we have a net gain in membership of fifty.

Inspection and Weighing.—At the last annual meeting, held in Kansas City in last January, the president was instructed to appoint a committee of three to confer with a like committee from the Kansas City Board of Trade, they to confer with the railroad officials with a view of bringing about needed reform regarding delayed switching and inspection after first inspection was made on arrival of grain. This committee will make a report, but in addition to their report I wish to state that out of 1,065 cars of grain handled during the month of November in Kansas City, only eleven were delivered on the same day they arrived. It took from one to thirty-nine days to switch the cars to the proper tracks to which they were ordered. You can see from this statement that there is no improvement in the situation at Kansas City, notwithstanding the fact the railroad companies claim to have increased elevator and track facilities.

Association Emblem.—The president was also instructed to appoint a committee to decide upon and obtain a suitable emblem, and the secretary was instructed to advise members of the emblem chosen and urge use of same. An emblem was decided upon and each member advised of the cost, but only a part of the members are to-day using them. If you were aware of the number of letters received at our office annually, asking if so-and-so are members of the Kansas Grain Dealers' Association, you would recognize the importance of the use of such an emblem.

Arbitration.—Arbitration is to-day recognized by all trade organizations as the best, cheapest and most suitable method of settling differences that arise between their members. I am sure that a number of our members do not take advantage of their rights under our arbitration rules. To illustrate: "A" advised me some weeks ago that the business he had had with "B" had not proven satisfactory, and insisted that "B" be ruled out of the Association for refusing to make good to him, under the terms of the contract on which the shipment was made. "B" contended that he was not at fault in the matter and was perfectly willing to submit the controversy to arbitration, but "A" refused, assigning as his only reason that he did not consider "B" on the square and wanted nothing further to do with him. Now, had "A" submitted the difference to three disinterested grain men, he would either have been convinced that he was at fault and that "B" was only standing for his rights, or received what was due him as claimed. Certainly an arbitration committee, composed of three or more men engaged in the same line of business, is better qualified to render a fair and equitable award than an average jury of twelve men, where it is the exception that they have any practical knowledge of the business. Under our present arbitration rules, either plaintiff or defendant has the right of appeal from the decision of the arbitration board to the arbitration committee of the Grain Dealers' National Association. As we are no longer affiliated with the Grain Dealers' National Association, and as comparatively little business is done with Eastern dealers, I would recommend that this Association elect one man from its membership as part of an appeal committee, provided the Texas and Oklahoma associations will do the same, forming an appeal committee, to whom any member of either of the three associations can appeal from the decision of the state committees, the decision of the tri-state committee to be final. The interests of the dealers in the three states are identically the same, and there is a constant interchange of business between the dealers in the three states.

Scale Inspection.—At the last annual meeting a motion prevailed that the matter of securing a scale inspector be left with the board of directors, with power to act for the Association. The board of directors instructed your secretary to correspond with scale manufactures and others, with a view of ascertaining the cost of such service to our members, and make a report to the Official Board. Two propositions were submitted: First—The employment of a man and to own our weights for testing scales, with the necessary tools for repairing and adjusting scales found out of order. We found that the cost of such weights and tools would be about $150, and to secure the services of a first-class scale inspector we would have to pay at least $100 per month and expenses and furnish him employment for the entire year. The second proposition was that the scale company would furnish the weights and tools necessary for the testing and repairing of scales and charge 40 cents per hour for the services of a mechanic for the time he was out. In addition to this expense would be the transportation of weights from one station to another, which in many instances would be by express, or the man would be tied up for an entire day at some station waiting for a local freight train.

I submitted my report to the Board of Directors, and they were unanimous in the opinion that the Association could not make any contract obligating the Association, unless we had the assurance that the members were willing to bear their proportion of the expense for the service performed. I then addressed a personal letter to every grain dealer located on the Union Pacific Railway in the state, advising the approximate cost of such service. Of 64 replies, 25 stated that their scales were giving satisfaction, and they did not care to go to any expense in having them tested. Ten stated that if the expense did not exceed $2 per scale, they wanted their scales tested, and 29 were willing to pay whatever the cost might be.

We naturally concluded from these replies that the majority of the grain dealers were satisfied with the weights taken from their scales. There is no doubt that more interest should be taken in the matter of keeping country scales in good condition, as it has been the source of endless loss to the purchaser. The only question being how to secure the services at a reasonable cost, it has been suggested that the state legislature create a scale department for the purpose of inspecting all public and private scales used in the state, when requested to do so by the owners, and when such inspection was made, caused to be placed in a conspicuous place card or plate, showing date of inspection, etc. The idea seems a practical one, from the fact that the state has an oil inspector, grain inspector, live stock inspector and numerous other inspectors, and if such an office was created it would furnish a few more appointments for hungry office-seekers. It would be necessary, however, that applicants for the position pass an examination and demonstrate their fitness to hold same.

Another plan would be for a group of grain dealers to purchase test weights, and at least once a year employ a scale expert to go over their scales, the expense to be prorated among the dealers in certain counties.

By adopting this plan you would avoid the expense of transportation of weights to and from Kansas City. This question is of such importance that I trust some plan will be worked out at this convention whereby all scales in the state may be tested at least once a year.

Private Seals and Seal Record.—Comparatively few of the grain dealers pay any attention to the sealing of loaded cars before leaving their stations, and few, indeed, keep a seal record. The chief weighmaster of the Kansas City Board of Trade advised me on January 1 that over 8,000 cars loaded with grain arrived in Kansas City during the past year without seals on end or side doors. During the month of December, out of a total of 3,671 cars of grain unloaded in St. Louis. 833 had no seals on side doors and 286 with end doors not sealed. Is it not possible that this accounts for many excessive shortages? If you had your own seals you would know positively that your cars were sealed before leaving your stations. Keep a record of your seals and also show your seal record on your invoice. If you can establish the fact that all of your cars are sealed before leaving point of origin, and the car or cars reach destination minus seals and you sustain a loss, you can then recover for any loss sustained.

A bill will be introduced at the present session of the legislature, making it the duty of the chief grain inspector to keep seal record and show on the inspection certificate the seal number or letter. We do not expect any opposition to this measure. These seals are inexpensive and no sealing irons are required. About 100 shippers in the state are now using them.

Association Officers.—Article 3, Section I, of our present Constitution, provides that the "officers of this Association shall consist of a president, vice-president, secretary-treasurer and a board of directors, consisting of the president, secretary-treasurer and three members of the Association." As our membership has increased since this Constitution was adopted, I would recommend that in addition to the president, vice-president, secretary-treasurer, four members be added, and that the state be divided into four districts, taking the sixth principal meridian as the dividing line north and south, and the third standard parallel as the east and west line, and that one man from each district be elected at each annual meeting to represent his district as a director. This change, if made, will avoid having all of the officers located in one part of the state.

Crop Report.—The past year your secretary issued two reports, the first in April, showing condition of growing crop and the amount of grain remaining in first hands and elevators; the second was issued October 2, showing the average yield per acre, per cent threshed, per cent damaged and per cent marketed. If members would be more prompt in filling out the blanks mailed them we could make the report of greater value to them. As grain dealers come in daily contact with farmers, the information they secure is certainly more reliable than information received from any other source. We must have your support in gathering the information on which the reports are based. Any suggestions from members as to how to improve this service will be appreciated.

Inspection.—I have little to say on this subject, but have this recommendation to make: Under the present inspection rules a certificate of inspection issued in Wichita, Wellington, Salina or any city in Kansas where an inspector is located, is not recognized by buyers at Topeka, Atchison, Leavenworth or Kansas City. To illustrate: A lot of wheat originates at some point west of Wichita, and on its arrival in Wichita grades No. 2, and the inspection fee of 40 cents per car is paid. It is sold to a mill in Topeka, and on its arrival a state inspector makes the grade No. 3, making another 40 cents charge. The seller refuses to accept this inspection and orders the car on to Kansas City, where final inspection is made and another 40-cent charge is tacked on, making the cost of inspection on a single car $1.20. Why not make the first inspection good at Topeka, Atchison, Leavenworth and Kansas City, unless the purchaser calls for reinspection, and, if he does and the original inspection is sustained, make the buyer pay for reinspection? Why make the seller pay for three or four inspections simply because one inspector made an error in inspection or was incompetent? Only a few days ago I brought this matter to the attention of one of the Kansas Grain Commission, a member of the legislature, and he agreed with me as stated. As the present inspection laws will be amended at the present session of the legislature, I would recommend the appointment of a committee to take the matter before the House and Senate, if necessary.

The Car Shortage—What's the Remedy?—There is little doubt that the car shortage has been the worst handicap shippers have had to contend with the past season. When cars get so scarce that a station agent in Western Kansas forgot what they are for, or even what they looked like, and telegraphed the division superintendent that there was a great big red box with iron wheels on his sidetrack, and he did not know what to do with it, one is safe to say that road needed additional equipment. The cause is variously attributed to unprecedented general business growth, lack of equipment, want of motive power, incompetent service, favoritism or discrimination, congestion at terminal markets and a hundred other things. One railroad man says it is the fault of the Wichita dealers, which is another indication of the vast importance of Wichita as a grain center. No doubt these causes differ. With one road it may be lack of cars; with another lack of motive power; with another this, and another that—all of which, taken together, has brought about this decidedly injurious result. But the remedy is what most interests the shipper. What can be done to remedy the situation? There are several answers. If we may believe the railroad officials, if it is because of the business growth all over the country, then every railroad needs thousands of more cars; if it is want of motive power, they should get that and get it quick; if it is lack of expert mechanics in railway shops, and this is evidently true in one case at least, that road had better settle this long drawn-out strike and get some of its "dead engines" busy, of which it has several hundred within the borders of our own state. Now, let's see if we are in any way at fault. Do you, shippers, load and bill your cars immediately? Are they billed and ready for the first engine that passes? If they are not, you are not doing your duty; you are partly at fault, and you, receivers and elevator men, do you give disposition of them as soon as they reach you? Do you unload them as soon as they are set on your tracks? Or do you allow some of them to stand around as long as "free time" will permit? If you don't do this, you are partly at fault. A half-hour's delay may not seem much to you, but that half-hour may prevent the agents and train crews from moving those cars for twenty-four hours, possibly longer. It is these many little items that amount to so much the country over, and every one of us [illegible] see to it that we are not a party to these delays.

Reciprocal Demurrage.—Several of the Western states, Kansas among the number, enacted reciprocal demurrage laws, with a view to compelling transportation companies to refund to the shipper $1 per day for each and every day they neglected or refused to furnish equipment after orders were placed, within a specified time. Section 4, Chapter 345, of the Kansas Railroad Law, provides that when cars are applied for, if they are not furnished, the railway company so failing to furnish them shall forfeit to the party or parties applying the sum of $1 per day for every car failing to be furnished, to be recovered in any court of competent jurisdiction, and all actual damages that such applicant may sustain. Several suits are now pending in the state courts to recover under the provisions of this law, but it will doubtless be a year or more before the Supreme Court will hand down a decision on the validity of this act. Then should the case be appealed to the Supreme Court of the United States, two or three years more will elapse before a decision is handed down finally determining the validity of the Kansas reciprocal demurrage law. By this time Kansas and the entire West may experience a partial or total crop failure, and extra equipment and additional motive power will not be needed.

A bill has been introduced at the present session of the legislature for the purpose of bolstering up the present railroad law. The new features of the bill are to increase the penalty from $1 to $5 per day, and to give the penalty to the shipper instead of to the state, and in addition an attorney's fee, so that the expense of the suit will be decreased to the shipper, and his efforts to enforce the law will be stimulated. Comparatively few shippers care to bring suits against railroad companies to recover what they consider justly due them, and they give as their reason that they are afraid to incur the ill-will of the transportation companies, fearing that they might be discriminated against in favor of other shippers. Shippers act as if they were of the opinion that when a law is enacted for their benefit it does not become necessary for them to demand their rights. This is a mistaken idea, and unles shippers will demand their rights they cannot expect to secure relief.

On January 4 a convention was called in Chicago, which is known as the National Reciprocal Demurrage Convention, consisting of delegates from different parts of the country, representing over forty associations. The convention declared for reciprocal demurrage, and a committee was appointed to confer with President Roosevelt, urging the advisability of sending a special message to Congress, requesting that a national reciprocal demurrage law be passed at this session of Congress. This organization was made permanent, and is to continue in the effort to secure national reciprocal demurrage. If a Federal reciprocal demurrage law would improve the situation and put into motion the thousands of empty and loaded box cars now standing on sidetracks and at terminal elevators throughout the country, all of the shippers are certainly in favor of it. This is one of the great problems of the day, and I trust this convention will conclude to take some action to relieve the present situation.

In General.—As secretary, I have endeavored to conduct my work in detail according to the policy outlined by the board of directors, with the general object in view of securing for the members all the legitimate benefits possible, by exercising our influence to secure improved conditions at terminal and country elevators, to elevate the standard of the moral responsibility of our members, to arrange peaceable adjustments of differences and to offer all the encouragement possible to prompt the interests of our members.

On motion of W. S. Washer, the report was adopted with the commendation of the Association.

The report was accompanied by a financial statement showing receipts of $3,662.90 and a balance on hand January 1, 1907, of $271.25.

Mr. Smiley was followed by J. W. Radford, chief grain inspector of Kansas, who made an address on "Uniform Inspection." Before proceeding with his address, Mr. Radford said: "I desire to make some explanation of what your secretary has just referred to. It might leave a wrong impression. We do not pretend, or expect, to be perfect in all of our work. I do not have any idea that there will ever be a time when we will. A case might be selected now and then where a car is graded in the interior of the state by one party or another and days afterwards, under different conditions, very frequently be graded differently. That is not only true in the matter of grading, but it is true in the question of analyzing or passing on many other things where you have to bring into use your judgment and do it under different conditions. The cases are very rare where there would be any excuse for shipping the grain at point one and having it stopped and inspected at point two and again at point three, but I say that that might happen and I am sure that it is not necessarily the fault of the department if it did. Mr. Radford then continued with his address as follows:

UNIFORM INSPECTION.

When I was invited to furnish a paper on the subject of "Uniform Inspection" I really hesitated to accept the task of furnishing anything to the Kansas grain dealers that would be considered new or interesting, principally for the reason that from time immemorial the word uniform has been misused and abused so much, and so many times adopted for the sole purpose of misleading and misguiding the unsuspecting individual, that I think there ought to be some radical steps taken to prevent further trampling of the term under foot. But on the other hand, when I call to mind the many conditions created and the many agencies brought into use that are uniform, but are used for the purpose of defeating uniform grades that in reality give some excuse for the word uniformity, I will confess that there is some excuse left yet, even out of wrecks of the past, to point to the remains and say: "There is uniformity," though it may be a uniform steal.

There was a time when each community designated or appointed some men to judge the value of or weigh an article by the touch of the hand or foot. In those days there was very little that could be said of uniformity, for every locality had a different man and used different standards. As time passed on the mind of man became more adapted to determining exactness in all things, and then a uniform weight was adopted; then a uniform measure. But I am compelled here to admit that a great lapse of time intervened between the adoption of those uniform methods and the date of any uniform requirements, in a percentage, such as amount of "unsound," amount of "dirt" or amount of "moisture," or amount of damaged grain permitted in any grade of grain; and I am again sorry to state that that has only been done in a few markets, and all within the last thirty days.

As you no doubt are aware, in the committee of the Uniform Grade Congress, held at Chicago last December 11, 12 and 13, there was a very bitter fight waged by the members of that Congress representing different inspection departments and markets of the United States; and while the "corn committee" succeeded in carrying out the government's recommendations, as contained in Mr. Shanahan's address on that occasion, as effects corn, and were able to come on the floor and defend it and secure its adoption by the Congress, which are now printed into rules and recommended for the general adoption of the United States, yet the proposition to so classify wheat met with defeat at the hands of the men who have been schooled and drilled with the idea that the inspector should be allowed all the discretion in determining grades; that he might be permitted to place after his grade of 3, 4 or rejected the word "damaged," without further qualifying or specifying, failing to say whether damaged by "spontaneous combustion," "by fire," by "water," "smoot," "dirt," or what not.

In fact, the terms have been so indefinite that they could be favorably compared with the methods employed by the early Indian traders at the first settlement of the country, when they would make a fair bargain for all the land that the sound of a gun coud be heard on, and then go back and invent a gun many times larger than anything known, and insist that they were complying with the rules governing the trade. That is just the kind of rules designed by the parties who can control the inspections, for the reason that the inspector, in favoring his boss, could, if called down, say that it is "reasonably clean," or "reasonably dirty," etc.; and that would let him out. But if you intend to be honest in trying to give uniform grades, why should you object to having the rules prescribing grade requirements to be definite? Is it because you are afraid you haven't the ability to pass judgment and want to hide under the cloak of meaningless terms, "tolerably," "fairly," "usually," "commercially," or "reasonably," etc.? If we would be content with such indefinite and meaningless terms, why not let the inspector look into the car and say that you had a reasonably good-sized car, and that you should have a reasonably fair price, and approximate its value? or a reasonably small car, or an extra big car? What is the use of trying to determine the weight within a pound, when you adopt no rules that would tend to determine other things just as essential to its value? Is that what you would call uniformity? That certainly has been the practice for all time, and up until three years ago there had been no definite steps taken to right this great wrong. The markets all seem to be content with rules of their own, each one trying to outdo the other in adopting some odd phraseology, and having its boards meet occasionally and decide that they will loosen up or tighten up on the grades, whichever they think best to do, and by those methods seek to divert the trade out of the ordinary channels, to create unnatural conditions—all of which I do not hesitate to condemn as petty practice that should have been abolished long ago, if you hope to properly and uniformly pass on everybody's grain alike.

There has been a lot of slop handed out to the trade, especially the producer, to the effect that the rules were not favorable to his interests, in many different ways, just as though it would improve his business if you would call his oats wheat, simply because wheat is selling for considerably more than oats. I want to insist that it makes very little difference what the rules are, as long as they are well established and generally known, for the damage lies in the interpretation or application of the rules governing grading. A buyer will come into the market this year and examine a standard sample of No. 2 wheat, and find that it must be sound, dry, reasonably clean and weigh 59 pounds to the bushel. Six months from now, we will say, he would come back to make another purchase and find that you had changed the standards. He would never be able to keep pace or keep posted with a system of that kind. But what we do need is uniform rules for ALL markets, based entirely on the per cent basis, and let them become well established and well advertised, and construed and applied uniformly; then we will have no trouble of this kind.

The meeting in New York on January 6, 1904, was prompted by the introduction of a bill in Congress, seeking to remedy the evil complained of in the lack of uniform grading; and the resolutions, a copy of which I have, practically admit the great necessity of uniform action, but protest against the operation of it by a uniform body.

I see my friend, Mr. Frasius, in a number of articles, has been advocating government inspection, and went so far as to quote a great many members of the Kansas City Board of Trade as being in favor of it; in fact, the language of his article is to the effect that all but three or four members were in favor of the government controlling the inspection; yet, within a few days from this announcement, Mr. Flack of the Midland Elevator Company, representing the Kansas City Board of Trade, in the Chicago meeting on the 11th of last December, wanted the Kansas City (Mo.) Board of Trade emphatically placed on record as opposing any government control, or even interference by the United States government with any inspection of grain whatever. In that case, the Kansas City Board of Trade has been quoted as uniformly favoring the inspection on one hand, and on the other they have been represented as not only being uniformly, but unanimously, opposed to just such inspection. I will confess that such changes of front would be hard to keep up with.

While endeavoring to make the grades under my department uniform, and to have all instructions to the men throughout the department uniform, it has been part of my duties in making complete inspection to do the weighing under the law, and to my mind there is nothing more important to the men interested than the weighing.

In relation to cars being coopered before getting to the elevator and the railway companies having it done, I take the railroad's side in this much, that I think the railroad ought to do that, and, in fact, they do do it. I have a man in each railroad yard who tries to meet all the trains, and he has a great deal of trouble, as the roads fail to place the cars where they should be. The man then can tell how much damage is done the shipper when a car bursts open. In my department, in looking after the cooperage, it makes it hard for us to find that out. The railroads do that. If there are cars reaching an elevator without seals, I think it is not always the case that those cars come any distance, or that they were taken off or left off by the party who sent them.

I know full well when I say this that I draw fire from places that I might escape if I chose to say nothing on that point. And further, my duties would be much less, my responsibility less than half and my remuneration just as much, if there was no weighing to do; but as long as I am called on to say anything in behalf of the improvement of the department, looking to uniform inspection, I consider that I would be dodging the question and shirking my duty if I would fail to point out the material and necessary questions that must be decided whether for or against the trade.

I have been surprised at the lack of understanding that some of the trade have of the importance of maintaining a representative to do their weighing, or see it done, for it needs only a glance at the work being done to convince anyone that it is highly important to have the weights supervised in the interest of the absent man. It is not only frequently the case, but it is the prevailing custom with many successful shippers, in selling at a terminal market, to specify that in case his grain fails to grade a certain grade, for them to wire him and hold disposition for orders. What is the result of that? Why, the advantage is that the shipper, though several hundred miles away, may be advised within a few hours after I inspect his car. He can, in turn, order some other party to go down and examine this car, or come in himself and do so, and in that case have a complete check on any incompetency, carelessness or crookedness at the hands of the inspectors, and he would always have a chance to establish his claim. But not so with his weights. When his grain gets into the modern elevator with the equipment of hopper scales, and the weight is recorded, there is no chance to hold it thirty minutes. One second after the hopper slide is open every chance to rectify the weight, if challenged, has been lost, as it goes at once to the interior of the house with other grain. Then the importance of the shippers having a representative can be appreciated, to avoid mistakes and accidents, and, if they happen, to have him report them. I don't think it matters whether any supervision of the weights is done at any point other than public houses, if the weights taken do not govern account of sales.

When I took charge of the department in 1903 I found but one weighmaster for the state, at each elevator. I found also one tally man, known as the Board of Trade employe; I found another one, known as the elevator weighmaster. I fail to see any chance to have uniform weighing done with arrangements of that kind. It was a member of the Board of Trade employing a weighmaster to do the weighing, and it was the same member of the Board of Trade, acting on a committee representing the Board of Trade, hiring the same man to watch the same scales. What benefit could there be in that system? I fail to see the justification of having the market at Kansas City burdened with two weighing departments, owned, controlled and operated by the same interests. The rules of the Board of Trade are sufficiently stringent to force all members to obey it to the letter in every particular, as I understand it—at least, that is what they advertise. Then, why should they not be able to make Mr. Elevator Man give honest weights without any expense to the shipper in fees for maintaining another set of weighers? They maintain a first-class weighman, or he could not hold his position; then, if there is any merit in their claim of taking care of the outside man's interest, why isn't it sufficient for them to order this Elevator Man to see to it that correct weights are returned, without the necessity or expense of maintaining another weighmaster employed by the operator of his elevator in conjunction with others? To my mind it is simply a multiple of men from, by and for the same interests, but paid for almost exclusively by the OTHER interest. So I very promptly decided if I wanted to know what was really being done I must at least employ another man and put him downstairs, which I did. And there is where I reaped after the sowing. A uniform howl went out. A case in the Federal court was instituted and a systematic and uniform persistence ever since to put the department out of business.

It has been my idea to give as good inspection to

PERRY N. ALLIN, DIRECTOR.

the foreign trade as we do to the local buyer, thereby building up the demand for our goods for the reason that we are honest in labeling them. As my experience has been that if we get the reputation of having applied false labels, it condemns our entire institution, and in trying to carry that out in practice I have a great deal of trouble, especially in making the OUT inspection. I have been importuned to lower the grade; have been abused for insisting on uniform standard OUT as well as IN; have been refused the inspection of thousands and thousands of cars, solely on the ground that I insist OUT inspections should be no more liberal than IN. And the climax to this all came last summer, when I had refused day after day to grade cars as No. 2 at a certain elevator in Kansas City, and finally they loaded out ten cars of excellent 60-pound No. 2 hard wheat, and I so graded it and reported and issued certificates. By my having weighmasters stationed at this elevator I was able to detect and finally stop the fraud in this case, as they set the cars back, unloaded them and loaded them out with a poor quality of wheat, sent my certificates to St. Louis to the buyer, and gave orders to give out no information as to destination of the grain.

In order to demonstrate what I have often contended, that fraud in different places existed, and would be practiced more if some vigilance was not maintained, I spent a great deal of money and time in running down and getting evidence that was conclusive in this case, and so presented it to the Federal court, to the effect that the St. Louis firm had not only affirmed my word of mouth, but I had their letters admitting that the deal was based on the certificates furnished, and that they had used the certificates and had sent them to Mexico, and that they had asked me to keep quiet until they got their money; and the St. Louis party recovered $1,300 as damages sustained by reason of the situation. And, as further proof that the deal was crooked, the Mexican miller received in settlement, after a drawn-out dispute, $500 for his damages, and only on account of the trouble and expense of maintaining a lawsuit did he consent to do this, as he considered his damages much more. The standing of the department and the Kansas product were discredited and always will be as long as you would mislabel and attempt to deceive the public in this way. Yet the Kansas City Board of Trade, to the surprise of almost everybody else, let this man off by suspending him for 90 days from the floor, thus treating it as a joke. I speak of these things to show you that if a man wants to be independent in doing his duty his path is not strewn with roses and his efforts often receive very little reward at the hands of the trade.

This same influence—the elevator men at Kansas City—have contributed nothing in the way of making the operation of my department a success. They have been as far from that as they have from obeying the law against deduction of one hundred pounds from each car. And, as some of you remember, Mr. Miller of Miller & Sons of Anthony said in a meeting of your body in the parlor of the Cary Hotel last year, that these same parties paid his expenses at Topeka during the legislature of 1905 for three weeks—and he was only one among many others—for the purpose of passing an amendment to the present law, and they assured him they would abolish the rule of 100 pounds' deduction in case it passed. Now, why do you think they made that promise? The same interests have raised money now and have employed some Judases, who have been very industrious in betraying the safeguards to the trade, as far as the outside dealer is concerned. It ought to be strengthened instead of weakened. I will have something interesting later on to say about this feature of the business.

Uniform work is all right in some places, but it makes a great deal of difference whose ox is being gored. There is no more reason why the inspection and weighing should be placed in the hands or under the control of the elevator men than there is that a man bringing suit should be allowed to select from among his special friends the jury to decide his case.

My report on track inspections at Kansas City, up to June 30, 1904, shows about three cars out of every hundred, on which, on reinspection, the grade was changed. I employ all the methods deemed best to improve the condition of things, with the result that for the last two years, ending June 30, 1906, the record shows that out of 72,312 cars inspected, the grade of only 1,286 cars was changed, which represents less than two per cent; and this amount, considering the conditions under which these first grades are to be made, such as being done in all kinds of weather, rain, snow, sleet, bright sunshine and extreme cloudiness, one car standing out in the bright sunshine and the next one in between two big, high furniture cars, I think shows a wonderful degree of accuracy, and, also, considering the inspection has got to be made in a hurry, it should be considered about as near correct as it would be expected to get it; in fact, it would compare favorably with the work of any inspection, though done under more favorable circumstances. The family doctor is not able to diagnose properly one hundred cases without making more than two mistakes, nor can the horse jockey, examining a horse, come that close to finding the defects, though in each case they have plenty of time and favorable conditions.

I am aware that the department has not been able to give entire satisfaction at all times. Indeed, I would consider it a marvel of perfection if it could do that; but my efforts have at all times been along the line of uniform rules—uniformity applied without fear or favor by competent, honest and responsible men. I first recommend the installation of track scales for the sole purpose of enabling one man to do the weighing and certify to what was in the car, with the view of having uniform treatment. That drew a lot of fire for my department. I have been hounded and harassed ever singe by parties seeking to have their own way without having any chance to be checked up on these matters.

Now, I am thoroughly convinced that the solution of uniform grade lies: First, in the adoption of rules with uniform phraseology, to be used in all departments; then for the inspection department to be clothed with authority to execute the rules without being dependent upon any part of the trade. Let them be entirely free from any influences that could cause them to lose their positions, or diminish their revenue on account of their work, so long as it was properly done. Have the law give sufficient authority to place them in control of their work without any interference whatever, and base all the rules on a percentage basis, so that any court of inquiry could determine what they were doing, and then, and not until then, will you ever succeed in having uniform work done of grading grain in different parts or even in the same markets.

The inspection department must not be used for the purpose of making the markets whole, or saving some class of speculators from the effects of a break. The department ought to be ignorant of all fluctuations in the market. The inspector should not know for whom he is doing the work. The consignee should be kept off of the cards. I take the position that the inspection department was not created or intended to guarantee the trade a profit, but to pass on grain as the inspectors find it.

Mr. Radford's address created a lively discussion, some points of which are considered in the following:

Question: Mr. Wilson said this morning that our claims should be well sustained if we proved the seals were broken. Would it not be possible for the inspector to state that these seals were broken so that we might know whether they came through intact or not?

Mr. Radford: I want to say that my men make a notation at any time a car is opened. This is done by the grain inspector who gets the sample, or grades the grain. Do not understand that I am in favor of having the seals taken off the cars. We had a proposition come up where they wanted the seal records. I told them I would be glad to furnish the seal records if they would designate a track where we could meet the cars. They promptly designated track No. 9. I issued orders to my men to take seal records in that yard of every door. They abandoned keeping the cars and stuff there. I followed them two or three tracks and then had to quit. I think there is some hope at this legislature of getting help enough to make a complete seal record. Hence I have adopted the serial seal record and have each inspector charged with the seals in that series. I can tell you what series of seals the Santa Fe man uses and so on. That is the basis I have been following.

Question: In case of a seal being broken, is it under the state superintendent of inspection or is it under the superintendent of railroads where you would make your claim when the car arrives at destination with the seal broken?

By the President: I think if you can prove that the seal has been broken before it arrives in the railroad yards—if you can establish that fact, I do not think there is a shadow of a doubt but that you can press the claim to a conclusion with the railroad company.

Question: All cars are sealed before they reach the station. When cars arrive at Kansas City, they break the seal, the inspection department of the railroad; and then they should put on a seal of their own. Consequently, when the seal is broken and another put on, no one can tell who is at fault if it is not on, or who breaks the seal?

Mr. Radford: Of course, we do not know who break the seals. It might be ourselves, or the Board of Trade, or the seal might have become broken in a number of ways. Of course, we have no way of knowing the original seals. If we find a seal broken, however, we do have a record of it in the office. We always apply a seal before we leave it. This seal has our name on it, and has a number. We are using something like 160,000 now.

Question: A car leaves the station with seals on both doors, and when it gets to Kansas City those seals are not on it; who took them off?

Mr. Radford: We keep a complete record of them at the elevator. Outside of that we are not able to tell. When the seal is off, the railroad company is up against it.

By the President: It is difficult very often to establish a seal record, when the seal has been broken in transit at any time. If you can establish that a seal is broken, or the cause of it, it is a very great help in making a collection for damages. But it is a very hard matter to establish that seal record. It is something that has been agitated a great deal. We hope the legislature will do something along that line to establish a way the seals can be checked up, that the shipper may know what has become of his grain.

Question: I want to ask a question in regard to inspecting a car of wheat. A car was delayed thirty days on one sidetrack. This was delayed at the loading point. Probably there was some low-grade wheat in that car and it was destroyed by that time. How would you grade that wheat?

Mr. Radford: It depends on the contract. No low-grade wheat, unless under very good conditions, would be taken. I do not see how you had any remedy unless you got after them for delay. If they accept that grade of wheat, they ought to get it through before it spoils.

Question: The question I wished to ask was, how you adjusted the grade on the car?

Mr. Radford: Our rules necessarily provide (we do it for the protection of the business trade and the department) that if in the judgment of the inspector the car has been plugged, he is supposed to make the grade of the lowest quality he finds. If you sent the car and notified the inspector how much of it was low grade, etc., and that you did not intend to plug it, then he would give you what it was worth outside of that.

Question: I stated in this case that one end of it was low grade, but I did not know how much. How would you adjust it when you got it?

Mr. Radford: It would be graded then as much as an average sample would show.

The next paper was by F. B. Bonebreak of Osage City on "Railroad Legislation in Kansas," the publication of which is postponed for the immediate present.

Mr. W. S. Washer of Atchison then offered the following: "I move that the board of directors be directed to correspond with the board of directors of our associations in Oklahoma and Texas; and, if they are agreeable, to have a member appointed from each of these states to work in conjunction with a member from this state, who shall act as a Board of Arbitration on Appeals, as suggested by Secretary Smiley; the president be instructed to appoint a member in Kansas, and the others to be chosen from each of their states, to constitute said Board of Appeals." The resolution was referred to the committee on resolutions, and subsequently it was reported favorably and then unanimously adopted.

The convention then adjourned until the following day.

WEDNESDAY—SECOND DAY—MORNING.

After some routine business, Mr. Carr W. Taylor, attorney for the state Railway Commission, made an address on railway regulation. Mr. Taylor said: "It gives me great pleasure to meet with you this morning. I consider Kansas raises one-seventh of all the wheat that is grown in the United States of America, so I know something about the magnitude of your business. My remarks this morning will be confined to railroad rate regulation. I have prepared a paper, or rather my address, which I have had written out in order that I may not be misunderstood or misquoted if the newspapers say anything about it:

RAILROAD RATE REGULATION.

The greatest question for our people as a nation to settle is the control and regulation of corporations by the state and government. There are two kinds of corporations known to the law: Private and public corporations. A private corporation is an association of individuals banded together in a corporate capacity for the purpose of conducting as one person any kind of business or manufactory. A public corporation consists of municipalities, such as townships, cities and states.

The private corporations I have just mentioned are divided into really three classes; corporations for business and profit; charitable corporations, such as lodges and eleemosynary institutions, that do not exist for profit; while there is a third, and most important, class of corporations which transact business with and for the public, and this class includes all common carriers, railroad lines, steamboat lines, hack lines, stage lines, telegrapn, telephone, gas, electric light, and waterworks companies, and even inn keepers are included in this list. These corporations are called quasi public corporations.

A corporation is an artificial person. It is created by the state. It can have no existence until the state breathes the breath of life into it. It follows that what the state gives it can take away; and it is also settled by the highest courts of this nation that the state has absolute control over corporations and can prescribe their conduct. There is only one limitation to this power, and that is that such control shall not amount to the confiscation of the property of the corporation.

It is not my purpose to discuss the relation of private corporations to the public. I only desire to say in referring to them that private corporations have had the right, practically without any restraint whatever, to issue stock in any amount, regardless of the cash value of the assets of the corporations. The fact that the law has not limited the issuance of stock to the actual value of the assets of the corporation has led to great abuses and an unlimited amount of fraud in connection with corporations in the United States.

The thinking people of this nation with an understanding of this question are amazed to-day that the law, in the first instance, did not limit the issuance of stock by a corporation to the actual value of its assets. With such a clause in the law, and with criminal statutes making it a felony to violate the provisions of such a law, any investment in corporate stock would have been reasonably safe even for the average uninitiated investor. It will occur to you that stock issued upon the basis of the actual value of the assets of a corporation would always remain at par, providing the properties of the corporation are managed in such a manner as to prevent their depreciation in value and to pay a dividend; such stock would increase in market value in proportion to the amount of dividends earned by it. Without going into this subject further, I will say that I believe that the people of this nation are almost unanimous in their demand for the passage of laws which will prevent the issuance of stock by corporations for a greater amount than the actual value of the corporation's assets, and are further unanimously in favor of laws making the officers and directors of a corporation guilty of a felony, and the corporation liable to heavy fines for the violation of such laws. The importance of this question is apparent to everyone when we consider that such law would also apply to all of the railroads and common carrier companies in the United States. This brings me to the principal subject of my discourse to-day: The Railroads of the United States.

The magnitude of the question of the regulation of railroads by the state is appreciated to the fullest extent by every person, when the fact is brought to our attention that we have in the United States of America an actual operated railroad mileage of 212,243.21 miles. The railroad companies of the United States do not only operate several trans-continental lines, but cover the face of the country like a net with their steel highways.

Before the time of railroads throughout this country, in its early life, and throughout Europe during the past centuries, traffic was carried on by means of the natural highways, such as rivers and artificial highways called canals, and by the old stage coach and freight wagons. The government from the earliest time was interested in the maintenance of public highways, suitable for the convenient and speedy transportation of freight and passengers over them, and those who have visited Europe are loud in their praise of the magnificient public highways of that country, which were built by the government and have been maintained in excellent condition from the time of their original construction.

The government, which is nothing more than a representative of the people, has always been intensely interested in maintaining suitable highways for the purpose of enabling its people to exchange and distribute all their superfluous products. The government has always had the right under our constitution to own and operate the railroad lines of this country, but it has never seen fit, and may never see fit, to exercise that power. Heretofore it has conferred that right and privilege upon private quasi public corporations, and in the manner provided by law. The state, in each instance, through a written charter, conferred its power upon such corporations to carry on the transportation business of the people, and with that great power it gave such quasi public corporations the right of eminent domain. This is perhaps the greatest power that can be conferred by a state upon any person. It is never given to a private individual; it is always given to a public corporation for the purpose of benefiting the public through the conduct and operation of transportation lines. Under this power of eminent domain the private property of any individual is taken for public use, without his consent. Under our constitution the private property of an individual can never be taken "for private use." Of course, the right can only be exercised by compensating the owner of the private property by payment in full of the actual cash value of the property taken, and the actual damages he sustains by reason of the taking. All the railroad corporations of the United States received their charter and the right of exercising the power of eminent domain from the state, and in turn assumed certain obligations to the public.

The first great obligation resting upon the railroad companies is to give to the public, which they serve, adequate and convenient service; and by adequate and convenient service I mean sufficient depots, freight houses, yards and terminal facilities, sidetrack, and passenger and freight train service as will conveniently and speedily care for and handle the normal transportation business of the public. It should be understood, that the railroads under the law have never had the right to prescribe the measure of their duty by asserting that they have done the best they can in furnishing sufficient equipment. Such an excuse is no excuse. The real fact is that the railroads have fixed the standard of money making for the purpose of paying dividends on watered stock and upon excessive valuations of their properties as the basis upon which they act, without regard to the matter of providing themselves with sufficient equipment, depots, yards and terminal facilities, and have thereby wilfully overlooked and refused to perform the duty they owe to the public in this regard.

I do not care to discuss at this time this first obligation, but have only this to say, that the legislatures of the respective states and the national Congress have the unqualified power to require by law the railroads to discharge this obligation. It is apparent that a weak law is but little better than no law upon the subject; that a law, in order to accomplish the desired result, must contain a penalty of sufficient severity to make it absolutely incumbent upon a railroad company to furnish adequate facilities for the purpose of speedily conducting the transportation business of the public. The failure of the transportation companies of the United States to fulfill this first great obligation, assumed by them when they accepted their charters, has resulted in countless millions of dollars of loss to our producers and shippers. Will our law-making bodies permit such conduct to continue, and ignore the demand of the public that they enact laws which will force the railroad companies to comply with this obligation resting upon them?

Sole Object of Control.—The second great obligation resting upon the railroads is to carry both freight and passengers at a reasonable price. You will observe, therefore, that the sole object of the regulation and control of railroad corporations by the state and nation is to compel such corporations to fulfill these great obligations to the public.

It has always been the settled law of this nation, and of each state therein, that an unreasonable charge for the carrying of passengers or freight is an unlawful charge. The individual shipper has always had the right to sue a railroad company for the difference between a reasonable freight charge and an excessive charge paid; but the remedy has always been impracticable, except only in cases where shipments were very large. There are millions of shipments made each year where the excess of each individual amounts to but every little, but which in the aggreate amounts to millions of dollars, and yet the individual would lose money by instituting an action for the recovery of the excessive charge because of the fact that the value of the time lost in the prosecuting of the action and his attorney's fees would amount to more than his claim for the excessive charge.

It early became known to shippers that the railroad companies would charge all that the traffic would bear; that the question of what is a reasonable charge for carrying freight was rarely considered by traffic managers, but the real question that was considered by them, was, how much can we charge and yet secure a movement of the product? Too great a charge would prohibit the movement; so it was necessary for the railroads to fix the rates so that the traffic would move and it has been this method of fixing rates which has given rise to the expression that railroad companies charge "all the traffic will bear."

You will observe, therefore, that the impracticability of the common law remedy for the recovery of excessive freight charges made it absolutely necessary, in order to protect the shippers of the United States, to regulate freight and passenger transportation by law. In the past this has been done in two ways; first, by the legislature itself, through the enactment of what is known as maximum freight laws, which provide that certain articles of freight and merchandise shall not be carried for a greater charge than the rate named in the law; second, by a railroad commission, usually composed of three members, which is the creature of the legislature and which investigates and acts for the legislature in altering, fixing and naming future rates to be charged. An order of a railroad commission is a law to the same extent that an act of the legislature is a law when signed by the governor and published. The remedies of the railroad company against an order of the board of railroad commissioners are precisely the same as they are against a law of the legislature.

The usual defenses by the railroad companies against such orders and laws are that they are made in controvention of the constitution of the United States and are confiscatory; and by confiscatory is meant that the law, or the order of the board fixing rates, if such rates are put into effect, will not permit the railroad company to make sufficient earnings upon its investment.

The producing and shipping interests of a state like Kansas are so great that in order that the people may be protected from excessive and extortionate freight rates the establisment of a railroad commission was deemed to be necessary. A railroad commission is the agent of the people. As I have heretofore stated, the railroads have the sole power to make and fix rates. Our Railroad Commission, under the present law, is given the power to alter and to amend any rate schedule or classification of any railroad company. If this power was not given to the Commission the people would have no redress against an extortionate rate, and the railroad companies could continue to charge excessive and extortionate rates. A railroad commission, therefore, in the fullest sense, is the agent of the people, invested with full power to compel the railroad companies to serve the people for a reasonable passenger and freight charge. The importance, therefore, of a railroad commission to the producing and shipping interests of the state, is impressed upon us. There can be no greater power conferred upon any body of men than the power conferred upon a railroad commission to act for the people in securing reasonable rates and in compelling railroads to furnish convenient and adequate service.

The opposition of the railroads to any interference by the railroad commissioners and legislatures in the making and fixing of rates is so tremendous that the only way that the producers and shippers of a state can secure fair play is by electing and installing into office commissioners and legislators not only of high character but men of ability, and who are known to have the courage to do what is right, regardless of the consequence to themselves.

As I have heretofore stated, the legislature has the constitutional right to confer any power upon the Board of Railroad Commissioners to carry out the great purpose for which it was created. The trouble with the administration of the Board of Railroad Commissioners in the state of Kansas in the past has been the disposition upon the part of such Board to do nothing and to assume that they had no right to proceed to correct the damaging transportation conditions existing in this state. Our people have lost millions of dollars during the past years because the railroads have succeeded in preventing official bodies, which have had the power to force them to perform the obligations they assumed, from compelling a performance.

The Basis for Fixing Rates.—The basis for the fixing of reasonable rates has been clearly outlined by the courts. Right here let me say that the courts, both state and United States, have never swerved from their full duty in upholding the law and in stating what are the obligations of common carriers to the public. In most cases the fault has been entirely with Congress and the state legislatures. Laws in many instances have been passed creating railroad commissions and not giving them the proper powers. Where sufficient powers and aids have been given the failure to make laws effective has been caused by commissions that have not had the courage to do their full duty under the law.

The courts have said, in substance, that a railroad company has the right to charge such freight and passenger rates as will enable it to earn its operating expenses, taxes, and second, a fair return upon the value of its property. In order that you may know that the statement I have just made is not my own, but is the law as laid down by the courts, I will now read to you an extract from the opinion of the United States Supreme Court in the case of Smyth vs. Ames, 169 U. S. 467, 18 Sup. Ct. 418, 40 L. Ed. 819, as follows: "A railroad is a public highway, and none the less so because constructed and maintained through the agency of a corporation deriving its existence and powers from the state. Such a corporation was created for public purposes. It performs the functions of the state. Its authority to exercise the right of eminent domain and to charge tolls was given primarily for the benefit of the public. It is, therefore, under governmental control, subject, of course, to the constitutional guaranty for the protection of property. It may not fix its rates solely with a view to its own interests, and ignore the rights of the public. But the rights of public would be ignored if rates for transportation of persons or property on a railroad were exacted without reference to a fair value of the property used for the public or of the service rendered; and in order simply that the corporation may meet its operating expenses, pay interest on its bonds, and declare dividends to its stockholders."

The rule is also very clearly stated in the case of Matthews vs. The Board of Corporation Commissioners, 160 Fed. 7, as follows:

"Railroads are the arteries of trade. Through them flows the life-blood of the community. The best statesmanship contributes to their maintenance and encourages their prosperity. What the remuneration shall be depends upon the circumstances of each case. Investments may be made in railroads, as in any species of property, so unwise as never to be remunerative. As was said in Covington turnpike case, supra, 'it cannot be said that a corporation is entitled as a right, and without reference to the interests of the public, to realize a given per cent on its capital stock.' A fortiori, a corporation cannot be entitled to compel the public to make profitable an investment which was unwisely inaugurated and badly executed. The basis of all calculation as to the reasonableness of rates is the fair value of the property used for the convenience of the public—not its cost, nor the amount of money expended for it, but its value as a producing factor, taking into consideration its location, character of the country through which it passes, and the reasonable expectation of business coming to it. The railroad company is entitled to a fair return upon the value of the property, ascertained in this way, and it is not entitled to exact from the public more than this."

There are many other cases supporting this doctrine, but I only quote from these two, in order that you may know that the law upon this proposition is settled.

You will therefore understand that the courts have explained to the law-making powers what they may do in the way of regulating public service corporations. The people should understand, once and for all, that a railroad company does not have the right under the law to do as it pleases with reference to furnishing equipment or to charge what it pleases for the carriage of freight. The people should understand that if a railroad company is permitted to do as it pleases, relative to these matters, it is suffered to do so because the law-making power refuses to exercise the right which it has to regulate the railroads.

Many of the great railroad system of the United States are at the present time over-capitalized, and all of such railroads, in the face of the law, are claiming that they have the right to earn reasonable dividends upon such over-capitalization. The railroad companies of the United States will not concede that they are entitled only to earn their operating expenses and taxes, and in addition thereto a fair return upon the value of their property; and in order to prevent the legislatures from passing maximum bills, fixing freight and passenger charges upon the basis laid down by the courts, the railroad companies, by means of strong lobbies, pass favors and other means, prevent any action that would bring about that result; and as a consequence of this, so far, apparently unconquerable power and influence, the people are continuing to pay excessive and extortionate rates, in order that the railroads may pay dividends upon watered stock.

Here is an illustration of how the railroad companies evade the law and continue to do as they please: The Santa Fé Railway Company, according to the specific report, filed by it with the Board of Railroad Commissioners in September 1906, has issued a total capital stock of $233,486,000 and has issued in bonds, $275,484,800, making a total amount of outstanding capital, stock and bonds, of $508,970,800. The financial papers of the United States say that the Santa Fé is over-capitalized. The total mileage of the Santa Fé Railway system is 8,878, but the mileage given in the sworn report, that I have referred to, is 9,887.99; and yet the Santa Fé Railway Company has called a meeting of its stockholders for the purpose of determining whether or not the road shall issue $98,000,000 additional of bonds and stocks. There can be no doubt that the issue of such an additional amount in bonds will be made, unless said company is prevented from so doing by law. If the issue be made, the capital of the Santa Fé Railway Company will be increased to 606 millions of dollars.

In the inquiry which was had before the Board of Railroad Commissioners on Monday afternoon, Mr. Hurley, general manager of the Santa Fé, was unable to specifically state what the money to be realized from such bonds, if issued, would be used for. He did state in a general way that it would be used for "improvement purposes;" but he also stated that a portion of the money so realized would be used for the payment of $110,000,000 worth of equipment ordered during the year 1906, and $9,000,000 contracted for the year 1907. Mr. Hurley also stated that no money is ever taken from the general earnings of the Santa Fé Company for the purpose of buying new equipment or motive power, nor for new ballasts, nor for new bridges, nor cement, nor stone abutments or piers; that all new betterments, tracks and structural work made by said company are paid for by new stock or bond issues.

You will observe, therefore, that all of the net earnings of the Santa Fé Railway Company are used for the purpose of paying dividends to stockholders and paying interest upon bonds and other fixed charges.

I want to say here, that this kind of management is not indulged in by all of the railroad companies of the United States. For illustration, the Illinois Central drafts from its income the cost of miles of extention and additional rolling stock. If the Santa Fé and other railroad companies would do the same, the increase of the indebtedness of such companies would cease, and there would be some hope that ultimately freight rates might be reduced. But the Santa Fé system insists upon charging such freight rates as will enable it to pay not only its operating expenses and taxes and interests on bonds, but to pay dividends upon all of its stock, when it is a well-known fact that its $102,000,000 common stock only realized the company at the time of its re-organization, in 1895, $10 for each 100 shares.

The sworn report of the Missouri Pacific Railway Company, filed with our Board of Railroad Commissioners, shows a capitalization of $148,966 per mile for its entire line; and it claims that it should be permitted to earn a dividend upon such an enormous capitalization.

Further illustrations are unnecessary. From what I have said you will observe that if a railroad corporation, which owes its life to the state and performs a function of the state and which is subject to legislative control, is permitted to earn only its operating expenses and taxes and a fair return upon the value of its property, none of the railroads in the state of Kansas, and I may say throughout this Western country, would ever be permitted to make further issue of stock or bonds. But if they were permitted to do so, the application of the rule laid down by the courts for determining what would be a reasonable rate, would prevent railroads like the Santa Fé and the Missouri Pacific and all other over-capitalized roads from ever paying any dividends at all upon its waterstock; and if new issue of stock or bonds were to be made, they would find no market, for the reason that they would have no value.

To refer again to the Missouri Pacific system in Kansas—its roadbed, in a great many places in the state, is in bad condition; its branch lines are all laid with light steel; its engines are small, and the service it gives is complained of at almost every point upon its lines in this state. All of these lines and rolling stock, in their present condition, could be reproduced for much less than $30,000 per mile; and yet it asks, insists, and requires the producers and shippers of Kansas to pay it a dividend upon an over-capitalization, in round numbers, of $118,000 per mile. I should say to you, that the Missouri Pacific stock earned 5 per cent dividend for the year, ending June 30, 1906.

Politics.—Now, I have come to the political part of my argument. It is a well-known fact that not only Congress but many of the legislatures in the United States have been and are refusing to recognize the facts that I have stated to you. The principal argument made by the railroad companies is, "to be let alone." President Ripley says the Santa Fé is worth every dollar that it is capitalized for, and nearly every other railroad company makes the same claim, but the people have come, at last, to know better. We know that it does not cost $51,000 per mile to build a railroad in the state of Kansas, like the Santa Fé Railroad Company. We know that the Missouri Pacific Railway Company in Kansas is not worth $148,000 per mile. And we know that rates ought to be fixed upon the basis of the value of the railroad properties. We know that expert contractors, who have been in the business of railroad building for years, and that civil engineers who have made a specialty of railroad construction, have recently testified, under oath, that railroads in Iowa in their present condition, can be constructed for $25,000 per mile without ballast, and at $28,000 with ballast. And we know the railroad construction in Iowa is much more expensive than it is anywhere in Kansas, for the reason that the streams run from the northwest to the southeast, and that the railroads cross such streams at right-angles, thereby requiring deep cuts and heavy fills in order to reduce the grades. It is also shown that the grades and curves in Iowa are deeper and more extreme than they are in Kansas, which fact adds to the cost of transportation. In the coal and wheat cases which I tried before the Board of Railroad Commissioners a year ago, W. C. Beckenridge, of the Burlington system, testified to the facts, relative to the costs of construction, which I have just given you, and his deposition is on file with the Board of Railroad Commissioners of this state.

The question is whether or not the producers and shippers of this state and of the United States will continue to pay excessive freight and passenger tolls to the transportation companies.

You should know that the railroad companies are more vigilant and determined than ever in their fight against the reduction of freight rates; but it is my experience that they will make no general reduction of freight rates that would be of benefit to the people until forced to do so by law; and a study of the history of railroad legislation throughout the United States leads one to the inevitable conclusion that the producers, merchants and shippers of the United States will never get relief until they force their respective legislatures and our national Congress to act. The fight is not between the railroad companies and the courts, but it is between the railroad companies and the law-making powers. So far the railroad companies have been able to control the law-making powers and to prevent such remedial legislation as would give to the people complete railroad regulation. No legislature in the United States of America meets to-day without there being present, organized for active service, a strong railroad lobby. Such a lobby is in Topeka to-day during this session of our legislature; and strong influence will be exerted by it to prevent the passage of needed amendments to our railroad laws giving additional powers to our Board of Railroad Commissioners.

The legislature ought to give our Railroad Commission and the attorney for the Board a large contingent fund for the reason that the work those officers have to do is of the very greatest monetary importance to our people. We might as well have no Commission as to refuse to give the Commission and the attorney for the Board an ample contingent fund. The railroad companies pay large salaries to their chief rate men. The state of Kansas should have a rate department in connection with the Board of Railroad Commissioners with a high salaried man who is as competent in rate matters as are the chief rate men of the railroad companies operating in Kansas. Such a man cannot be procured for a small salary. Inasmuch as the Railroad Commission is the agent for the people in securing for the people reasonable rates, it should be given all of the aids by law that will enable it to accomplish the desired result.

One of the proposed amendments to our present railroad law authorizes the Board to ascertain the value of all of the railroad properties in this state, and authorizes the Board to employ such engineers and other experts as may be necessary to ascertain such value. The information obtained in this proposed amendment, if it becomes a law, will be of incalculable benefit in the matter of taxation of railroads, as well as for enabling the Board to determine what is a reasonable rate; and I will say that if the legislature of Kansas does not make these needed amendments, we might as well have no Railroad Commission and attorney for the Board. Less than complete regulation is, in a measure, a farce.

There should be no politics in this question. The citizens of overwhelmingly democratic states are as intensely interested in these problems as are the citizens of overwhelmingly republican states. Party lines should not be drawn upon these questions in the legislature; but regardless of party politics every legislator should do everything within his power to make railroad regulation complete. If the legislature fails in doing what it should do, by the passage of proper laws, to give our people relief, every man failing in his duty should be retired from office. The time for temporizing is gone by. The time has come when the individual citizen should take a hand in selecting his candidates for representatives, state senator, congressman, United States senator, and state officers, to the end that he may finally receive the consideration to which he is entitled to under the law. Namby-pamby, nerveless men, who can be influenced to inactivity or passivity, should not be nominated to office in this state.

Let me say here that no one desires to injure any railroad operating in this country. We desire all railroad companies to earn a sufficient amount of money from reasonable freight and passenger tolls to give us the best equipment that can be invented and that adequate and convenient service which every community demands and is entitled to. But all of these things can be accomplished by giving such railroad companies a fair return upon the value of its property. To permit the present conditions to continue means to sacrifice that sovereign power which is inherent in us under our form of government. When the British Parliament was seeking to place a tax upon tea, Edmund Burke said in substance, in opposition to the tax, "it is the principle involved and not the question whether or not the American colonists are able to pay three pence." They are in the same position that John Hampton was in when he refused to pay a six shilling shipping tax. Would the payment of six shillings have impoverished John Hampton? No, but the payment of one-half that sum upon the principle it was demanded would have made John Hampton a slave.

The people of this state are prosperous; they are growing richer every day; our bank deposits will continue to increase; and our cities will continue to grow in a natural way, and we can pay the excessive freight rates that are charged us to-day; but if we consent to do so, we thereby consent to the confiscation of our money to the extent that the rates now charged are excessive; and for the individual citizen to sit supinely down and premit such a confiscation to continue, when he has a quick and speedy remedy through the election of the right men to the legislative offices, he sacrifices, to a certain extent, his sovereignty and becomes a slave to the transportation companies.

Continuing, after the conclusion of the reading of his manuscript Mr. Taylor said:

"I believe that I know what kind of a law would be perfect and which would be universally satisfactory to the state and to the courts. I want to refer to the reciprocal demurrage clause. I have never believed that as a matter of fact anything should be given to the shipper. The true theory of penalties is that a penalty should be given to the state. The state said to the railroad companies: 'We have the right to own and operate the railroad companies, but we do not choose to exercise that right. We choose to confer that right upon you by charter.' The railroads said: 'All right; we will accept it.' The state says: 'But if you expect that right from us to conduct the transportation business of the country, we propose to punish you if you do not furnish adequate and convenient service to the public. For every instance in which you fail to furnish cars to shippers, we will impose a fine upon you of ten dollars or twenty-five dollars.' The new bills which have been introduced contain a penalty of twenty-five dollars. The state says, 'If you do not do it, we will punish you by making you pay a ten-dollar fine, and if there is a million of those failures and it bankrupts your road, we will appoint a receiver and sell your company to someone who will do it.' Do not misunderstand this. The trouble in the past has been the failure of our legislative bodies to do anything. They do not thoroughly understand the relation of the railroad companies to the people.

"I will say that the amendments which are suggested provide for a forfeiture of five dollars per day to the shipper for a failure to furnish cars. It does not give any penalty to the state. The language used in the act is that the railroad companies shall pay as liquidated damages to the shipper the sum of five dollars per day. The legislature could make it twenty-five dollars per day and it would be legal. Do not forget the United States Supreme Court has settled the law on that question. The legislature has the power to prescribe the penalty and it has the discretion to give that penalty either to the shipper or to the state. There ought to be no trouble about it when people understand the proposition; but I want to say to you that it is not the purpose of the railroad companies to enlighten the people upon these great questions. And I want to say to you, further, that there are a great many lawyers who have no occasion to give these matters special study. They know that certain fundamental principles exist; that certain things have been decided by the court in a general way; but they have no knowledge of the subject in a definite manner. This is all I have got to say about the subject of cars."

Question: Now, when the shipper fails to load the equipment in the forty-eight hours, shall he pay the railroad company five dollars per day for his failure?

Mr. Taylor: Yes, sir. The reason is that the railroad company has the right to demand that the cars be released as soon as possible. You see the rate has to be reciprocal. It is absolutely just and equitable to require the shipper to get his cars unloaded and get them back to the railroad company. There is no use to try to pass unconstitutional acts, so this had to be inserted, as also a clause that if the railroad company is prevented from furnishing cars from some unavoidable cause, they shall have the right to show that. The railroads claim that they are short of cars because the shippers hold them so long. I have a theory that this shortage has been caused by a desire of the railroads to raise their stock to par. In other words, they have taken all the dividends to pay charges, and they have not used any of their income for the purpose of buying new equipment.

Question: What causes will excuse the shipper from the penalty?

Mr. Taylor: Any unavoidable cause would be an excuse; otherwise the act would not be reciprocal.

It was moved and carried that a vote of thanks be extended to Carr W. Taylor for his paper and the concise information given the Association.

Papers were then read by Senator J. A. Noftzger on "Railroad Companies' Liability to Shippers —From a Legal Standpoint," and by C. A. Smith of Wellsville on the same topic, but "From a Shipper's Standpoint," which will be published in a later number.

The morning session was concluded by an address by John D. Shanahan, grain standardization expert of the Bureau of Plant Industry, Washington, on "What the Government Is Doing About Grain Inspection and Why?" which was received with marked interest.

Adjourned to 2 o'clock p. m.

FINAL SESSION OF SECOND DAY.

The final session was devoted mainly to routine matters, like arbitration committee decisions (published on another page with legal matters) and reports of minor committees.

Resolutions were adopted thanking Carr W. Taylor, the Commercial Club of Topeka, the Missouri & Kansas Telephone Co., Wichita Board of Trade, also the following:

We, the grain dealers of Kansas, in convention assembled, do hereby unanimously, earnestly, endorse the efforts of Carr W. Taylor, attorney for Board of Railroad Commissioners, in his fearless fight, without money or expert assistance, before the the Board of Railroad Commissioners and the courts to better shipping facilities and to secure a reduction of rates in Kansas; and we unanimously request that he be reappointed as attorney for the Board of Railroad Commissioners, believing that his retirement at the end of his term would be detrimental to the interests of the shippers of Kansas.

Among the resolutions referred to the committee and reported unfavorably by that body was the following, introduced by F. W. Frasius:

Whereas, Representatives of some thirty organized bodies met in Chicago, on December 11, 1906, for the purpose of formulating rules for the uniform inspection of grain throughout the United States; and

Whereas, The territory growing the celebrated hard winter wheat, the great Southwest, comprising nearly one-half of the winter wheat grown in the United States, was not represented; and

Whereas, This so-called Uniform Inspection Congress assumed the right to establish the grades for nearly two hundred million bushels of winter wheat grown annually, of which that territory represented by said grain Inspection Congress does not produce a single bushel; and

Whereas, Gross discriminations against Southwestern winter wheat growers is apparent; therefore, be it

Resolved, That the members of the Kansas Grain Dealers' Association, in convention assembled, jointly with the visiting grain dealers and growers to this convention, hereby attest their disapproval of the grades fixed upon hard winter wheat by the alleged Uniform Grades Congress; and be it further

Resolved, That this convention asks the honorable Grain Inspection Commission of the state of Kansas to prevent this discrimination and to reduce the test weight of the several grades of hard winter wheat at least one (1) pound per bushel at its next meeting to fix grades; and be it further

Resolved, That copies of these resolutions be transmitted to the members of the Kansas Grain Inspection Commission and to the Secretary of the Grain Dealers' National Association, John F. Courcier, Toledo, Ohio.

Mr. Frasius opened the debate supporting the resolution rejected by the committee.

The Chairman: The committee on resolutions has given the matter consideration and recommend that it be not adopted.

A Member: I move that the report be accepted.

Another Member: I believe the report ought to be adopted. It is one step toward getting universal grades. I think there is a misconstruction. I believe that every miller and every experienced grain dealer, laying aside all bias and prejudice, will honestly say that a bushel of red wheat testing fifty-eight is equal to a bushel of No. 2 hard wheat testing 59 pounds. I think for the benefit of the soft wheat growers that it is not an injustice to them. I think it will be accepted by the majority of the mills. I think this is one step toward getting universal grades of inspection.

Mr. Shanahan: While I am not particularly interested in this question, I think it incumbent upon myself to make a little explanation. I attended this uniform inspection meeting at Chicago. I went there purposely and solely for the purpose of informing them as nearly as I could what the United States Department of Agriculture was doing on the question; and among other things I told them that we were looking up the advisability, or the practicability, of making grades for the country on a percentage basis. Now, that looks very simple; but this question has occurred to me: They immediately took the cue from that and went ahead and formulated a grade. They ran through it hurriedly, and, of course, did not give it the time it should have had. In fact, if you gave it the time it should have, it would take at least four or five years to formulate the proper grades. However, I give them credit for being entirely honest in their efforts; but perhaps they went a little too far without the proper sounding and depth. I told them it was commendable, at least, and as it was the consensus of opinion they made an effort to formulate a grade that would have a basis, as at the present time they had none. I think their action was commendable. I am quite sure that no discrimination was meant against anyone. I know that the grades they adopted there are not fair and equitable. As I say, they went a little bit too fast. Their grades upon corn were made up upon a report of the department two or three years ago. That bulletin did not say that it was positively right or equitable or did not recommend that, but merely showed the figures and data that were gotten together in that investigation at that time. Therefore, gentlemen, you can see from what I say that the Department of Agriculture took no responsibility in the matter of formulating the grades. The credit is due the National Grain Dealers, and I think it is a step in the right direction.

A Member: Mr. President, this uniform grade as I understand it is all right, but I can see no reason why Kansas grain should build up somebody else's territory.

A Member: I move you as a substitute that the resolution be laid upon the table.

Mr. Robb: I second that motion. I have been down in Galveston several times during the last year and I have seen several cargoes of wheat loaded for Europe. I want to say that it was a disgrace for the stamp of the inspector to be put on that wheat as No. 2 hard wheat. Most of it would make a poor No. 5. My partner has from 1,000 to 250,000 bushels of grain of low grade wheat and he has been unable to handle it and cannot do it. I venture to say he cannot sell it. Now, why is that? It is because seventy-five per cent of his wheat is loaded out No. 4 rejected and low grade. Twenty-five per cent 3 and 2, low grade.. This wheat that is loaded out has the inspector's seal as graded No. 2, and I want to say that it is a poor No. 4. Now that thing works against us, and I am in favor of Government inspection for Kansas, Oklahoma and Nebraska.

Motion to lay Mr. Frasius' resolution on the table prevailed.

The committee on trade rules reported, recommending the adoption of the trade rules of the Grain Dealers' National Association, and said report was adopted.

The committee on constitution and by-laws recommended the adoption of this document as amended by the directors, which report was adopted.

The closing action of the convention was the election of the officers for 1907. On motion of W. S. Washer of Atchison, the name of L. Cortelyou of Muscotah was placed before the convention, in nomination for the presidency, but Mr. Cortelyou declined the honor with thanks. He said he had served in that capacity for seven years, and, while he enjoyed the work and appreciated the honor, he felt that it was time to pass it around. A. Aitken of St. John was then chosen president by a unanimous vote.

R. L. Cox of Elsmore was elected vice-president, also by a unanimous vote.

For the tenth consecutive time, E. J. Smiley of Topeka was chosen secretary, and a vote of thanks was given for his efficient service in the past.

Directors were elected as follows: W. A. Miller of Anthony, Perry N. Allen of Coffeyville, S. J. Thompson of Holton, and Joseph Blackshaw of Wilson.

A telegram was received from the Topeka Commercial Club, assuring the members of the Association that they would be well entertained if they would but call their next annual meeting to assemble in Topeka, and a Kansas City delegate

extended an invitation to the Association to hold its June meeting in that city.

The meeting then adjourned.

NOTES OF THE MEETING.

At the directors' meeting, held Wednesday night, the arbitration committee for 1907 was named as follows: A. H. Bennett, Wichita; Mr. Pribble of Salem, and C. A. Smith of Wellsville.

On motion of S. J. Thompson, a committee, consisting of the president and secretary, was instructed to watch the Kansas legislature; and, if deemed necessary, they were empowered to draft a larger committee to appear before the legislature while in session, with a view of protecting the interests of the millers and grain dealers.

Following are the names and addresses of the majority of those in attendance. It was impossible to secure the names of all, for various reasons: L. Cortelyou, Muscotah; E. J. Smiley, Topeka; W. L. Scott, Wichita; C. A. Baldwin, Wichita; A. H. Bennett, Topeka; C. E. Winthrope, Wichita; Miss Nell Hilliker, Kansas City, Mo.; M. Toomey, Americus; J. G. Goodwin, Kansas City, Mo.; Chas. Moody, Atlanta, Kan.; A. L. Williamson, Clay Center; Wm. Murphy, Kansas City, Mo.; C. F. Prouty, secretary, Enid, Okla.; P. G. Kroker, Cheney, Kan.; J. C. Bradley, Roseville, Kan.; S. C. Wilson, Ottawa; W. F. McCullough, Wichita; H. Kauffman, Grossburg; J. R. Baker, Hutchison; Paul Gano, Hutchison; H. D. Yoder, Hutchison; M. N. Randalls, El Reno, Okla.; H. W. Kueker, Niles; L. Noel, Galsco; B. U. Raymond, Haven; S. J. Thompson, Holton; P. M. Kelly, Hiawatha; W. A. Miller, Anthony; B. F. Smith, Anthony; M. S. Graham, Zurich; A. Aitken, St. John, Kan.; R. R. Sherrar, Preston; W. S. Washer, Atchison; H. Work, Ellsworth; T. L. Hoffman, Enterprise; J. S. McCaulley, Wichita; A. R. Clark, Wichita; W. E. Clark, Sawyer; R. E. Cox, Elsmore; H. M. Loyd, Sterling; E. N. Bailey, Baileyville; H. F. Probat, Arkansas City; H. A. Probat, Arkansas City; T. M. Van Horne, Kansas City, Mo.; S. P. Hinds, Kansas City, Mo.; J. W. Radford, Kansas City, Kan.; J. R. Mentzer, Kansas City, Kan.; A. D. Crotts, Kansas City, Kan.; G. M. Cassity, Tonkawa, Okla.; O. W. Hutchinson, Tonkawa, Okla.; B. W. Fenquay, Tonkawa, Okla.; F. A. James, Burden, Can.; John W. Ledlie, Burden, Kan.; Joseph Latshaw, Wilson; L. E. Raymond, Sawyer; C. C. Smith, Conway Springs; E. M. Elkins, Wichita; C. W. Binkley, Wichita; W. T. McCauley, Wichita; F. C. Dymock, Wichita; D. C. Kolp, Oklahoma City, O. T.; J. A. Woodside, Wichita; F. D. Stevens, Wichita; S. C. Groth, Ellsworth; E. E. Rohen, Kansas City; J. R. Senter, Clearwater; R. F. Coats, Wichita; C. L. Wagoner, Mount Hope; J. R. Wagoner, Mount Hope; David Heenan, Wichita; E. K. Nevling, Wichita; J. R. Hargis, Hazelton; P. M. Kelly, Corwin; Walter Ulrich, Hamelton; John T. Snodgrass, Kansas City; Angus McLeod, Peru, Ill.; G. C. Canaan, Kansas City; John D. Shanahan, Washington, D. C.; E. M. Flickinger, Wichita; F. L. Fairchilds, Wichita; Geo. W. Crowell, Alva, O. T.; J. C. Robb, Wichita; W. F. Bort, Wichita; D. F. Pjassek, Kansas City, Mo.; L. A. Dockum, Garden City; W. A. Watson, Wichita; Martin H. Nelson, Gueda Springs; D. P. Lorenze, Kansas City, Mo.; D. L. Croysdale, Kansas City, Mo.; A. S. Barr, Wichita; Frank Barnett, Kansas City, Mo.; C. S. Miller, New Kirk, O. T.; F. G. Olson, Wichita; J. F. Skinner, Coats; J. S. Strickler, Ramona; H. W. Gorvin, Wichita; John Herzer, Wichita; H. Herzer, Wichita; J. B. Miltner, Wichita; F. B. Downs, Belle Plain; H. Hatfield, Belle Plain; J. F. Shotts, LaCrosse; Rollie Watson, Alton, Ill.; J. A. McKinney, Alton, Ill.; Lee Fuller, Kansas City, Mo.; F. D. Logan, Kansas City, Mo.; C. A. McCotter, Indianapolis, Ind.; Fred Strong, Riverdale; H. I. Merrill, Furley; F. P. Evans, Kansas City, Mo.; J. A. Pribble, Salina; C. C. Fields, Wichita; Ed. Boots, Isabel; H. H. Haines, Gainesville; Ed Ordway, Kansas City; D. H. B. Crowell, Attica;

B. F. Kelsey, Oxford; E. G. Swayze, Pamona; A. Logan, Kansas City, Mo.; G. E. Cooper, Kansas City, Mo.; P. H. Pelkey, Wichita; C. B. Gaunt, Wichita; C. A. Smith, Wellville; J. T. Dale, Douglass; Allison Barry, Kansas City, Mo.; Hammell & McCarty, Bronson; M. M. Cubbinson, Bayard; R. T. Williams, Hiattsville; A. M. Brandt, Severy; W. E. Edgar, Sacksman; J. A. Lyons, Langdon; J. D. McCord, Fredonia; A. R. Norton, Norwich; F. X. Rexford, Thayer; D. D. Wiechen, Garden Plain; W. K. McMillan, Hutchinson.

INSPECTION IN MINNESOTA.

Chief Inspector Eva of Minnesota has sent his annual report to the Railroad and Warehouse Commission. It is for the year ended August 31, 1906, and shows inspection of 235,422 cars, of which 146,864 were of wheat, 4,409 of corn, 26,277 of oats, 2,948 of rye, 23,969 of barley and 30,955 of flaxseed. The revenues of the office were $200,131.36 and the disbursements $245,448.90, making net loss of $45,310.54, which was taken from the surplus of the previous year. Continuing, the report says:

Reinspection and Appeals.—Out of a total of 297,902 carloads of grain inspected "on arrival" and "out of store," 43,445 cars were held out for reinspection, with the following results: In 18,184 cases the original grade and dockage was confirmed; grades were raised in 15,779 cases, lowered in 3,303 cases, and in 6,179 cases the dockage was changed. Appeals to the Board of Grain Appeals were made in 18,716 cases, in 12,251 of which the decisions of the chief deputies were confirmed, and in 6,465 cases changed.

Bad Order Cars.—The number of cars received at the terminal points and found in what might be termed "bad order" were 12,230 cars out of a total of 235,422 cars; of these, 4,549 cars were without seals, 1,174 with seals broken; 876 open end and side doors; 1,652 leaky grain doors; 222 with leaky end, side and bottom; 1,486 with no fastenings; 1,848 were poorly fastened, and 123 with no doors.

Dockages.—Of the 140,546 carloads of spring wheat inspected "on arrival" at the several terminal points during the year, 7,981 were docked one-half pound per bushel; 37,951, one pound; 33,823, one and one-half pounds; 25,875, two pounds; 9,784, two and one-half pounds; 9,936, three pounds; 9,737, over three and at an average of four pounds; and 477 without any dockage. The net average dockage on total receipts at all points was 27.9 ounces per bushel, as against 18.6 ounces the previous year.

The report also contains a "Brief History of the Minnesota Inspection at Superior, Wis.," which is a fair statement of the Minnesota side of the Duluth-Superior inspection row of a year ago, and is particularly happy in the exposure of the ignorance of all things concerned with official inspection of Senator McCumber of North Dakota, who aspires to be the author of a law for the national inspection of grain. We may refer to this part of the report at another time when our space is less crowded.

N. I. GRAIN DEALERS.

The Northeastern Indiana Grain Dealers' Association held a meeting at Fort Wayne on February 5, in the rooms of the Commercial Club. New officers elected for the year are as follows:

President—R. A. Brown of Huntington.

Vice-President—T. P. Riddle of Fort Wayne.

Secretary-treasurer—C. F. Davison of Bluffton.

Resolutions were adopted as follows:

Resolved, That the Northeastern Indiana Grain Dealers' Association indorses the bills introduced in the state Senate, and known as Senate bills Nos. 194 and 195.

That we use our best endeavors with our senators and representatives to secure their support for said bills, believing that the present conditions of traffic are an injury to the producers of grain and that relief must come through legislation along this line.

That a copy of these resolutions be sent to the chairmen of committees on railroads in the Senate and House of Representatives and to the members of both houses from Allen County, Adams, Whitley, Wells, Huntington and Blackford counties.

IN THE LEGISLATURES.

Legislatures in many states are now at work, and in the West and Northwest there is enough threatening legislation on hand to warrant a warning to the trade to keep a watch on general assembly proceedings. A brief statement of the matters brought to our notice appears below:

MASSACHUSETTS.—A bill for a law has been offered which provides for fine and imprisonment of anyone operating a bucket-shop in that state.

TEXAS.—The Texas senate has passed a bill providing that the railroads must furnish cars for the shipment of live stock within six days of the time a written demand is made for them or pay a heavy penalty.

KANSAS.—There are two grain weighing and inspection bills before the Kansas legislature, one by Chief Grain Inspector Radford, who says the bill introduced by Representative Creech in one of the sections provides that grain consigned to the Kansas City markets shall be weighed by the state department unless the consignor specifically demands that it shall not be weighed. Mr. Radford said of this provision: "If they get that bill through it will end state weighing. The consignor would be bulldozed into asking that his grain be not weighed by the Kansas department. The consignor would be told that his grain could not be handled unless it be sent with the understanding that it should not be weighed."

On February 6 W. Y. Morgan introduced in the House a bill fixing maximum rates on grain and grain products. In round figures it reduces existing rates about 25 per cent.

ILLINOIS.—Representative Behrens has a bill to prevent discrimination between shippers in the furnishing of cars. It gives the Railroad and Warehouse Commission authority to hold public hearings when complaint of discrimination is made and to lay down rules for the future distribution of cars.

MISSOURI.—Senator Humphreys has introduced a bill for a law empowering the governor to appoint the Chief Grain Inspector, now appointed by the Railroad and Warehouse Commission. Such a law would substantially remove the inspection and weighing functions from the control of the Commissioners.

Another bill before the Missouri legislature is one known as the Avery bill, inspired by the Railroad and Warehouse Commission. It would enable the Commission to inspect and weigh all grain shipped to mills or to market in Missouri, whether on cars, boats, barges, on track or in wagons. At present the Commission may weigh grain only at the public elevators in the state. This bill the grain exchanges of both St. Louis and Kansas City will oppose for the following reasons, as formulated by Edward Devoy, chairman of the St. Louis Merchants' Exchange grain committee:

Our desire is to have the Exchange and Warehouse Commission work in harmony and perfect understanding. Up to four years ago, when our weighing bureau was established, there was no weighing done except by the Commission. The bureau was organized at the request of 90 per cent of all the men who ship grain to St. Louis. Now the Commission only weighs grain in public elevators, of which there are five in St. Louis. It does not do anything at all in this direction with the private elevators. Our bureau weighs grain in private elevators, and provides also supervisors for the weighing in public elevators. Shippers generally are opposed to the proposed legislation, for the reason that they demand that the Exchange supervise the weighing of all grain, as such good results have been obtained from this supervision. Chicago, Baltimore, New Orleans and other important grain centers conduct weighing and supervision, as it is practiced by the Exchange bureau.

Since the establishment of our bureau complaints have been reduced to a minimum. Fully 90 per cent of the shippers have agreed to pay our fee in addition to that exacted by the state Railroad and Warehouse Commission. The Exchange appoints inspectors who inspect the condition of cars before the railroads place them on side tracks or at the elevators, to find leaks or other defects.

Last year the bureau inspected some 45,000 cars, of which about 19,000 were discovered to be faulty. The bureau works in perfect harmony with the railroads and the roads accept the Exchange weighing in computing freight charges. The railroads also co-operate with our inspectors in finding leaky cars. The weighing bureau is maintained by the Exchange at a cost of from $8,000 to $10,000 per year. It has numerous advantages which could not be obtained by state weighing and supervision. The bureau operates on the East Side as well as in St. Louis proper, while in Illinois the state Commission has no authority whatever.

The St. Louis Merchants' Exchange addressed a communication to the Railroad and Warehouse Commission on this bill, and also sent a delegation to Jefferson City to protest; but on February 6 the joint committee on agriculture unanimously recommended the passage of the bills providing for state weighing of grain and state inspection of hay.

IOWA.—Representative Stillman of Greene County has introduced in the Iowa house a bill for a law to prohibit grain dealers and elevator men from "combining to prevent free competition in the buying of grain." The bill is the Nebraska law with a new label, and aims to knock out the case card system of quoting prices. The bill provides that it shall be unlawful for any person or company engaged in handling grain to enter into any agreement with others handling grain, for the pooling of prices of different and competing dealers or buyers or to divide between them the aggregate or net proceeds of the earnings of such dealers, or for agreement upon regulating or fixing the price which any other grain dealer shall pay for grain and to form, enter into, or maintain any trust pool, combination, or association of persons which has for its objects the prevention of free competition among buyers or sellers or dealers in grain. In case of such a pool, the bill provides, the offender shall be liable to those injured for the full amount of damages sustained. For violation of that act a penalty is also made of a fine not less than $500 nor more than $2,000, and half the fine imposed shall go to the person who shall furnish information on which conviction shall be found, and imprisonment in the county jail not exceeding six months or both fine and imprisonment.

Senator Saunders of Council Bluffs has offered a bill creating a state department for the inspection of grain, which is intended to oust Omaha Grain Exchange Inspection at Council Bluffs and repeat the miseries of a dual inspection, now such a nuisance to the trade at Kansas City and St. Louis.

NORTH DAKOTA.—Senator Johnson has a bill before the North Dakota legislature by which it is hoped to stop the annual outward flow in grain in the spring, when the elevators empty their bins to avoid paying taxes on the grain. Very little tax is paid by the elevator companies on grain in store under the present law, and the repeal of the tax (which the bill would do) will decrease tax collections only a nominal amount. The heavy annual shipment of grain in the spring, it is believed, lowers the price materially and works a hardship on the farmer.

There is a bill before the senate requiring that all packages of seeds must be labeled, stating nature of seed, mixtures and place of growth. A statement of the year's crop must be published according to the present provisions of the bill.

Senator Cashel has introduced a resolution urging the withdrawal of opposition on the part of Duluth to the establishment of an equitable grain grading and inspection system at Superior; and asking that the laws of Minnesota and Wisconsin be amended to accord with the best interests of the grain growers of the Northwest in regulating terminal elevators and grain inspection; that suction draft be prohibited before the grain is weighed and dockage taken, and that the value of the dockage be paid to the owner of the grain; that car inspection be established and that, in the event that the grievances are not redressed, farmers and grain growers co-operate for the building of local and terminal elevators.

A bill is before the house providing that all railroads shall maintain stations at all sidings where shipments of grain and merchandise are made.

An amendment has been proposed to the license law providing that public grain warehouses shall take out licenses for two years, or for a term to expire on August 1 of each odd-numbered year, the license fee to be $8 for warehouses of a capacity of 12,000 bushels or less, and $10 for warehouses of a capacity of over 12,000 bushels and not to exceed 25,000 bushels, and $12 for all warehouses over 25,000 bushels' capacity for each public grain warehouse.

MINNESOTA.—Senator Wilson of Hennepin County has introduced in the Minnesota legislature a joint resolution asking the Congress to abolish the tariff on wheat.

Senator Thorpe of Willmar has introduced a bill providing that any person purchasing, selling or storing grain in Minnesota state shall use the bushel as the unit. No other number of pounds per bushel shall be used than the number of pounds provided by law as the standard weight of the kind of grain in question. The Railroad and Warehouse Commission is authorized, after a hearing, to cancel the license of any person found guilty of violating this provision or who may be found guilty of entering into any trade agreement or contract to control, directly or indirectly, the price to be paid for grain. After canceling a license the Commission may refuse to grant a new one for a period of one year. The bill provides further, that each warehouse man shall make a detailed report of his business to the state Railroad and Warehouse Commission by July 15 of each year, which report shall contain an itemized statement of all of the business transacted by him as such public warehouseman during the preceding year, and shall state the grade, gross weight and dockage of all of the grains of various kinds in his warehouse at the beginning of the year, of all received and shipped during the year and of that remaining at the end of the year. The report shall give the shortage also in any kind of grain arising during the year and shall state the weight basis upon which all grains have been received or shipped. The commissioners also are authorized to require special statements at such times as they may deem expedient.

A resolution calling for an investigation of the Minneapolis Chamber of Commerce and the Duluth Board of Trade was passed by the house on January 15. The resolution was introduced by J. A. Gates of Kenyon and calls for the appointment of a committee of five to make an investigation into the organization, rules, methods, policies and practices of the two named bodies. The committee is given power to subpœna witnesses and to employ the necessary clerical help. No debate was offered on the resolution and it was passed without opposition. The speaker will announce the appointment of the commission in a short while.

Senator Schaller has introduced a bill making the Railroad and Warehouse Commission's recent rate-reducing order the maximum tariff permissible in the state, thus taking the matter out of the jurisdiction of the federal courts.

Senator Dale of Madison County has introduced a bill for a law authorizing municipal corporations to pass ordinances prohibiting the establishment or maintenance of bucket-shops within their corporate limits. The bill provides that when any ten electors petition the common council of any municipal corporation for the enactment of such an ordinance it shall be submitted to the voters at the next general or special election; that municipal corporations may prohibit by ordinance the maintenance of any bucket-shop, the penalty being a fine of not to exceed $100 or imprisonment in the county jail for not more than ninety days. There is a provision in the bill that it is not necessary to commit the offense mentioned in the act that both buyer and seller shall agree to do any of the acts prohibited, but the crime shall be complete against the corporation or individual offering to sell or pretending to buy, whether the offer to sell or to buy is accepted or not.

PENNSYLVANIA.—Senator Tustin has introduced a bill for the creation of a railroad commission to be known as the State Commerce Commission and to consist of five persons, to be appointed by the governor, for six years, at $8,000 a year each. The expense is to be apportioned among the common carriers of the state. The Commission shall have power to regulate rates, articles to be transported, transportation agencies and facilities, switch-connections and passenger stations. It shall forbid the offering, granting or receiving of rebates or the pooling of freights by competing companies. It shall investigate all complaints against railroads, and may send for witnesses and papers. It may compel the publication of joint rates or the rates for through transportation. Free passes or free transportation is forbidden except to railroad employes. No passenger station can be abolished without the consent of the commission. Penalties are provided for violation of any of the provisions.

NEBRASKA.—A bill is before the Nebraska legislature to outlaw bucket-shops.

A resolution of Representative Weenes, calling for the appointment of a committee to investigate the low grain prices in Nebraska as compared with those in adjoining states, was smothered by the House on January 25. The resolution had been referred to the railroad committee, which brought in a recommendation that the speaker appoint a special committee to take charge of it, as the railroad committee did not know what else to do with it. Chairman Marsh did not personally favor an investigation, for, he said, it was plain to "any sensible man" that a state situated closer to market than Nebraska would naturally get higher prices for its grain. The resolution was tabled.

Representative Cone has a bill before the House that provides for the creation of a state grain weighing and inspection department. Mr. Cone believes that "all inspections are bad," and he is quoted by Omaha papers as saying that, "the grain trust is operating to-day just the same as it had always operated, and we rewarded the man who says he busted the trust by sending him to the Senate."

ALABAMA.—Two bills have been introduced into the Alabama legislature to do away with bucket-shops in that state. The bills follow very closely the measure which was passed by the Georgia legislature recently, and which the United States Supreme Court has upheld.

INDIANA.—Senator Kimbrough of Muncie has introduced a bill in the Senate to regulate the car service of state railways. The bill was prepared by the legislative committee of the Indiana Manufacturers and Shippers' Association and has been indorsed by many similar organizations, including the Retail Lumber Dealers' Association, the Hardwood Lumber Dealers' Association and the Indiana Grain Dealers' Association. The bill gives the state Railroad Commission power to enforce its rulings; provides for reciprocal demurrage; requires commodities to be moved a given minimum miles per day; stipulates for credits for prompt loading and unloading; forbids discriminations; aims to prevent the stealing of cars by connecting roads, etc.

CANADIAN.—The Grain Growers' Association desires the Winnipeg Grain Exchange's charter amended, along the line of removing the Exchange's power to suspend a firm from the privileges of the floor without the concurrence of the Minister of Agriculture. The Exchange naturally opposes any change in its charter, and has made to the government the following declaration: "Members of the Exchange cannot conduct business without the provision of the charter they now hold. We do not want the charter amended. If this committee intends to do so, we will ask to have it cancelled. We shall ask for the appointment of a receiver, for our assets to be distributed, and we will do the best we can without an Exchange." The Manitoba Minister of Agriculture is a member of the Exchange.

WISCONSIN.—An amendment will be introduced in the Wisconsin legislature to turn the inspection over to the Railroad Commission, with a view to enabling that body to take control of the Superior elevators and direct their operation.

TENNESSEE.—The legislature has a bill before

it prohibiting any trading in cotton or grain for future delivery.

CANADIAN GRAIN COMMISSION.

The Royal Grain Commission resumed its inquiries in the Canadian West at Moosomin, Sask., on January 10, where the most interesting information elicited was the fact that train crews have taken advantage of the car famine to hold up shippers. The prevailing price seems to have been $10 per car.

At Regina, next day, the car shortage continued to be the theme. The farmers complained that frequently the 1,400-bushel cars were set out for them when they had only 1,000 bushels to ship and that they had either to pay for the 400 bushels' waste or miss their turn and go down to the bottom of the list on the order book.

At Weyburn there was complaint of short weights, and the following colloquy, among others, took place: Mr. McNair—"Do you consider there are honest elevator men?" Witness, H. W. Boden of Lang—"Yes, I have met one." Mr. Miller—"Under the present system, do you consider it is possible for a farmer to get just weights?" Witness—"No."

Thomas Montgomery of Glen Ewen recommended government weigh scales at every shipping point; that the weighing be made compulsory, and that a moderate charge be levied to pay expenses. Railways should be made responsible for any loss in transit.

On January 23 the Commission returned to Winnipeg and took testimony bearing on the relations of the Winnipeg Grain Exchange to the trade. The Exchange presented a printed argument on its own behalf, which was read in part and filed. Then a deputation from the Grain Growers' Association asked that the powers of the Exchange be limited 'so that the business would be conducted on an equitable basis between the buyer and the producer." Mr. Bonnar, solicitor for the Association, presented the following suggestions for the guidance of the committee in taking action:

That the Grain Exchange set no limit as to the number of persons which may enjoy its privileges. Every reputable person, firm or corporation engaged in or proposing to engage in the grain trade and willing to bear his share of the cost of maintenance of the organization, must be eligible for membership therein; and since the question of reputation might be made a barrier, the question of reputability shall be decided by the majority of the members.

It is also asked that a firm or corporation must be eligible for membership irrespective of registration under a membership held by an individual; that is, a membership which has been purchased for the use of said corporation and so declaimed shall confer all privileges of exchange upon that firm or corporation.

Also that the right to membership shall include the right to delegate the trading powers to anyone in the employ of the firm or corporation.

Also asked that the arbitrary interference with the business methods employed by individual firms or corporations and the inquisitional inquiry into such must be prohibited.

Also that the penalties and disabilities against those breaking the common rules and maximum price rule should be abolished.

Also that the right to define the eligibility of a person as an employe of any person, firm or corporation or fix a limit to salary in any way must cease.

Also that the expulsion of no member shall be final until assented by the minister of agriculture.

Also, that all by-laws shall receive the assent of the lieutenant-governor-in-council before becoming legal and binding.

Also that the government shall have full access to the minute books and papers and accounts of the Grain Exchange.

Also that the public shall have access to a gallery overlooking the trading room during the progress of a session so that the transactions occurring there may be observed and the prices may disseminate through the public press.

Also that gambling in future be made a criminal offense.

Amendments were asked by the Association to the grain act—that elevators be required to make

uniform rates for services performed; that they be required to have cleaning machinery; that a permanent inspection survey board be appointed; that the government take full control of the elevators at Fort William and Port Arthur; that storage elevators should be established in the interior by the government.

Then the Commission turned its attention to the affairs of Geo. Wood, who, Frank G. Simpson, of Simpson & Hepworth, commission merchants, intimated, had approached him on a pure bucket-shop proposition, Mr. Manahan, law partner of Mr. Bonnar, counsel for the Grain Growers, was counsel for Wood, who had said, so Simpson testified, that he had been run out of the United States. Wood is now the Canadian Stock and Grain Company. Mr. Wood was examined in detail, who, in answer to Commissioner McNair, said: "We buy and sell on option. Our profits do not necessarily depend upon the rise and fall of the price of grain. Our profits are derived from commissions, which is one-eighth per cent, never more and never less." "Are the contracts placed by you with the Wisconsin Stock and Grain Company actually carried out?" was asked Mr. Wood, who said that he was unable to answer.

It was shown that there was a connection, more or less intimate, between Wood and the Wisconsin Stock and Grain Company of Superior. Wm. H. Holton, now in the employ of a Winnipeg firm, but who had been prior to his present engagement in the service of the Wisconsin Stock and Grain Exchange, which worked with the Superior Board of Trade, said: "I firmly believe it is a combination, from the knowledge I derived when employed in Duluth in the service of the Wisconsin Stock and Grain Exchange, to run a bucket-shop." He said he thought Edwards-Wood company was fictitious. "I have been on the floor of the Wisconsin Stock and Grain Exchange three or four times," said Mr. Holton in answer to a question from the Commissioners as to the proceedings there. "There were usually seven or eight people present. They went through actions and talked as if for the purpose of deceiving the public into the idea that the transactions were bona fide." "As a matter of fact," asked W. Manahan, counsel for Mr. Wood, "do you really know whether those transactions were real or not?" "I do not."

In brief, the examination disclosed the following state of facts: The Canadian Stock and Grain Company operates under a Manitoba charter. Neither the company nor any of its members are members of the Winnipeg or Minneapolis or Chicago exchanges or boards of trade. Mr. Wood himself is a member of the Superior Board of Trade. His company did business through the Wisconsin Stock and Grain Company, but Mr. Wood did not know whether these people were members of any board of trade or exchange. Parties buying and selling through his company had absolutely no guarantee as to whether their orders were placed or not. Quotations as to the price of Fort William wheat sent out by the company to their country branches were quotations received by them through the Wisconsin Stock and Grain Company from the Superior Board of Trade. Mr. Wood objected to giving names of shareholders and directors, and to producing the books of the company, but was told by the Commission that he must do as the others had done. It has been learned that several of the provisional directors of the company were clerks in the attorney-general's department.

On January 29 the Commission finished its work in Canada. A short ad interim report will be made immediately, and then the Commissioners will take a vacation. Early in the spring they will meet again and go to Halifax, St. John, N. B., Portland, Me., and New York, where further evidence will be taken, after which the members will sail for Great Britain to inquire into all the conditions there which affect the Canadian grain trade. A full report of the Commission will not be presented to Parliament until next session.

PUBLISHED ON THE FIFTEENTH OF EACH MONTH BY

MITCHELL BROS. COMPANY

(INCORPORATED.)

OFFICE:

Manhattan Building, 315 Dearborn Street,
CHICAGO, ILL.

HARLEY B. MITCHELL..................................Editor
A. J. MITCHELL..............................Business Manager

Subscription Price, - - - - $1.00 per Year
English and Foreign Subscription, - 1.60 " "

ADVERTISING.

This paper has a large circulation among the elevator men and grain dealers of the country, and is the best medium in the United States for reaching persons connected with the trade. Advertising rates made known upon application.

CORRESPONDENCE

We solicit correspondence upon all topics of interest connected with the handling of grain or cognate subjects.

CHICAGO, ILL., FEBRUARY 15, 1907.

Official Paper of the Illinois Grain Dealers' Association.

LANDA-LATTIN DOCTRINE.

It was predicted in these columns, several years ago, when the decision in Landa vs. Lattin appeared—which sustained the contention that banks handling drafts on bills of lading become liable to the drawee for the quantity and condition of the shipment itself—that unless this doctrine were modified, it would eventually break down the entire system of making collections on order bills of lading. Common sense advised that it is absurb to expect a bank, which has no interest in the commodities represented by the bills of landing drawn against, further than the amount of a small fee for making the collection, to be held liable for the character of a shipment made by a drawer over whom it could have no control, but who might take advantage of the ruling to sophisticate a shipment for the purpose of swindling the drawee and leave the bank in the lurch. It is strange that so many of the state courts passing on this question rejected this common-sense view and held to the doctrine of the decision from Te_as. Drafts have since been collected by the banks, in spite of this ruling; but, as the reader is well aware, some banks of late have been giving notice of a change of method and taken the precaution to disavow responsibility, while a few others have refused to handle such paper at all; and such might ultimately have been the general rule among them.

However, the Tennessee Supreme Court, in a decision very fully abstracted on another page of this number, has completely rejected the Landa-Lattin doctrine and returned to a common-sense view of the transaction in question. The decision so ably presents this view of the subject that it can hardly fail to impress other courts with the soundness of the reasoning, and become a new authority. The decision is a righteous one, and one that will be welcomed by the grain and hay trades, particularly, as relieving their banks of an improper burden of responsibility, that will restore the former relations of banks to such paper.

MR. GOEMANN RESIGNS.

While admitting the sufficiency of Mr. Goemann's reasons, the grain trade will regret the resignation of Mr. Goemann as president of the National Association. Made chairman of the executive committee at Buffalo at a time when the Association had neither a secretary nor funds and but few friends, he immediately entered upon the work of resuscitation with an energy and wholeheartedness that permitted no slighting of his duty to the Association in favor of his private interests. Going wherever called, ready to say the right word and do the right thing whenever and wherever needed, and doing all with singular wisdom and effectiveness, within the year he had rebuilt the Association and made it a militant body, which since his election to the presidency has become a strong and powerful trade organisation, with an efficient secretary and working capacity for good, limited only by the supineness of a certain portion of the trade who support nothing in the way of trade utilities, that takes the form of supplying funds.

Mr. Goemann retires with the affection of all members of the Association, who can but envy his executive ability and success and admire his cordial and self-sacrificing response to the calls of duty as he saw it.

TESTING COUNTRY SCALES.

The Kansas Grain Dealers' Association turned down a proposition to spend money for testing the condition of country station scales. There is a well-founded suspicion in the minds of the informed that the Association in this matter acted without sufficient knowledge of the average condition of grain elevator scales in the country. Not that the scales in Kansas are worse than grain scales elsewhere, for, of course, they are not. Unfortunately, they are doubtless for the most part in like condition to scales in other states; which is equivalent to saying that probably not 5 per cent of them weigh correctly.

With all due respect, then, it may be said that of all men who find it absolutely necessary to use scales all the time, few men know less about them, their care and their condition after a few weeks or months of use, than country grain dealers; and it is the exception when a disinterested owner on examination does not find such scales out of order in some respect, after having been some time in use.

Wherefore, if dealers prefer to use a scale out of condition and are satisfied with an approximation of the amount they buy and prefer to be uncertain that they are not stealing from themselves or from their customers, why, then, there is nothing more to be said.

The duty of the adviser of the dealer ends when he reminds the latter that in 95 per cent of the cases he is relying on a scale that is not true, if it has not been adjusted within, say, the year.

QUEER OFFICIALS.

It certainly is discouraging enough to honorable business men, at a time when the demagog hysteria seems to be so infecting the community that a perfectly normal mind is coming to be a rarity, that this infection should take hold of men presumably so well trained to calm as well as judicious thinking as the Governor and the Attorney-General of a great state like Minnesota. Yet the latter official, in his biennial report to the Governor, declares that in his opinion, and he is endorsed by the Governor in his message, that—

The grain trade of the state has fallen into the hands of two close monopolies, one situated in Minneapolis and the other in Duluth. These institutions have the absolute control of the grain market of the state, and they assume to have, under the law, the power to exclude from membership in their organizations anyone considered undesirable, and the person so excluded is absolutely barred from embarking in the grain trade by reason of its concentration within the organizations referred to.

It hardly seems credible that a man in this official position does not understand the true functions of such bodies as the grain exchanges named, yet to acquit him of ignorance would be to convict him of misrepresentation. The true status of the public exchanges need not be explained to this reader, who surely must understand how essential—how indispensable—they are to the marketing of grain, hay and the other commodities that must be bought and sold on change if the producer is to obtain for them the highest prices the world will pay. That the Attorney-General has been unable to differentiate between the exchanges per se and any alleged abuses, operating outside and wholly apart from the exchanges themselves, that certain handlers of grain may or may not have been guilty of, is a serious reflection on the commercial education of the Attorney-General. If Minnesota farmers were to take this lawyer at his word and should undertake to protect themselves "against such monopolies," what form other than another similar exchange would it be possible for this Attorney-General to suggest?

BARLEY CULTURE.

The article by Dr. Wahl, printed on another page, is commended to the barley trade, in spite of its apparent length, because of the importance of the subject treated; and its wide circulation among farmers is strongly advised.

Barley culture in the United States has been hitherto but an incident of farming, rarely a distinct aim, and the crop has been only what may have been expected. Naturally also its habitat has changed frequently, in recent years, with consequent disturbance of the malting industry. Now, however, that the range of American barley lands has been traversed, the crop in the future will be confined to certain states, or parts of those states. That fact predicates a change in cultural methods if the crop is to become a permanent one. Dr.

Wahl's address is, therefore, a contribution of great value to the science which hereafter must dominate the growing of high-grade barley.

That scientific farming applied to barley will be profitable to the farmer goes without the saying, considering how such culture influences the regularity of the crop and the volume of grain produced, as well as its quality, so distinctly required by the demands of the brewing industry, which every year, as population and the consumption of beer increase, will demand a greater and still greater supply of choice brewing grain.

THE OLD STORY AGAIN.

The Indiana dealers adopted a resolution expressive of their belief that the off-grades should be sold by the receiver to the highest bidder and not applied on contracts with a penalty. In Kansas, Mr. Radford told the dealers they should sell on bids with the understanding that all off-grade stuff should be turned over to the shipper's commission man to be sold on his account by sample.

Both propositions seem entirely fair and practicable. But if dealers who sell on track bids will take the trouble to read the contract carefully and with a view to its legal meaning, it will be seen that the document is entirely a jug-handled one. The bidder has absolute control of the grain consigned to him, and can do as he pleases with it, even to holding it for his disposal until such time that the plans above proposed would avail nothing. Receivers, for obvious reasons, rarely enforce all the rights they have under this cut-throat form of contract, so commonplace that probably not 25 per cent of the dealers who sell under it realise its nature and their own helplessness in the hands of one who would be disposed to exercise all his rights; but it is safe to say that neither the Indiana nor Kansas proposition will ever obtain until dealers themselves demand a radical revision of the form of the card contract itself, to give a mutuality of rights under it.

HUMBUG IN IOWA.

It is a score of years, or more, since Herbert Spencer published his fascinating "Study of Sociology"—the reasons why thinking men should study the new science (?). Not in the way of the parlor sociologist, who is responsible for an infinitude of misery born of a factitious discontent, but to get a grasp of the invisible forces that move men and create the currents that fashion social phenomena. One striking thought one remembers out of this mass of learning and the remorseless logic of this greatest thinker of his age—the omnipresence, we had almost said the omnipotence, of humbug as a potential force in society.

The performances of certain gentlemen in Iowa are strikingly in point, illustrative of this power of humbug persistently and consistently adhered to, which Barnum put into practice with so much profit to himself. Like Barnum, and with the same end in view, the co-operative promoters use this same old force to convince Iowa farmers they are in

the throes of financial dissolution. Here is C. G. Meserole, secretary of the co-operatives' state association, and editor of the Co-operative Journal, who is brother to one of the traveling men of a Chicago commission house now working the co-operatives; then the treasurer of this organ of the movement, the Co-operative Journal, is brother-in-law to another Chicago house working the same trade, while two other representatives of the same two firms do the oratorical stunts—quite a nice little family party.

Now, this happy family arrangement would be all right—if the game were fairly played. But it isn't. Like the parlor sociologists, this coterie of relations are stirring up a discontent in the state that is not justified by conditions, simply to get business that might otherwise go in other directions—creating distrust of the class of business men to which they themselves belong—befouling their own nests and encouraging adverse legislation that threatens to put the grain trade into restrictive harness, when in fact it needs greater liberty and freedom of action. It is all tommy rot that farmers need protection from themselves or from grain dealers. What they do want is what the grain trade wants—a freedom from discriminations by railways in favor of the line companies, a restoration of the public elevator system and competition of buyers on 'change, a chance to do business on a broad and not a narrow scale, and the self-emancipation of the country grain dealer from the track-bidding system, as well as freedom from this everlasting preachment of misrepresentation and humbug and the artificial creation of discontent.

COLLECTING CLAIMS.

C. S. Wilson of Ottawa, Kan., in a paper read to the Kansas Grain Dealers' Association, and the Bassett Grain Co., in a letter on another page, throw out some valuable hints to shippers on the procedure in the matter of collecting claims. Mr. Wilson's paper this writer especially enjoys and commends, as it is an elaboration of the hints repeatedly thrown out to shippers in these columns, while Mr. Bassett's letter cites a concrete illustration.

Railroad offices are systematic—to a large degree they are entirely impersonal in their treatment of men; and those who deal with them in a matter of a claim for the payment of money must be methodical also. Railroads understand their liability even better than most shippers understand it, and are prepared to defend themselves against claimants who are but half-prepared to substantiate their claims, no matter how well founded. Introduce system into your business records and you will not have serious difficulty in collecting righteous claims for losses.

Mr. Bassett's letter presents a variant, however, but only a variant; and the case he cites proves the truth of our former and present contention—that if a shipper is prepared to back his claim by absolute proofs, even the grab of ½ or 1 per cent shrinkage will be waived. The thing is to be able to prove your

case—not to your own satisfaction but to convince a court or jury, and then stick to your case.

MUTUAL FIRE INSURANCE.

Both the insurance and the daily press are frank enough to give notice that the old-line insurance companies propose to begin a combined campaign against the mutual companies and the wholesome competition they are making with the old-liners. Many insurers do not realise the nature of this competition fully, even when they are friendly to the mutuals. They do not realise that being mutual in form they can never practice anything like a hold-up, rates being limited to the actual losses and expense necessities, and that these are limited by the insured themselves, whose individual care and protection of their own premises inevitably lowers the rate.

The union companies well understand all this, as well as the other strong points of mutual insurance; and in some states have already secured laws that make it practically impossible to organize mutual companies, and are endeavoring to enlarge the area of prohibition by the capture of other states. Grain men, therefore, should be on their guard against this subtle movement—should keep watch of bills in the state legislatures; and where such prohibition laws now exist they owe it to themselves to work for their unconditional repeal.

NEW ORLEANS INSPECTION.

This paper holds no brief for the New Orleans inspection department, but as a suggestion to the Illinois dealers who have apparently inspired the attacks on the department that appeared recently in central Illinois papers, it may be said that it is not improbable the failure of Illinois corn to grade in the Gulf market is due to the excess of moisture it carries. Expert Shanahan, with his moisture tests in the Western markets, invariably found an excess of moisture in new corn; and this was true at Decatur, where he demonstrated to local shippers that none of the corn from which samples had been taken for the tests was grain that they could expect to grade high, however good it might be in other respects. Besides, cold corn shipped in a winter will condense moisture in a warmer climate as soon as it comes in contact with the outer atmosphere. We can but repeat, therefore, what has often been said here before—that the means are now at hand for easily ascertaining the exact amount of moisture in their corn. They should realise that any amount above 13 per cent, approximately, will put corn into the unsafe class until the excess is removed, either naturally on the cob in the crib or artificially in the drier.

A co-operative company at St. Cloud, Minn., complains that it can't compete with the St. Cloud mills. Well, if the mills pay the farmers more for wheat than they can get for it elsewhere, one would naturally think it the height of folly for them to make an effort to keep up a fight against the mills.

Editorial Mention.

Mr. Frasius and his back-number ideas on inspection have had their day in Kansas.

Gasoline that freezes in the feed pipe this winter must be more heavily watered than even oil stock.

The tip to the train man to drop an empty is spreading—even the Canadian West complains that that is the only way cars are to be obtained nowadays.

A big Chicago shipper of corn labels its cars with a card about 12x15 inches in size, bearing the legend "New Corn—Perishable." Not a bad idea, eh?

The Warehousemen's Association are trying to push through the legislatures the association bill to unify the warehouse laws of the various states. We are sure grain men will sympathize with this movement and lend their aid to its consummation.

It is, of course, true that the marketing of grain and hay directly robs the land of its fertility; but farmers must remember that it cannot all go from the farm in the form of stock—men must eat cereals in other forms than meat, milk, butter and cheese.

Grain dealers who are so "cock sure" their scales are "right," may be surprised to learn that of 88 country scales examined in 1906 by the Chicago Board of Trade weighmaster's men, only six were right, and of the first eleven examined in 1907 ten were wrong.

The co-operative company of Joice, Ia., by advertisement notifies its members, "If you have sold any grain to any other elevator other than the above named, call on our manager and settle without delay; otherwise you will forfeit your shares." A good bluff; but one would like to see it called in the courts.

The announcement of the abandonment of the uniform bill of lading with its 20 per cent extra charge for insurance is offset by the filing with the Commerce Commission of a declaration by the uniform bill carriers that they will hereafter add 20 per cent to their rates for insurance—another way of peeling a cat! Of course, their right to do this will be contested under the Carmack amendment to the Hepburn act.

Among the features of the Corn Growers and Stockmen's Convention at Urbana in January was a lecture to the students and farmers there on grain inspection by Sam. H. Smith of the Chicago department. Mr. Smith is master of the subject and a good talker, and the brief report of his address before us is conclusive evidence that his talk was well worth while. Farmers need practical talk of this kind to show them why so much of their corn goes wrong and what they can do to make it grade better and bring them a better price; and it would be a great benefit to the grain trade and to the farmers as well if Mr. Smith

could be sent regularly around the circle of the Institutes held every winter in this state.

Mr. Chandler of Mississippi, who led the fight for the free seed graft, said he "could not go back and look his dear old farm friends in the face," after the increase of the salaries of the congressmen, if free seeds were not to be had. Of course not—if that's the kind of "dear farm friends" Mr. Chandler represents.

George H. Morgan of the St. Louis Merchants' Exchange recently completed his fortieth year as secretary of that body, but in spite of the modern theory of Oslerizing men over forty, the Exchange is so well satisfied with Mr. Morgan's indispensability that he has been re-elected, and is now entering on his forty-first year of continuous useful service.

The Chicago Commercial Association has gone on record as opposed to reciprocal demurrage as a remedy for car shortage. This position is not, as we understand it, a sop to the carriers so much as it is an expression of belief that the remedy proposed would be a failure. What is more needed, as we understand the position of that Association, is a law to require commodities to be moved promptly and continuously to their destination. This is, of course, the real thing, but shippers will differ as to the best course to pursue to bring this about.

It is announced that the Rock Island, Frisco, C. & E. I., C. & A., St. Paul, B. & O., Erie, Harriman System, Pennsylvania, Santa Fe and I. C. roads have formed a car pool and have appointed a committee to arrange the details of a freight clearing-house. The roads named own about one-third of all the freight cars in the country. The pool system has been suggested as a remedy for car famines, as every car of each road will be regarded as "at home" so long as it is on the rails of any other road in the pool. Of course, the operation of the pool would be supervised by the Commerce Commission.

Farmers in the Canadian West are certainly taking the bait of the "new civilization" of the parlor socialists quite greedily. The latest fad there is the government-owned elevator—a sort of concern paid for by All-of-us, but operated for the sole benefit of Some-of-us. The idea doesn't sound just right; and so far as human experience is a precedent, it does not promise to. But, after all, with the three great railways of the Canadian West all leasing their elevators to private companies, and so fastening on that new country the abominable system of slugging the independent or small private merchant in grain, that has prevailed for so many years in the United States, and from which we are now escaping only by slow degrees, after much tribulation, it is no wonder the small Canadian dealer cries to be saved. Having in mind American experience, it is no surprise he objects to being compelled to pass his grain through elevators owned by

competitors who are directly interested in putting him out of business at the earliest possible moment, and whom the railways put in the ideal position to that very thing.

The trade will agree heartily with ex-President Warren that, "it seems incredible that the Chicago Board would think for one moment of abandoning its fight on bucket-shops." To do so now, when it has full legal power to prevent the use of its quotations, would be pusillanimous and be a step itself backward into the ranks of that gentry.

The daily record of inspection substantiates the information obtained from receivers, that Illinois corn is arriving at terminal markets in a very dirty condition. The difference in grades means a loss to the shipper and farmer of 1 to 4 cents a bushel, which in 90 per cent of the cases is due wholly to dirty condition of the grain at loading or to carelessness in loading. This penalty, it would seem, should be enough to warrant the dealer in cleaning his corn and taking pains to load so as to distribute what dirt is unavoidable well through the car and not have it occur in spots, as is too frequently the case.

The reorganization by Governor Deneen of the Railroad and Warehouse Commission will be gratifying to the grain trade, more especially as it involves the appointment of B. A. Eckhardt of Chicago, who while naturally in sympathy with the shippers is a man of broad views and experience and not likely to be stampeded by sophistries. Under his lead the Commission may be expected to resume the exercise of the functions the law put upon it, and will act as the defendant of the shippers as well as conservator of the rights of the carriers, while also acting as a whip to spur the latter to a recognition of their duties to the public.

One of the most amazing performances by an intelligent body of men is the resolution engineered through the meeting of farmers' elevator company representatives at Salina, Kan., on January 15, presided over by C. W. Peckham of Haven, president, and E. C. Dowling, the secretary. It is no less than one protesting against a movement in Kansas City to induce the postoffice to issue a fraud order against the so-called National Board of Trade, probably the largest, most far-reaching and arrogant gambling house in this country, and a concern which, as this resolution attests, is doing immense moral damage to the community of the Southwest. Surely the gentleman named must have gone daft to imagine, even should the worst they may say of the Kansas City Board be true, that this very precious crowd of gamblers and their dummy at the National Elevator can help them in any respect. The National Board of Trade is a standing disgrace to Kansas City and would be to any self-respecting community; and that it should have been able to impress itself on the confidence of well-meaning farmers and other shippers is the best evidence of its insidious wickedness and a double condemnation of the police of Kansas City that permits it continued existence.

A conference was held the other day at Kansas City by the railroad claim agents and representatives of the Board of Trade upon the rule the railways have enforced hitherto of taking 1 per cent shrinkage in settling grain claims. No one seems to know how the rule originated, nor whether 1 per cent is too much or too little shrinkage. Like many other things it just simply grew, like Topsy. It was agreed, however, that the claim men should investigate the question of natural shrinkage and report in about sixty days. Meantime, the elevator and grain men should do likewise—too many cases cannot be included to strike a fair average.

Representative Stillman is making a good deal of cheap stir in Iowa by a bill for a law to make it unlawful to pool prices or to restrain competition in the buying and selling of grain. Mr. Stillman says the testimony before the Commerce Commission established the fact that there was a pool, etc. The Commission found nothing of the kind. It did find that a certain man sent out a card showing the prices offered for grain in Iowa by track bidders; but the country dealers, at whom Mr. Stillman directs the lightning of his bill, what had they to do with that? Mr. Stillman but adds to the volume of petty humbug that now is rampant in certain circles of Iowa.

Instead of complaining against the free handling of grain by the railways at Kansas City, the dealers of Atchison should turn their attention toward forcing free handling there also. The purpose of the grain men now should be to force the railways to abandon at every terminal the practice of leasing their houses to private corporations. It is tough on Atchison dealers that grain and feedstuffs are handled free at Kansas City while they are required to pay for such service, but so long as the fight is on, it should be to a finish and not to secure a temporary palliative that is likely in the long run to work a greater evil than a temporary suspension of business even.

Now an Iowa legislator has been infected by the grain inspection craze, and proposes to erect another double-barreled inspection nuisance at the Missouri River by asking for a state inspection law for use at Council Bluffs. Of course the Council Bluffs newspaper, which ought to have more sense, is pushing the bill because "it would be great advantage to this city." Horace Greeley used to have something to say about the long suffering of God, who in his inscrutable wisdom permitted a certain class of men to edit democratic newspapers in his time; but one is sure the caustic pen of the great editor would be impotent to characterise the legislators and editors of this day who, in this matter, persist in "darkening" counsel by words without knowledge." Council Bluffs has no exchange to handle grain, and inspection there would be simply a superfluous interference with the free

sale of the grain on the Omaha Grain Exchange, on Omaha inspection, and in so far would be a detriment to Council Bluffs as a handling point and not a benefit, just as the Wisconsin tomfoolery at Superior, Wis., has practically killed its grain business or turned it over to the tender mercies of bucket-shop gamblers. Besides, what business has the state of Iowa to meddle with private business, any way?

The committee sent by the shippers' conference last month from Chicago to call on President Roosevelt in the interest of reciprocal demurrage was cordially received and informed that a bill would be prepared and sent to Congress with a special message. It is not, however, at all probable that this message will go to Congress at this session. This will leave the year to December 1 next for agitation of the question. The experience of the country with the rate bill goes to show that it is more the pressure of public opinion on Congress than a Message that drives the members to the legislation the public demands. Thus, with all due respect for the power of the President's view and his influence on Congress, his hands must be upheld by the public or even his best intentions will fail, however those intentions may comport with the public desire.

When the Manhattan Stock and Grain Dealers' Company was raided at Jersey City, it was found that several big gamblers were in it to the tune of $10,000 each and that the manager was a graduate of a New York insane asylum, where he had been "under treatment," having shot a man at Albany. He wasn't so crazy on money matters, though. The concern had correspondents in Yonkers, Peekskill, Fort Plain, Syracuse, Albany, Middletown, Rochester, Utica, Auburn, Poughkeepsie, Scranton, Newark, Elizabeth, Trenton and Pittsfield, and was making from $500 to $2,500 a day. Yet, even so, it was too dirty mean to pay the winners! We haven't as yet heard that the "independent grain dealers" of Kansas have filed a protest against the raid, but having given a similar Kansas City outfit of gamblers a good send off, it is up to them to be consistent and kick for "Big Tim" Sullivan, the Mayers, and the rest.

Latest advices from Washington are to the effect that there will be no more railway legislation at this session of Congress. In the meantime the Commerce Commission is groping after a basis for the calculation of the reasonableness of rates upon which it may predicate redresses of grievances against the carriers. It should not be anticipated that complaints can all be redressed offhand; a vast amount of preliminary work will have to be done, and the Commission is now hard at work building such substructure by the collection of data. The public must needs be patient; but in the meantime, it does not seem unreasonable to expect that certain gross violations of the spirit of the law, like the allowances contracts, the absorption of railway elevators by private corporations, and the

inequalities of the demurrage laws, might be corrected without overturning business in other respects.

E. H. Culver, as all who know him will agree, fully merits the confidence reposed in him by the Toledo Produce Exchange, which the other day reappointed him chief inspector. Culver is a big man in every way—fair, intelligent, honest and charged with the "forward spirit." He is given carte blanche, so to say, at Toledo, but he does not abuse his commission as the advance agent of Toledo, whose interests he never forgets for a moment. For one must confess that especially in these later years he has broadened greatly, so that while he never forgets the interests of the Toledo market, he is able to see that a friendly attitude toward other markets need not interfere with his strict duty to Toledo. Professionally, Mr. Culver, like other big men, is growing, and, what is more, his personality makes him an influence for good wherever he goes; and he is welcome everywhere.

There is no state in the Union better situated for the intelligent growing of oats than Iowa. A large feeder, the greater part, perhaps 70 per cent, of the crop is consumed on the farms, while for the remainder there are the two monster cereal mills at Cedar Rapids ready to take every pound of milling oats the state is prepared to market; and, as a rule, pay a premium for them. Yet we find, as a matter of fact, that oats of all sorts are grown in the state, so that a large part of the farm surplus is penalised in price because it will grade only as the lowest class for feed. In order to correct the anomalous condition, the Iowa Dealers' Association a year ago began to agitate a change of method on the farms, in which the management was joined by the agronomists of the Ames College, more especially Prof. Holden, who has become famous in connection with his corn lectures and who is equally well prepared to take up this matter of oats. But because those people initiated this reform movement, the Co-operative Journal and all the orators of that happy family, the Chicago Board of Trade co-operative junta have seen fit to disparage it and to refer to it sneeringly as a "grafting" proposition. In spite of this questionable attempt to queer a praiseworthy movement, however, the Association and the Ames professors have gone ahead, and besides giving short courses in the study of oats at the College, they have induced the secretaries of the institutes to take up the study of improving the oats crop by urging the selection and cleaning of the seed, by using the formaline treatment for smut and making better preparation of the seed bed. Further, they have arranged for a seed oats special train to run during March over a portion of the lines of the C., M. & St. P. Ry. This is but a beginning, but like the work of the same people on corn in the immediate past, it is a beginning that, in spite of all obstacles thrown in its way by stupid selfishness, will eventually revolutionise oats culture in Iowa, to the lasting benefit of Iowa farmers.

TRADE NOTES

W. K. Miller is now representing the Huntley Manufacturing Company in New York City, having succeeded J. W. Perrine.

The Millers' Mutual Fire Insurance Association of Illinois is represented in Chicago by M. W. Fugit, with offices at 740 National Life Building.

The J. C. Robinson Seed Company of Waterloo, Neb., has ordered an "Ideal" Hess Grain Drier to be shipped at once and to be added to its equipment at Waterloo. The company reports frequent receipts of corn out of condition, and also intends using this machine to preserve any seed corn which may be on hand in the spring.

The Main Belting Company have some interesting literature on the subject of belts which they will send free upon request. They make the celebrated Leviathan Belt, which is used in a large number of grain elevators. This belting is suitable for power transmitting, bucket elevating and conveying and is sold on its merits.

Monarch Attrition Mills, made by Sprout, Waldron & Co., Muncy, Pa., are sent on trial to responsible elevator men, and the manufacturers pay charges both ways in case the mill does not make good. They will be glad to confer with grain men on the subject of feed grinding and have some interesting literature on the subject.

A very attractive book, entitled "The Horse," which contains suggestions for the proper care of the horse in and out of the stable, is published by the Joseph Dixon Crucible Company of Jersey City, N. J. This book will appeal to all who own or handle horses and will be sent free to those requesting a copy. Write the publishers at the above address.

N. A. Grabill, grain elevator architect of Daleville, Ind., reports the grain elevator building season at opening well this year. He has been very busy since January 1 and has a number of contracts on hand. The elevators which he puts up are of popular type, designed for economical handling of grain, and have given the best of satisfaction to the owners.

The Burrell Engineering & Construction Co. of Chicago report inquiries for new elevators the largest they have ever experienced at this time of the year. They are well equipped to care for a large business, but in order not to disappoint the trade they are still further preparing for the extensive building business that is due to come from present outlook.

Rowe & Nubson Company, builders of grain and rice elevators, are prepared to handle contracts rapidly and thoroughly. They are well organized and are well known in the grain elevator trade. They guarantee their rice elevators to be as satisfactory as their grain houses. The company may be addressed at either Clarksville or Kensett, Iowa.

The roller feed mills made by Barnard & Leas Manufacturing Company are very popular with elevator owners because they enable them to add a side line that is decidedly profitable. The line includes Williford's Light-Running Three-Roller Mill and Barnard's One, Two and Three Pair High Mills. These mills grind fine meal for table use, as well as all kinds of feed.

The progress and change of methods made by progressive shippers is manifested in the large increase in the use, last year, of private car seals. Orders for the Tyden Seal, made by the International Seal & Lock Company of Hastings, Mich., reached very large proportions and the factory was kept unusually busy supplying the demand. This seal costs about ⅓ cent per car, and is self-locking, requiring no sealing iron. Each seal bears the shipper's name and a consecutive number, and

there is thus protection against loss while loading, in transit and while unloading. The various railroads and associations that have adopted the seal have found a great saving in its use. Chas. J. Webb, 617 Railway Exchange Building, Chicago, is general sales agent for the seal.

A machine that cleans both grain and flax is a desirable one for elevators in the Northwest. Such a cleaner is the "Clipper," made by A. T. Ferrell & Co., Saginaw, W. S., Mich. The Nos. 9, 10 and 77 "Clippers" are especially suitable for this work and may be operated with little power. The makers will be glad to send full particulars to those who will write for them.

Fred W. Kennedy, Shelbyville, Ind., manufacturer of Kennedy's Patent Car Liner, reports an increasing demand for his specialty. The low cost of lining a car and the resulting saving in the prevention of losses from leaks makes the investment a profitable one for grain men. Mr. Kennedy announces that the cost of lining a car with his liner is but $1.30, and that elevator men who are using it are effecting a big saving.

The line of receiving and cleaning machinery made by the Huntley Manufacturing Company of Silver Creek, N. Y., is doing service in a great many elevators and warehouses and is constantly increasing in popularity with the grain trade. A feature of the line is machines of all-steel construction, which are built for fireproof houses. The company has representatives in all the principal cities and the latter will be pleased to hear from interested parties.

S. K. Humphrey, Boston, Mass., reports sales of Humphrey Employe's Elevators as follows: One for a new mill in Talachuano, Chili, South America; Hartline Mill & Elevator Company, Hartline, Wash.; Maple Leaf Flour Mills Company, Kenora, Ont., Canada; the Kaffrarian Steam Mill Company, King William's Town, South Africa; the H. W. Leighton Company, for Elevator "K," Twenty-ninth Street, Minneapolis, Minn. A new circular, recently issued by Mr. Humphrey, shows that this elevator is in use in all parts of this country and Canada, and that it is finding its way into countries all over the globe.

THE SHRINKAGE SYSTEM.

Although in July, 1905, the Commerce Commission investigated and subsequently condemned the shrinkage-of-the-rate system obtaining at Louisville, the old trouble will not down, and is now nearly as acute as two years ago; and it is likely the Commission will be again called on to adjust rates. The immediate question is, whether the railroads should charge six cents for grain sent to Louisville from East St. Louis for local consumption, and only four when it is sent to Louisville destined for Southeastern or Carolina territory.

The other crossings oppose the shrinkage system in toto as open to abuses and manipulations of the rate by the unscrupulous; and should the Commerce Commission take up the question again it will be asked to abolish the system altogether.

"Local shippers have no objection to doing this," said a prominent Louisville shipper to a press agent recently. "The present system means that when the roads are competing for the movement of grain sent to a point where there is competition, they give a rate to meet that competition, and where the grain is shipped for local consumption they raise the rate. If they can afford to carry the grain in the through transportation for one rate, they are able to handle it for the same rate on local business."

Another suggestion is the establishment of a clearing house to prevent manipulations and the application of the shrinkage on grain sent to the Southeast, which originates in Indiana; or the use by other dealers of fictitious destinations in the Southeast, in order to get the benefit of the adjustment, which enables them to ship it at a profit to the Southwest.

BOWSHER COMBINATION MILLS.

A business career extending over eighteen years, each one of which has shown a steady increase in sales over the preceding one, is a record that any firm may well be proud of. This, at least, is the opinion of the N. P. Bowsher Company of South Bend, Ind., makers of the Bowsher Combination Feed Grinding Mills.

In commenting on their successful record they say that every cause has its effect; likewise every effect has its cause. The "cause" to which they attribute this continued success is the fact that from the beginning these mills were constructed on logical, common-sense principles, and in all their years of experience building these machines they have spared no effort or expense to make a mill that is lastingly satisfactory in every respect. Any customer can rest assured that there is no cheap "clap-trap" work in the Bowsher Mills.

One of the fundamental principles of these

THE BOWSHER COMBINATION MILL.

mills is the conical shape of the grinding parts. This cone shape presents a large area of grinding surface and still does the work close to the center of the shaft, thus securing a maximum output with a minimum amount of power. The conical shape also reduces the end pressure of the shaft fully one-half, thereby effecting another great saving of power. Moreover, it makes a construction possible which allows the mill to run empty without injury to the grinders.

This is only one of many reasons which the Bowsher people will be glad to explain fully to any inquirer, why in principle, as well as in actual performance, the "Combination" is a winner. It will be noted from the cut shown herewith that elevators can be furnished with the mills if wanted. They come in either sacking or wagon box style, as desired. Free illustrated catalogue describing seven different sizes from 2 to 25 horsepower may be had for the asking.

A. P. Carrithers, for many years manager of the Shearer Grain Co. at Weston, Ill., has severed his connection with the firm and departed for the West. J. P. Shearer is looking after the business for the present.

Frederick Mayer, president of the Toledo Produce Exchange and chief executive of the Ohio Grain Dealers' Association, recently came near being killed by a live electric wire. As he alighted from a street car he came in contact with the wire, which had fallen across the street, and was rendered semi-conscious for a time. Mr. Mayer was badly burned by the heavy current.

RECEIPTS AND SHIPMENTS.

Following are the receipts and shipments of grain, etc., at leading receiving and shipping points in the United States for the month of January, 1907:

BALTIMORE—Reported by H. A. Wroth, secretary of the Chamber of Commerce.

Articles.	Receipts.		Shipments.	
	1907.	1906	1907.	1906.
Wheat, bushels	193,864	358,105	514,457	48,000
Corn, bushels	2,844,922	7,691,607	2,213,450	6,698,368
Oats, bushels	291,409	450,293	660	2:5,610
Barley, bushels	....	38,056	....	....
Malt, lbs	....	....	....	....
Rye, bushels	109,338	203,031	....	81,429
Timothy Seed, bushels	1,595	3,499	....	7,917
Clover Seed, bushels	830	8,454	678	2,254
Hay, tons	7,315	7,711	2,309	3,328
Straw, tons	....	....	....	....
Flour, bbls	289,210	138,581	121,421	111,540
Mill feed, tons	635	414	28	50

BOSTON—Reported by Daniel D. Morss, secretary of the Chamber of Commerce.

Flour, bbls	186,714	134,661	95,535	74,205
Wheat, bushels	1,596,688	1,835,410	854,695	1,879,178
Corn, bushels	607,018	548,799	558,103	325,187
Oats, bushels	376,267	530,394	1,300	71,072
Rye, bushels	2,797	600	....	....
Barley, bushels	28,941	397,524	65,665	288,627
Flax Seed, bushels	....	1,160	30,800	....
Mill Feed, tons	1,079	1,881	30	638
Cornmeal, bbls	6,225	3,707	1,481	1,507
Oatmeal, bbls	18,745	12,702	8,170	15,162
Oatmeal, sacks	8,080	7,285	7,190	6,881
Hay, tons	14,710	17,970	330	3,594

BUFFALO—Reported by F. Howard Mason, secretary of the Chamber of Commerce. Navigation closed.

CHICAGO—Reported by Geo. F. Stone, secretary of the Board of Trade.

Wheat, bushels	1,692,462	992,896	1,076,119	753,356
Corn, bushels	11,488,023	8,735,964	5,672,548	6,234,449
Oats, bushels	6,739,675	8,124,750	4,918,494	7,617,711
Barley, bushels	2,621,058	2,152,922	678,730	1,043,016
Rye, bushels	218,628	165,967	205,781	121,254
Timothy Seed, lbs	1,555,590	1,171,520	2,275,936	1,671,299
Clover Seed, lbs	771,650	584,641	745,520	422,102
Other Grass Seed, lbs	1,565,105	1,513,600	2,244,627	2,535,410
Flax Seed, bushels	138,690	137,800	5,378	8,020
Broom Corn, lbs	1,621,651	828,570	1,307,227	489,659
Hay, tons	85,321	20,757	10,012	1,778
Flour, bbls	859,039	740,970	704,165	567,665

CINCINNATI—Reported by C. B. Murray, superintendent of the Chamber of Commerce.

Wheat, bushels	191,090	232,574	80,428	248,038
Corn, bushels	828,562	773,566	370,174	561,964
Oats, bushels	371,030	790,920	231,870	723,639
Barley, bushels	117,284	252,750	10,000	215,110
Rye, bushels	74,440	78,396	17,350	49,696
Malt, bushels	204,630	182,340	104,430	36,082
Timothy Seed, lbs	1,130	499	2,858	751
Clover Seed, lbs	6,093	5,836	1,889	1,610
Other Grass Seed, lbs	10,166	12,320	9,390	9,771
Hay, tons	15,537	24,509	12,338	18,625
Flour, bbls	95,429	137,684	54,015	94,984

DETROIT—Reported by F. W. Waring, secretary of the Board of Trade.

Wheat, bushels	78,148	87,169	25,701	28,886
Corn, bushels	449,378	836,293	210,750	361,456
Oats, bushels	132,359	228,027	15,569	44,924
Barley, bushels	103,950	356,078	....	3,562
Rye, bushels	27,440	19,248	34,584	59,764
Flour, bbls	9,200	28,700	4,200	19,000

DULUTH—Reported by Chas. F. MacDonald, secretary of the Board of Trade.

Wheat, bushels	1,475,653	2,847,337	48,637	91,235
Corn, bushels	....	....	....	1,358
Oats, bushels	145,345	1,039,483	89,922	198,869
Barley, bushels	39,948	447,357	26,493	196,843
Rye, bushels	58,477	41,089	2,318	3,277
Flax Seed, bushels	615,790	1,305,599	*388,910	58,889
Flour, bbls	53,490	56,045	41,855	48,185

*324,887 bus. afloat.

GALVESTON—Reported by C. McD. Robinson, chief inspector of the Cotton Exchange and Board of Trade.

Wheat, bushels	....	....	487,620	243,443
Corn, bushels	....	....	805,801	2,864,647
Oats	....	....	....	....
Barley, bushels	....	....	....	....

KANSAS CITY—Reported by E. D. Bigelow, secretary of the Board of Trade.

Wheat, bushels	2,235,000	2,139,000	1,930,000	1,167,000
Corn, bushels	1,117,000	3,092,000	1,005,000	2,063,000
Oats, bushels	669,000	675,000	591,000	616,500
Barley, bushels	33,000	95,000	9,000	19,000
Rye, bushels	10,000	33,000	4,000	20,000
Flax Seed, bushels	7,200	....	8,200	....
Bran, tons	1,575	800	3,855	2,670
Hay, tons	11,140	17,700	8,360	6,790
Flour, bbls	24,600	....	111,800	98,000

MILWAUKEE—Reported by Wm. J. Langson, secretary of the Chamber of Commerce.

Wheat, bushels	671,000	647,680	298,273	177,075
Corn, bushels	737,000	616,550	710,688	478,143
Oats, bushels	1,038,800	973,600	750,081	862,263
Barley, bushels	1,887,600	1,982,200	727,497	986,942
Rye, bushels	143,100	99,200	105,747	51,923
Timothy Seed, lbs	159,077	1,008,964	257,085	247,585
Clover Seed, lbs	648,820	660,541	858,970	813,585
Flax Seed, bushels	81,800	37,920	1,060	....
Hay, tons	3,882	2,062	829	314
Flour, bbls	117,250	98,225	179,543	168,945

MINNEAPOLIS—Reported by L. T. Jamme, secretary of the Chamber of Commerce.

Wheat, bushels	5,937,100	8,916,610	1,398,330	1,700,120
Corn, bushels	859,890	558,210	374,490	439,410
Oats, bushels	1,610,530	2,012,200	1,701,790	2,426,320
Barley, bushels	825,250	1,214,100	917,100	1,358,870
Rye, bushels	113,760	150,530	148,820	154,280
Flax Seed, bushels	587,660	1,442,360	327,640	780,080
Hay, tons	1,870	3,219	170	100
Flour, bbls	16,072	21,929	1,279,688	1,054,290

MONTREAL—Reported by George Hadrill, secretary of the Board of Trade.

Articles.	Receipts.		Shipments.	
	1907.	1906.	1907.	1906.
Wheat, bushels	52,906	108,576	....	500
Corn, bushels	24,439	37,984	11,200	1,200
Oats, bushels	255,496	73,671	8,000	1,300
Barley, bushels	45,891	11,691	8,200	3,850
Rye, bushels	....	717	....	....
Flax Seed, bushels	9,500	15,949	....	....
Flour, barrels	14,859	20,836	38,290	85,700

NEW ORLEANS—Reported by H. S. Herring, secretary of the Board of Trade.

Wheat, bushels	167,000	310,000	274,964	129,500
Corn, bushels	2,004,000	7,744,000	1,619,000	5,847,484
Oats, bushels	271,000	270,000	183,295	429,189
Barley, bushels	....	....	....	....
Rough rice	....	....	....	....
Clean rice pockets	....	....	....	....
Hay, bales	51,480	60,600	1,494	501
*Flour, bbls	37,054	34,950	48,531	221,380

*Through consignments of flour to Europe not included in receipts.

OMAHA—Reported by Edward J. McVann, secretary of the Omaha Grain Exchange.

Wheat, bu	742,800	331,100	628,000	431,200
Corn, bu	3,424,400	3,577,200	2,429,000	3,770,400
Oats, bu	1,366,400	1,107,200	1,852,500	1,252,800
Barley, bu	17,000	18,000	....	11,000
Rye, bu	22,000	35,000	32,000	27,000
Flour, bbls	....	....	....	....

PEORIA—Reported by John R. Lofgren, secretary of the Board of Trade.

Wheat, bushels	58,500	64,300	24,500	38,800
Corn, bushels	1,678,300	1,058,100	1,037,200	545,600
Oats, bushels	872,500	1,097,800	908,500	1,555,600
Barley, bushels	380,000	300,200	75,200	253,400
Rye, bushels	30,000	26,700	6,000	4,100
Mill Feed, tons	3,116	1,530	3,713	3,739
Spirits and Liquors, bbls	....	....	....	....
Syrups and Glucose, bbls	....	....	....	....
Seeds, lbs	30,000	30,000	90,000	120,000
Broom Corn, lbs	300,000	345,000	480,000	232,500
Hay, tons	4,283	8,490	1,820	460
Flour, bbls	80,850	80,300	88,930	70,575

PHILADELPHIA—Reported by L. J. Logan, secretary of the Commercial Exchange.

Wheat, bushels	1,612,454	404,189	1,578,800	444,401
Corn, bushels	1,361,607	4,027,464	947,185	3,424,354
Oats, bushels	361,664	1,750,927	1,914	1,475,232
Barley, bushels	13,000	53,600	....	....
Rye, bushels	2,400	32,800	....	....
Timothy Seed, lbs	1,439	....	....	....
Clover Seed, lbs	1,439	425	....	....
Flax Seed, bushels	113,600	100,600	....	....
Hay, tons	8,446	8,570	....	....
Flour, bbls	312,197	237,158	133,138	149,755

SAN FRANCISCO—Reported by Wm. B. Downes, statistician of the Merchants' Exchange.

Wheat, centals	102,218	....	50,626	....
Corn, centals	7,209	....	1,061	....
Oats, centals	91,527	....	372	....
Barley, centals	475,822	....	297,577	....
Rye, centals	1,130	....	....	....
Flax Seed, sacks	425	....	....	....
Hay, tons	16,439	....	1,194	....
Flour, bbls	70,268	....	27,455	....

ST. LOUIS—Reported by Geo. H. Morgan, secretary of the Merchants' Exchange.

Wheat, bushels	799,000	1,596,950	827,870	1,202,750
" sacks	2,229	329	....	1,200
Corn, bushels	4,636,500	2,665,000	3,125,700	1,588,550
" sacks	2,722	328	3,975	63,670
Oats, bushels	2,652,800	2,354,400	2,002,880	1,657,490
" sacks	....	....	3,190	43,195
Barley, bushels	491,800	410,000	8,350	74,080
" sacks	....	....	....	504
Rye, bushels	52,000	106,000	47,945	79,900
" sacks	....	....	....	....
Hay, tons	25,055	23,850	11,355	8,415
Flour, bbls	237,230	190,390	324,240	225,950

TOLEDO—Reported by A. Gassoway, secretary of the Produce Exchange.

Wheat, bushels	208,000	143,000	71,020	127,250
Corn, bushels	932,900	810,000	817,200	560,900
Oats, bushels	284,600	386,100	566,100	538,950
Barley, bushels	....	500	....	....
Rye, bushels	6,200	12,200	1,180	17,665
Clover Seed, bags	5,242	5,814	9,904	76,370

FLAXSEED AT CHICAGO.

The receipts and shipments of flaxseed at Chicago during the 18 months ending with January, as reported by Charles F. Lias, flaxseed inspector of the Board of Trade, were as follows:

Months.	Receipts.		Shipments.	
	1906-07.	1905-06.	1906-07.	1905-06.
August	106,200	359,200	137,580	76,344
September	152,100	189,000	82,999	42,760
October	389,300	342,400	55,083	8,633
November	412,000	579,400	10,115	5,785
December	289,700	291,400	9,635	4,789
January	132,690	144,000	2,378	15,661
February	....	134,100	....	11,481
March	....	91,800	....	3,601
April	....	122,137	....	2,590
May	....	160,600	....	34,839
June	....	45,900	....	44,887
July	....	40,500	....	29,801
Total bushels	1,457,990	5,210,437	300,790	281,131

Arthur Hecker of Summerfield, Ill., has tendered Governor Deneen his resignation from the Illinois Grain Inspectors' Bureau at East St. Louis, where he has been since it was established in 1896.

VISIBLE SUPPLY OF GRAIN.

The following table shows the visible supply of grain Saturday, February 9, 1907, as compiled by George F. Stone, secretary of the Chicago Board of Trade:

In Store at	Wheat, bu.	Corn, bu.	Oats, bu.	Rye, bu.	Barley, bu.
Baltimore	317,000	1,398,000	191,000	182,000	....
Boston	346,000	122,000	11,000	....	2,000
Buffalo	3,398,000	102,000	379,000	488,000	786,000
do. afloat	3,253,000	....	1,460,000	145,000	358,000
Chicago	10,109,000	1,180,000	1,140,000	528,000	232,000
do. afloat	....	....	....	....	....
Detroit	319,000	188,000	44,000	22,000	....
do. afloat	....	....	....	....	....
Duluth	3,486,000	....	765,000	163,000	198,000
do. afloat	....	....	....	....	....
Ft. William	2,145,000	....	....	....	....
do. afloat	326,000	....	....	....	....
Galveston	675,000	271,000	....	....	....
do. afloat	....	....	....	....	....
Indianapolis	309,000	281,000	39,000	....	....
Kansas City	3,758,000	486,000	90,000	....	....
Milwaukee	560,000	231,000	716,000	2,000	383,000
do. afloat	....	....	....	....	....
Minneapolis	5,816,000	618,000	3,886,000	66,000	545,000
Montreal	20,000	30,000	107,000	1,000	49,000
New Orleans	292,000	622,000	126,000	....	....
do. afloat	....	....	....	....	....
New York	1,546,000	523,000	808,000	5,000	50,000
do. afloat	....	....	....	....	....
Peoria	217,000	550,000	1,058,000	14,000	....
Philadelphia	921,000	354,000	56,000	....	....
Port Arthur	2,134,000	....	....	....	....
do. afloat	164,000	....	....	....	....
St. Louis	2,980,000	703,000	382,000	37,000	14,000
do. afloat	....	....	....	....	....
Toledo	853,000	410,000	758,000	20,000	....
do. afloat	....	....	....	....	....
Toronto	24,000	....	10,000	....	....
On Canal	....	....	....	....	....
On Lakes	....	....	....	....	....
On Miss. River	....	....	....	....	....
Grand total	44,568,000	8,169,000	11,511,000	1,623,000	2,617,000
Corresponding date 1904	47,783,000	15,327,000	26,327,000	2,412,000	4,828,000
Weekly Inc	....	853,000	....	....	....
Weekly Dec	289,000	....	337,000	86,000	25,000

WHEAT RECEIPTS AT PRIMARY MARKETS.

Receipts of wheat at winter and spring grain markets for 31 weeks, since June, with comparisons, in bushels, compiled by the Cincinnati Price Current:

	1907.	1906.
St. Louis	12,389,000	17,111,000
Toledo	4,280,000	4,254,000
Detroit	1,669,000	1,666,000
Kansas City	31,727,000	33,458,000
Winter wheat	50,065,000	56,489,000
Chicago	26,998,000	20,778,000
Milwaukee	6,288,000	5,949,000
Minneapolis	49,321,000	69,932,000
Duluth	34,477,000	31,741,000
Spring wheat	117,034,000	128,400,000
Aggregate, 31 weeks	167,099,000	184,889,000

Total receipts of winter and spring wheat at primary markets 31 weeks since June, 1906, with comparisons:

	Winter.	Spring.	Total.
1906-07	50,065,000	117,034,000	167,099,000
1905-06	56,489,000	128,400,000	184,889,000
1904-05	50,086,000	112,972,000	163,058,000
1903-04	57,055,000	118,572,000	175,627,000
1902-03	64,322,000	139,796,000	204,118,000

The Frisco has restored a reconsignment charge on hay at Kansas City.

Minneapolis on January 28 received only 96 cars of wheat, the lightest day's receipts for years.

C. S. Barrett, president of the National Farmers' Union, is quoted as saying: "The whole custom of free seed distribution, by the government, is a graft pure and simple. It is based upon the false assumption that the farmers can be controlled by a few seeds distributed by the government, and the farmers themselves have answered this time and again by taking emphatic position against this form of graft. They see clearly through this vote-getting game. It has played out and the money could be appropriated much more advantageously by giving it to agricultural schools and good roads."

Through an error the following interesting news item failed to appear in our January edition: "The Cincinnati Grain Co., Cincinnati, O., received December 21 the largest car of oats that has ever arrived in the Cincinnati market, same being shipped by G. W. Voris of Stewardson, Ill., and containing 2,437 bushels and 12 pounds. Not only does this car break the records as far as the size of the contents is concerned, but it also established a high water mark for quality, grading No. 1 mixed. This car was sold to the Van Leunen Co., wholesalers and retailers of Covington, Ky., at 38 cents per bushel, which is also the record price for this season's crop, and about ½ cent premium over No. 2 mixed."

ELEVATOR AND GRAIN NEWS

EASTERN.

R. R. Frink has purchased the grain business at Kent, Conn., from C. S. Smith.

E. Libby & Sons have installed an electric motor in their elevator at Gerham, N. H.

George P. Blair has sold his grain house at West Danville, Vt., to William Fitzgerald.

The Lunger Grain & Elevator Co. of Netcong, N. J., is the successor to G. H. Lunger in the flour trade.

A concrete elevator of 20,000 bushels' capacity will be constructed at Lynn, Mass., for the Butman & Cressey Company.

The Albert Culver Co., dealers in grain and coal at Rockland, Mass., has advanced the wages of all its employes 12½ per cent.

Jennings & Fulton, grain dealers of Boston, Mass., have dissolved but both members of the firm will remain in the grain business.

R. H. Soule of South Windham, Me., has built a temporary warehouse where his burned elevator stood and is still in the grain business.

M. Stone, L. J. McGhie and C. W. Huff have incorporated the Pittsburg Grain Co. at Camden, N. J., with a capital stock of $250,000.

An elevator of 20,000 bushels' capacity is being built for the Albert Culver Co. at Rockland, Mass. It will be 70 feet high and contain 20 bins.

Repairs have been made on Abner Hendee's grain warehouse recently damaged by fire at New Haven, Conn. About $1,500 was expended.

J. B. Eshelman & Son will build a grain and flour warehouse at Lancaster, Pa., which will measure 80x190 feet and be four stories high.

Articles of incorporation have been granted the W. P. Whittemore Co., grain and flour dealers of Roslindale, Mass. It is capitalized at $50,000.

The Pennsylvania Railroad Co. has commenced driving the piles for the foundation of its new 1,000,000-bushel elevator at Cowden Station, Baltimore, Md.

E. A. Cowee of Hudson, Mass., has sold his grain store to William Rodeniser, who but lately sold his interests in the Marlboro Grain Co. to his partner, James F. Steele.

All the personal property of the Union Coal & Grain Co. at Concord, N. H., was sold at auction lately. The settling of the affairs is now in the hands of Joseph S. Matthews.

The Singer Grain and Elevator Co. of Netcong, N. J., was incorporated last month with a capital of $35,000. The incorporators are Gilbert H. Singer, Ira Mawery and Edgar A. Montfort.

A permit is sought by the Northern Central Railway Company for the erection of a grain elevator to the rear of No. 3. Elevator at Canton, a suburb of Baltimore, Md. The dimensions are 225x112 feet.

The Faramel Manufacturing Co. of Buffalo, N. Y., is a new grain and feed concern, capitalized at $50,000. The directors are C. A. Strangmann, Moses Shire and C. H. McLaughlin, with offices in the Board of Trade Bldg.

ILLINOIS.

The Northwestern Hay & Grain Co. of Chicago, Ill., is dissolved.

A new elevator will be built in the immediate future at Manning, Ill.

Eugene E. Sapp has purchased the grain business of Pratt & Pratt at Sciota, Ill.

John Guild has succeeded Albert W. Weimer & Co., grain merchants, at Geneseo, Ill.

R. Dale Fuller, a grain dealer of Gardner, Ill., is a voluntary petitioner in bankruptcy.

The Neola Elevator at Ohio, Ill., has been sold to the Farmers' Elevator Co. for $8,000.

Tom Abrams of Tuscola, Ill., will increase the capacity of his elevator to 20,000 bushels.

The Monticello Grain Co. of Monticello, Ill., is contemplating a new elevator and corn cribs.

An increase of $10,000 is noted in the capital stock of the Highland F. M. B. A. Elevator Co. at Highland, Ill.

William McQuillen, proprietor of two grain warehouses at Apple River, Ill., has acquired the old mill property there. It is a three-story frame building and was owned by L. T. Ziegle of Warren.

The Stonington Farmers' Grain Co. of Stonington, Ill., has increased its capitalization from $12,000 to $14,000.

E. J. McCabe, P. F. Pickrell and others are interested in the formation of a Farmers' Elevator Co. at Lanesville, Ill.

J. S. Grove, for many years a grain merchant at Bentley, Ill., has disposed of his elevator and business to Sim Walton.

R. A. Hasper & Son have purchased Elevator "A" and the Peerless Roller Mills at Flat Rock, Ill., from G. T. Taylor & Sons.

The Mahomet Grain Co. at Mahomet, Ill., has handled 80,000 bushels of oats and 67,000 bushels of corn during the past six months.

An increase of $5,000 has been made in the capital stock of the Monica Elevator Co. at Monica, Ill. The capitalization is now $10,000.

The Turner-Hudnut Co. will erect three additional grain tanks at Meyers Station, Ill., similar to the three now in use. Each will be of 40,000 bushels' capacity.

Ervin Bros. of Tuscola, Ill., have installed a 25-horsepower motor in their elevator and are greatly pleased with their change to electricity for driving power.

Articles of incorporation have been secured by the Walnut Grain Co. at Walnut, Ill., which is capitalized at $6,000. E. A. Woolley, W. J. Fisher and A. P. Allen are among those interested.

The Minier Grain Co. of Minier, Ill., has incorporated with a capital stock of $10,000. The directors are O. J. Brenneman, Henry Eisenberger and Christian Hiser. The Buehrig & Quincy Elevator has been purchased.

The H. J. Hasenwinkle Co. has been incorporated at Bloomington, Ill., with a capital stock of $10,000. The directors are H. J. Hasenwinkle, Henry Hasenwinkle and A. V. S. Lloyd. A number of other gentlemen are stockholders.

It has been decided by the El Paso Elevator Company of El Paso, Ill., to buy or build an elevator at Enright at once. Omar North was re-elected president of the company; George Patton is secretary and John Cleary treasurer.

S. W. Strong, secretary of the Illinois Grain Dealers' Association, has issued a bulletin calling attention to the following changes: Bartlett, Kuhn & Co. succeed the Holzman-Bennett Grain Co. at Sollitt and Grant Park; Coon Bros. (mail Rantoul) succeed W. H. Weatherooks at Reilly and Morrison & Grindley at Royal; Claudon Bros. succeed Wm. Murray at Ludlow; J. W. Bettendorf succeeds Bettendorf Bros. at Sublette; Miles & Bicketts is a new firm at Fisher; Mansfield & Co. succeed the Knight Grain Co. at Monticello; J. W. Puott succeeds J. C. McCord at Rolder; Bailey Bros. & Kearney of Lanton receive mail at Lavington.

IOWA.

A new elevator may be built at Wellsburg, Iowa.

A new farmers' elevator will go up at Alta, Iowa.

It is reported the new elevator at Omega, Iowa, is receiving grain.

Huska & Pepperling are erecting a commodious elevator at Bradford, Iowa.

William Schnepf of Merrill has purchased the grain elevator at Danbury, Iowa.

A movement is on foot to organize a farmers' elevator company at Conrad, Iowa.

The Bosch-Ryan Co. of Cedar Rapids, Iowa, will resume the rebuilding of its elevator.

Work on the new Whiting Elevator at Washington, Iowa, is progressing rapidly.

A meeting was held at Akron, Iowa, February 2, to organize a Farmers' Elevator Co.

An increase in capital has been made by the Farmers' Elevator Co. of Palmer, Iowa.

A new corn crib has been built for the Theodore Sund Grain Co. at Lake Park, Iowa.

Bosworth & Huber will build a 30,000-bushel elevator at Meltonville, Iowa, in the near future.

Work on the new elevator for the Farmers' Grain & Coal Co. at Pocahontas, Iowa, has been completed.

Farmers near Ireton, Iowa, have organized a stock company to conduct a grain business on $15,000 capital.

Should the new Farmers' Elevator Co. at Charles City, Iowa, fail to get either the Hunting Co.'s plant or the one belonging to Helgen & Sons, for which it is negotiating, a new elevator will be built.

The Wheeler Grant Coal Co. of Fort Dodge, Iowa, will occupy the new elevator just completed at Harcourt, Iowa.

Palmer & Hasty succeed O. L. Manott at Kalona, Iowa, where the latter has conducted a successful grain business.

It is proposed to organize a farmers' elevator company at Forest City, Iowa. N. H. Bailey, S. C. Gardner and J. N. Hangen are on the committee.

M. Parrott, F. S. Scott and T. W. Hartigan are among those interested in promoting a farmers' elevator company at Aurelia, Iowa. More than $4,000 has been subscribed.

F. L. Gitchell is building a 25,000-bushel elevator at Alburnett, Iowa, which will be 50-feet high, have twelve bins and a 36-foot cribbing. It will be equipped with automatic hopper and scales.

It is possible the Farmers' Elevator Co. at Eagle Grove, Iowa, will erect another elevator at that point. The one built last fall is not able to accommodate the grain owing to the car shortage.

Sam Scotten has not yet sold the B. & M. Elevator at Burlington, Iowa, one of the largest in that section, though he is considering several offers. The Gazette of that place suggests it be converted into a modern hotel.

Metcalf & Cannon of Paulina, Iowa, are planning to rebuild the Cannon and Haase Elevator at Granville, Iowa, and ask the "American Elevator and Grain Trade" for suggestions that will make the new 100,000-bushel plant an ideal one.

The Mystic Milling Co. at a recent meeting voted to remodel the old Sioux Milling Co.'s mill at Sioux City, Iowa, into a terminal elevator. It will be newly equipped with the most modern machinery. W. H. Matthews of Ada, Minn., is president; H. J. Hutton, vice-president; C. J. Zeller, secretary, and E. L. Matthews, treasurer, of the company.

Incorporation papers have been granted the Watkins Grain Co. at Watkins, Iowa, which is capitalized at $10,000. The company has bought out the Northern Grain Co. and takes possession February 20. James Harrington is president; William Riesser, vice-president; J. T. McGuire, secretary and treasurer, while other prominent citizens are interested.

MISSOURI, KANSAS AND NEBRASKA.

F. A. Wright & Sons, grain dealers at Frederic, Kan., have assigned.

The Goehner Elevator Co. of Seward, Neb., recently re-elected its officers.

The Duff Elevator at Turlington, Neb., is in active operation in the future.

The Farmers' Elevator Co. of Burr, Neb., has purchased the Holden Elevator Co.'s plant.

O. H. Eggleston, a grain dealer of Murdock, Neb., is reported as a petitioner in bankruptcy.

The W. R. Hall Grain Company, capitalized at $50,000, is a new incorporation at St. Louis, Mo.

Repairs have been made on the Gibbons Elevator at Kearney, Neb., including a new foundation.

Articles of incorporation have been granted the Farmers' Grain & Supply Company at Hoisington, Kan.

The Pickrell Farmers' Elevator Company of Beatrice, Neb., will soon install a 600-bushel hopper scale.

Articles of incorporation have been presented the Overbrook Elevator Company at Overbrook, Kan., with a capitalization of $10,000.

Bell & McCune have closed their elevator at Stromsburg, Neb., leaving but three in the field. They have opened an elevator at Durand.

H. C. Banta of the Oberlin Roller Mills at Oberlin, Kan., is building a 3,000-bushel grain elevator as an addition to the one he now has.

A new farmers' elevator is contemplated for Elm Creek, Neb. Among those interested are J. S. Canaday of Minden, L. S. Deets, O. G. Smith of Kearney and others.

It is reported the Pittsburg Elevator Co. of Pittsburg, Kan., is shipping large quantities of corn to France, Italy and Germany. Two or three ships are reported to be receiving it at Galveston, Texas.

James Pinkerton is president of the Snell Mill and Grain Company which was organized at Clay Center, Kan., in January, to succeed the Snell Mill and Elevator Company. It is capitalized at $75,000. S. S. Wilson is vice-president and H. H. Starkweather is secretary and treasurer. The company takes over all property and expects to increase the business.

Bailey & Connett, grain dealers at Axtell and Balleyville, Kan., have dissolved partnership. E. N. Bailey takes the elevator at Balleyville and H. H. Connett the one at Axtell.

Articles of incorporation have been granted the Flour Mills Grain Co. of Kansas City, which is capitalized at $7,500. Christian Bernet, Marcus Bernheimer, H. G. Craft and others are the incorporators. During January the Flour Mills Grain Company was organized at Kansas City, Kan., for the purpose of buying wheat for flour mills. C. F. Sparks of the milling company bearing his name at Alton, Ill., was chosen president and Marcus Bernheimer, head of the milling company at Kansas City, is vice-president and secretary. C. Bernet is second vice-president and treasurer, while F. C. Hoose is assistant secretary and W. E. Simison, formerly office manager for the Banner Mills of Clinton, Mo., is assistant treasurer. The business of the new grain company will be in charge of Messrs. Hoose and Simison, both of whom are members of the Kansas City board.

THE DAKOTAS.

Lear, N.D., is promised a 50,000-bushel elevator.

Louis Falk will build an elevator at Heaton, N. D.

Adrian, N. D., may have a new farmers' elevator.

M. King's new elevator at Stickney, S. D., is in operation.

Grain is being received at the new elevator in Buford, N. D.

A farmers' elevator company is being organized at Warner, S. D.

It is reported a farmers' elevator will be built at Manchan, N. D.

The Atlas Elevator Co. is constructing a warehouse at Pierre, S. D.

O. F. Edwards has purchased the Bagley Elevator at Groton, S. D.

Two new elevators will be erected at Crosby, N. D., by A. A. Gad of Dazey.

Wait & Dana of Howard, S. D., are building a line of elevators on the Milwaukee line.

A. H. Betts of Mitchell has acquired the J. S. Sammelson Elevator at Cuthbert, S. D.

A new elevator has been completed by the Imperial Elevator Co. at Wetonga, S. D.

It is possible the Great Western Grain Co. may select a site for an elevator at Heaton, N. D.

Ben Fiddler and H. O. Malone of Salem, S. D., have acquired the plant of the Canova Grain Co.

C. W. Thompson and Fred Way of Parker, S. D., have purchased the Hunting Elevator at Marion.

The Farmers' Elevator Co. of Kampeska, S. D., has been organized with a capitalization of $25,000.

A new 40,000-bushel grain elevator will be erected at Eldridge, N. D., by the Powers Elevator Co.

Three new elevators are scheduled to make their appearance at Brentford, S. D., in the near future.

Peter Jall will erect elevators at Hoven, Lowry and Tolstoi, S. D., new towns on the M. & St. L. extension.

Claude Thompson has leased the Hurley Flour Mills at Hurley, S. D., and will operate the plant as an elevator.

A $15,000 elevator will be built at Broadland, S. D., by a farmers' company, of which a Mr. Price is president.

Kludt & Raugust of Emery have acquired Paul Tscheller's interest in the grain business at Bridgewater, S. D.

The Aurora Farmers' Elevator Co. of Aurora, S. D., will not buy the Western Elevator, but will build one of their own.

A company is being organized by citizens at Church's Ferry, N. D., to build a line of elevators along the St. John's extension.

O. F. Edwards, a former grain merchant of Verdon, has purchased the George C. Bagley Elevator Co.'s business at Groton, S. D.

A new 10-horsepower engine has been installed by the Farmers' Elevator Co. in the elevator at Bruce, S. D., the old one being too small.

Recently the Salem Elevator Co. of Salem, S. D., acquired the Western Elevator. J. W. Gibson is president of the farmers' corporation.

A 50,000-bushel elevator is an important adjunct to the new 350-barrel flouring mill just completed by the Chaffee-Miller Milling Co. at Cassel-

ton, N. D. The elevator is one of 30 tributary elevators in the state, which are owned by the company. The plant is to be opened this month.

In connection with the new 500-barrel mill the Russell-Miller Milling Co. is about to commence at Minot, N. D., will be a 130,000-bushel grain elevator.

The Farmers' Elevator Co. at Aurora, S. D., will erect an elevator in the near future. Thos. O'Brien is president of the company and C. S. Ripley, secretary.

A farmers' elevator company is under organization at Vermillion, S. D., and an effort will be made to purchase the Truax Elevator, or a new building will be erected.

A farmers' elevator company may be organized to build a 40,000-bushel elevator at Park River, N. D. J. A. Harris, D. E. Towle, D. G. McKay and others are interested.

The Hall-Steiner Elevator Co. of Upham, N. D., has been incorporated with a capital stock of $6,000. John D. Hall, J. L. Steiner, Christ Smette and Carl Smette are interested.

H. M. Miller, the new owner of the elevator at St. Lawrence, S. D., was refused a spur by the C. & N. W. Co. and the matter is now in the hands of the railroad commission.

There is a movement on foot to organize a farmers' elevator company at Elliston, S. D. The committee having the matter in charge includes C. E. Peterson, Wm. Kaemper and A. C. Colburn.

Raugust & Kludt of Emery, S. D., recently purchased the Hofer & Tichelter Elevator at Bridgewater, which gives them three elevators. They contemplate disposing of the one at McClusky, N. D.

Recently the Farmers' Terminal Elevator and Grain Co. was organized at Hankinson, N. D., with a capital stock of $15,000. Walter Biggs, James Shea, Herman Prachman and others are the incorporators.

Fred Megley has sold his elevator and feed store at Williston, N. D., to Adam McCormack for the consideration of $6,000. The business was established two years ago and a large elevator was built last year.

SOUTHERN AND SOUTHWESTERN.

An elevator is being built for E. J. Wagner near Lamar, Colo.

J. A. Pryor of San Antonio will enter the grain business at Suling, Texas.

John Simon and F. Wartenbach are conducting a grain business at Mason, Texas.

R. E. Stewart and A. G. Lewis are organizing a $10,000 company at Glendale, Ky., to build and operate a 40,000-bushel grain elevator.

M. P. Engle, Louis Pizitz and J. Seligman of Birmingham, Ala., have incorporated the Alabama Grain Co. with a capitalization of $8,000.

The McDonald Engineering Co. of Chicago has begun work on a concrete storage annex for the Climax Milling Co. of Hopkinsville, Ky.

The Rock Island and the St. Louis & San Francisco railroad companies contemplate building a 1,000,000-bushel grain elevator at Galveston, Texas.

The elevator and warehouse of the Mosca Milling and Elevator Co. at Del Norte, Colo., is being dismantled and moved to Los Animas for the use of the Mullen Company.

The Farmers' Co-operative Co. has been incorporated at Sterling, Colo., with a capital stock of $50,000. L. T. Collier, J. T. Chapman and A. R. Youngquist are interested.

Recently the Seldomridge Grain Co. was incorporated at Colorado Springs, Colo., by C. B. Seldomridge, H. H. Seldomridge and A. D. F. Armstrong. The capitalization is $75,000.

Articles of incorporation have been secured by the Phelps-Donahue Grain Co. of Denver, Colo., which is incorporated for $60,000. Those who are interested are J. L. Donahue, T. D. Phelps and Fred Faulkner.

The Mansfield Grain & Elevator Co. of Mansfield, Texas, has been incorporated with a capital stock of $16,000. H. Waldo, Dewitt Waldo, Joseph Edwards, of Mansfield, and Martin Balweg of Cedar Hill are the incorporators.

Articles of incorporation have been granted the Oblapq Grain and Cattle Co. of Norman, Okla., and Ottawa, Ill., which is capitalized at $300,000. The incorporators are J. P. Gonigan and John McMullin of Ottawa, G. A. Hayman of Peoria, Ill., J. B. Dudley and John H. Mosier of Norman.

James S. Fraser has acquired a controlling interest in the Neil & Shofner Grain Co. at Nashville, Tenn., and with the retirement of the two members whose name the company uses,

will become its president. W. W. Waterfield will retain the secretary's office with the company.

The Glendale Grain Co. of Glendale, Ky., has been incorporated with a capital stock of $8,500.

CANADIAN.

A stock company with a capital stock of $8,000 will be formed at Cupar, Sask., to build an elevator.

The Medicine Hat Milling Co. of Medicine Hat, Alta., will erect a large elevator, making the fourth built by them in recent years.

The new annex to the G. T. R. grain elevator at Depot Harbor, Ont., has been completed, giving the 1,000,000-bushel structure an additional capacity of 500,000 bushels.

Recently the Board of Trade at Vancouver, B. C., passed a resolution calling on the Dominion government to build a 250,000-bushel elevator at that point, to store Alberta wheat.

The Medicine Hat Milling Co. is negotiating with the city government to secure a loan of $7,000 to erect a grain elevator at Medicine Hat, Sask. The company already owns three warehouses.

A concrete mill of 5,000 bushels' capacity and an elevator building of reinforced concrete with 750,000 bushels' capacity have just been completed for the Lake of the Woods Milling Co. at Keewatin, Ont. The McDonald Engineering Co. of Chicago, Ill., were the engineering firm and contractors.

Rumors at Fort Arthur, Ont., are to the effect that the Grand Trunk Pacific Co. is contemplating the largest grain elevator ever erected. The report has it that the plant will have a capacity of 10,000,000 bushels and will be constructed of concrete, steel and tile, making it entirely fireproof. If the elevator is to be built as the report says, it will be located at the mouth of the Mission river at Fort William and will be so arranged as to allow four trains to discharge their grain into the house at once, while ships are loading. It would be the fastest grain house yet constructed.

MINNESOTA AND WISCONSIN.

A new stack graces the elevator at Washburn, Wis.

It is possible a farmers' elevator will be built at Humboldt, Minn.

A farmers' elevator is assured for Nerstrand, Minn., in the spring.

James Lorne is operating the old Farmers' Elevator at Jackson, Minn.

The Farmers' Elevator Co. at Canton, Minn., will lease its elevator this season.

A Farmers' Elevator Co. at Kenyon, Minn., is being organized to build an elevator.

Tis reported the Cargill Elevator Co. will rebuild the elevator at Rockville, Minn.

Lahr Bros. have disposed of their grain business at Conger, Minn., to Gustave Krueger.

It is reported the St. John Grain Co. closed its elevator at Douray, Minn., on February 1.

The Farmers' Elevator Co. of Lamberton, Minn., will build a corn crib adjoining the elevator.

Incorporation papers will be secured by the Farmers' Produce & Elevator Co. at Park Rapids, Minn.

A. W. Swinton has sold his elevator at Stanton, Minn., to N. T. Austinson. Possession is given April 1.

A press dispatch states the Woodworth Elevator Co. will close its plant at Kensington, Minn., and expects to tear down the building.

The Northern Grain Co., owner of 106 grain elevators, will move its general offices from Cedar Rapids, Iowa, to Minneapolis, Minn.

Recently the Northwestern Grain Co.'s elevator at Janesville, Wis., was leased to the New Richmond Roller Mill Co. of New Richmond.

The National Elevator Co. closed its house at Wheatville, Minn., the last of January. O. B. Hoven, the agent, was transferred to Tolna, N. D.

Six elevators and two "scoopers" are doing a lively business at Brown's Valley, Minn. J. L. Paul and R. H. Christian are buying on the street.

The Sauk Rapids Elevator at that place, Minnesota, which has been operated for the past year by the farmers' exchange, has been closed. About 1,000 bushels of oats and 200 bushels of wheat on hand have been sold to local parties.

A new grain firm will be known as the Reinganz-Wolf Grain Co. of Milwaukee, Wis. The principals are former employes of the Charles A.

Krause Grain Co., who will capitalize at $10,000. The Krause Company has retired from business.

An elevator will be built at Ormsby, Minn., by the Farmers' Elevator Co., now being organized.

Recently the Peavey Co. sold its interests at Blue Earth, Minn., to the Central Grain & Coal Co. The Pfeffer Elevator Co. will be in charge for the present.

Charles Bollenbach, F. R. Kauffman, John Knauss and others are forming a farmers' elevator company at Nerstrand, Minn., and may build an elevator.

F. W. Sanborn has purchased P. Luff's interest in the grain business at Ortonville, Minn., and will in the future conduct the business in partnership with Charles Luff.

State Senator Thorpe has introduced a bill in the legislature authorizing the railroad commission to fix the time when local warehousemen shall keep their warehouses open for business.

The new Globe Elevator (Pv.) at Rice's Point, Duluth, Minn., will be 193x72 feet in size and 172 feet high. It is being constructed of fireproof material and will be completed in about sixty days.

Articles of incorporation have been granted the Clark Grain and Fuel Co. of Chippewa Falls, Wis., which is capitalized at $75,000. Among those interested are Robert B. Clark, W. S. Congdon and W. M. Bowe.

Incorporation papers have been given the Terminal Elevator Co. of Minneapolis, Minn., which is capitalized at $100,000. W. W. Cargill of La Crosse, Wis., J. H. McMillan and D. D. McMillan of Minneapolis, are interested.

The Minnesota Mutual Elevator Co., of which E. I. Leland is president, will move its offices from Minneapolis to Marshall, Minn. The company was organized two years ago and has plants in Fenton and Dolliver, Iowa; Ceylon, Triumph, Minneota, Taunton and Porter, Minn.

OHIO, INDIANA AND MICHIGAN.

W. C. Hawk is erecting an elevator at Mongo, Ind.

Elmer Sheets is building an elevator at Wapakoneta, Ohio.

Charles Pierce has purchased the McMillen grain elevator at Van Wert, Ohio.

Shug & Horn are now in possession of the Mason Elevator at Monroeville, Ohio.

A receiver is in possession of the Princeton Elevator Co.'s property at Princeton, Ind.

The Urmston Grain and Elevator Co. of Frankton expects to build an elevator at Alexandria, Ind.

Frank Menefee has bought the elevator property and business of Finck & Freeman at Dayton, Ohio.

C. C. Coon of the J. J. Coon Grain Co. at Toledo, Ohio, has disposed of his interests and gone to California.

Edgar T. Jones & Co. of Lafayette, Ind., have incorporated their grain business under the name of E. T. Jones & Co.

E. M. Mossburg has sold his interests in the Warren Elevator Co. at Huntington, Ind., and will retire from the trade.

Plans are being prepared by N. A. Grabill for two elevators at Fort Wayne, Ind., of 17,000 bushels' capacity each, for Nathan & Levy.

William W. Adler of Lafayette, Ind., has sold his grain business to Fred G. Heinmiller, who has been employed by him during the past four years.

Conrad Erne has leased the Vandalia Elevator at Columbia City, which has been idle since Horace L. Combs discontinued business a year ago.

James K. Rhode of Winthrop has acquired Ora Thomason's interest in the Chatterton, Ind., elevator and will operate it in conjunction with John Thomason.

John Howell has completed an 8,000-bushel grain elevator at Camac, Ind. It was equipped with B. S. Constant machinery and was built by N. A. Grabill, architect.

The new 40,000-bushel grain bins being erected by the Quaker Oats Co. at Battle Creek, Mich., are constructed entirely of fire-clay tile, each block being 4x12 inches, on a concrete foundation. They will be 60 feet high and 15 feet in diameter.

The Union Grain and Coal Co.'s elevator at Anderson, Ind., was expected to be completed about the middle of February. It has a capacity of 50,000 bushels, and a meal plant in connection has a capacity of 60 bushels per hour. It is equipped with Skillin & Richards Manufacturing Co.'s machinery and a Sprout & Waldron Meal Mill. The house was built by N. A. Grabill of Daleville, Ohio.

William Gray Jr. has purchased the grain business of Bliss & Bartholomew at Romeo, Mich.

N. A. Grabill, the well-known elevator builder of Daleville, Ind., has just completed a 15,000-bushel grain elevator for W. C. Hile at Versailles, Ohio. It was equipped with the Weller Manufacturing Co.'s machinery and a B. S. Constant Sheller and Drag.

E. W. Elmore of Chicago, Ill., recently acquired the Interior Transfer Elevator at South Bend, Ind., from the syndicate formerly operating it and has reopened it after an idleness of eight months. William C. Buck of Toledo, Ohio, is again in charge as manager.

WESTERN.

A farmers' elevator company may be organized to build an elevator at Edwall, Wash.

The Pacific Grain Co. has bought the Farmers' Warehouse Co.'s plant at Elberton, Wash.

THE EXCHANGES

The Nashville Grain Exchange has secured new and larger quarters.

Julius H. Barnes is the new president of the Duluth Board of Trade.

Eugene Blackford Jr. has succeeded John W. Snyder as a member of the weighing committee of the Baltimore Chamber of Commerce.

It is announced that the Norfolk Hay and Grain Association has been merged with the Board of Trade of that city, under the latter style.

The directors of the Clearing House Association of the Duluth Board of Trade have decided to clear trades in No. 1 Durum. Heretofore nothing but No. 2, the regular contract grade, could be cleared.

George S. Jackson has resigned as chairman of the corn committee of the Baltimore Chamber of Commerce and J. Collin Vincent, vice-chairman, has been elected to fill the vacancy. Edwin Hughes is now vice-chairman.

A proposition to purchase and retire Chicago Board of Trade memberships from the general fund, which is to be swelled by the additional $25 per annum levied for 1907, was recently defeated by a vote of 368 to 259.

At the annual meeting of the New Orleans Board of Trade, held on January 14, officers were elected as follows: Henry B. Schreiber, president; C. H. Ellis, first vice-president; Charles Dittmann, second vice-president; A. F. Leonhardt, third vice-president; H. S. Herring, secretary-treasurer.

The Omaha Grain Exchange will be moved from the Board of Trade to the new Brandeis Building, and a considerable number of the active traders will find offices in the same structure. The trading room of the Exchange will be on the seventh floor of the building and will be 36x80 feet in size.

W. E. McHenry has been defeated in the Appellate Court in his mandamus suit brought against the Chicago Board of Trade to compel it to transfer his membership to a prospective buyer. McHenry was expelled from the Board in 1902, and subsequently sought to sell his membership.

Two petitions dealing with the delivery of No. 3 corn on contracts have been turned down by the directors of the Chicago Board of Trade. The first asked for the abolishing of the rule making No. 3 deliverable at a penalty of 5 cents, and the second sought to permit the delivery of No. 3 on the payment of a 3-cent penalty.

The St. Joseph (Mo.) Board of Trade has been incorporated with a capital stock of $2,000. Among the purposes of the board are to furnish weighmasters correctly to weigh the grain shipped in and out of St. Joseph, to certify to the correctness of warehouse receipts, to furnish daily market reports as to the condition of grain, stocks and produce, and to assist generally in building up the grain and produce business of St. Joseph.

The annual report of the directors of the Chicago Board of Trade for 1906 shows the membership to be 1,727, or 48 less than that of the preceding year. During the year 44 memberships were retired, the average price paid to each retiring member being $2,650. The bonded indebtedness of the Exchange is $1,198,300, maturing in 1927, and bearing interest of 4 per cent. Members who died during the year were Albert H. Farnum, John Dwyer, John Prindiville, Marshall Field, Thomas W. Hallam, Anderson Fowler, Henry Meyer, George A. Hellman, Thomas E. Barrett, Corwin H. Spencer, John F. Howard and Elisha A. Hancock.

At the first meeting of the newly-elected committee of management of the Montreal Corn Exchange consideration was given to the decision reached at a special meeting of the Corn Exchange that everything possible should be done to secure united action in order to get a ruling from the Railway Commission enforcing the principle of reciprocal demurrage. The secretary was instructed to communicate with other interested commercial organizations in order to secure their co-operation to this end.

Following are the inspection and standing committees of the Toledo Produce Exchange for 1907: Wheat inspection committee—C. L. Cutter, F. J. Reynolds, Geo. B. McCabe, F. O. Paddock, J. C. Keller, Fred. Mayer, W. W. Cummings. Corn, oats and rye inspection committee—E. L. Southworth, H. L. Goemann, W. H. Haskell, J. E. Rundell, H. W. De Vore, James Hodge, C. L. Reynolds. Seed inspection committee—F. W. Annin, E. W. V. Kuehn, J. C. Keller, F. W. Jaeger, C. S. Burge, R. L. Burge, W. E. Cratz. Transportation—A. L. Mills, F. J. Reynolds, W. H. Morehouse, E. L. Southworth, F. W. Rundell. Publicity—F. I. King, W. H. Morehouse, W. W. Cummings. Quotations—Wm. W. Cummings, F. I. King, C. S. Burge. Claims—C. S. Burge, F. O. Paddock, C. L. Cutter. Rules, floor and call—W. H. Morehouse, F. J. Reynolds, C. S. Burge. Rooms, supplies and employes—J. E. Rundell, C. L. Cutter, F. I. King. Telegraph—F. J. Reynolds, F. I. King, W. W. Cummings. Finance—W. H. Haskell, E. W. V. Kuehn, H. L. Goemann. Judiciary—H. L. Goemann, C. S. Coup, E. L. Southworth. Elevators—E. L. Southworth, F. O. Paddock, W. H. Morehouse. Harbor—C. L. Cutter, E. L. Southworth, J. E. Rundell. Weights—E. W. V. Kuehn, C. S. Coup, Wm. W. Cummings.

Geo. F. Stone has been reappointed secretary of the Chicago Board of Trade, for the twenty-third consecutive year. H. A. Foss has been appointed weighmaster; Samuel Powell, manager of the clearing house; J. F. Lee, assistant; John A. Tobey, registrar of provisions; J. T. Canbin, flour inspector; R. P. Kettles, chief grain sampler, and A. R. Ware, assistant grain sampler. Standing committees for the year are: Executive, Zeiss, Andrews and Stream; finance, Pettit, Bunnell and Bunch; real estate, Bunnell, Bennett and Rice; rules, Baker, Griffin and Pettit; legal advice, Bradley, Rogers and Baker; room, Sullivan, Bennett and Boore; membership, Andrew, Zeiss and Wickham; warehouse, Griffin, Rogers and Keller; grain, William N. Eckhardt, C. B. Pierce, E. L. Glaser, H. Mueller, John J. Keller, J. C. F. Merrill and George A. Wegener; clearing house, White, Pettit and Griffin; market report, Bradley, White and Boore; violation of rules, Rogers, Stream, Rice, Sullivan, Bradley and Wickham; transportation, Stream, Pettit, B. A. Eckhart, Griffin, Frank M. Bunch, E. L. Glaser, E. L. Merritt, W. N. Eckhardt and Frank B. Rice; weighing, Keller, Andrew and White; claims, Wickham, Boore and Baker; meteorological observation, Boore, Sullivan and Rogers; provision inspection, Zeiss, Bunnell, A. S. White, Paul Tietgens and John Roberts; flour inspection, Rice, B. A. Eckhart, A. B. Black, I. Horner and V. J. Petersen; flaxseed inspection, Bunch, P. B. Eschenburg, T. M. Hunter, George E. Alt and J. H. Milne; other inspection, Boore, Stream and Bunch; arbitration committee on grass and field seeds, A. L. Somers, F. E. Winans, Charles A. Heath, G. S. Green, Adolph Gerstenberg, George Wegener and T. M. Hunter; insolvencies, Bennett, Baker and White; call, George R. Nichols, William N. Eckhardt, G. B. Van Ness, E. L. Merritt and S. T. Graff.

MONTREAL CORN EXCHANGE ELECTION

The officers elected to preside over the affairs of the Montreal Corn Exchange for 1907 are: President, Joseph Quintal; treasurer, Norman Wight. Committee of management—Charles R. Taylor, T. R. McCarthy, H. D. Metcalfe, R. W. Oliver, James S. Norris, A. E. Labelle and D. Mahaffey. Board of review—Edgar Judge (chairman), Charles McLean, J. B. McLea, H. W. Raphael, James Carruthers and A. G. Thomson. As Mr. Thomson refused to act, it will devolve upon the committee of management to elect a member of the board of review in his stead.

Thomas A. Crane, the retiring president, stated that the grain exported from Montreal exceeded in volume last year the shipments of any year since 1900. The export of grain during the season of 1906 had been 56,812,000, an advance of 23 per cent over the season of 1905, when the quantity exported was only 21,750,000. The increase had been chiefly in flaxseed, of which over 3,000,000 bushels had been exported, as against only 250,000 bushels in the previous year. The volume of grain handled had been lessened somewhat by the difficulties of securing prompt transportation, as the demand made upon the railways to carry general merchandise had been in excess of the equipment, and much suffering had resulted to merchants in the grain trade through inability to secure early delivery of their purchases.

ANNUAL ELECTION AT TORONTO.

The annual meeting of the grain section of the Toronto Board of Trade was held on January 17, at which time the following officers and committees were chosen: Chairman, C. W. Band; vice-chairman, A. V. Pearce; secretary-treasurer, F. G. Morley. Executive committee—John Carrick, A. Cavanagh, L. H. Clarke, J. L. Fisher, E. Hannah, F. W. Hay, J. L. Love, W. D. Matthews, D. Plewes, D. M. Spink, C. B. Watts. Complaint committee—C. W. Band, D. O. Ellis, C. Goode, S. McNairn, Hedley Shaw. Market report committee—C. W. Band, John Carrick, E. J. Hannah, D. Plewes, W. Stark. Membership committee—D. O. Ellis, J. L. Fisher, George Goldie, C. Goode, J. N. Hay, E. J. Hannah.

PEORIA'S ANNUAL ELECTION.

The officers elected by the Peoria Board of Trade for 1907 are: President, T. A. Grier; vice-presidents, E. Roberts and Daniel Mowat; secretary, John R. Lofgren; treasurer, Walter Barker. The directors are: A. G. Tyng, W. R. Buckley, C. C. Miles, Peter Casey, R. W. Van Tassell, J. H. Ridge, George C. Clark, J. M. Quinn, Frank Hall and Geo. Breier. Following are some of the committees: Arbitration—W. H. Mills, W. T. Cornelison, E. S. McClure, W. B. Kingman, C. H. Feltman, D. D. Hall. Appeals—L. H. Murray, George A. Smith, J. Wachenheimer, I. W. Donmeyer, F. H. Rockwell, F. W. Arnold. Inspection—W. R. Buckley, A. G. Tyng, J. H. Ridge, C. C. Miles, R. W. Van Tassell. Rules—J. M. Quinn, W. H. Buckley, Peter Casey. Weights—C. C. Miles, G. C. Clark, R. W. Van Tassell.

NEW OFFICERS AT WINNIPEG.

The annual election of the Winnipeg Grain Exchange resulted in the selection of the following: President, W. J. Bettingen; vice-president, J. F. Fleming; secretary-treasurer, C. N. Bell; council, John Fleming, B. McBean, Robt. Muir, G. V. Hastings, W. A. Black, H. N. Baird, J. C. Gage, G. R. Crowe, J. G. McHugh and W. L. Parrish.

Arbitration committee (by acclamation): S. Spink, J. C. Gage, W. L. Parrish, G. R. Crowe, Robert Muir, Donald Morrison and W. A. Matheson.

Committee of appeals (by acclamation): S. P. Clark, E. W. Kneeland, H. N. Baird, W. A. Black, Thos. Thompson, A. R. Hargraft and J. M. McHugh.

Retiring President Tilt delivered the annual address and President-elect Bettingen spoke on the progress of the Exchange, after thanking the members for his election.

ELECTION AT PHILADELPHIA.

James L. King was unanimously elected president of the Philadelphia Commercial Exchange on January 29. Edmund E. Delp was named as vice-president and Samuel C. Woolman was re-elected treasurer. The following directors were chosen: S. F. Scattergood, Watson W. Walton, William M. Richardson, William H. Donahue, John A. Killpatrick and W. S. Woodward.

In his inaugural address on January 31 President King made a demand for better grain-handling facilities. He said, in part:

"Philadelphia is admirably located for the prompt handling of its full share of the export grain trade of this country, but the terminal facilities we now have are not sufficient to permit of any large expansion in this business.

"The greater portion of the grain received for several months has arrived over the Pennsylvania Railroad. But on its arrival here the lack of elevator room and equipment, the scarcity of docks and the poor condition of the docks we now have caused the grain to be handled at considerable disadvantage to receivers.

"We need to keep the steamship lines now operating in Philadelphia actively engaged, and we need more steamship lines if we are to keep up with the growing commerce of the country, but we cannot invite or expect additional steamship service if the docks and wharves are not adequate or in proper condition.

"It is, therefore, very necessary that the docks should be properly dredged without delay, and that more docks and more wharf facilities be given to enable Philadelphia to increase her trade as it should be increased.

"By reason of the large volume of grain that is coming to Philadelphia over the Pennsylvania Railroad, it is absolutely necessary that we should have additional elevator facilities connecting with this company. To my mind, one of the greatest needs of the grain trade tributary to Philadelphia at this time is that there should be erected here at the terminus of the Pennsylvania Railroad a modern, first-class elevator, properly equipped and of sufficient capacity to accommodate and handle the business of the present day and to provide for the increase of the future.

"I call your attention to these great needs in order that the members of the Exchange may unite to secure them, and I promise every effort of my administration to urge that these improvements be made and additional facilities installed."

BOSTON'S ANNUAL MEETING AND ELECTION.

The annual meeting of the Boston Chamber of Commerce was held on January 15, at which time officers were elected as follows: President, John F. Crocker; first vice-president, Frank A. Noyes; second vice-president, James J. Storrow; directors for three years, John Shephard, William A. Bancroft, George T. Coppins and Edward P. May.

The report of the board of directors made one notable suggestion in connection with the grain department. The board finds that there must be some readjustment of the railroad rates on grain to Boston if the city is to compete in the exportation of this product with the gulf ports. On this question the board says:

"The operations of the grain department for the year have been disappointing. In pursuance of the understanding had with the railroad companies at the time the fees for inspection were raised from 30 to 50 cents per thousand bushels, a reduction to 40 cents was made, taking effect January 1, 1906. This change in the rate, combined with a reduced volume of business, are the causes for the lessened revenue. While it is not possible to make a proportionate reduction in expenses, the committee on grain have cut their force down as low as practicable by accepting the resignation of one of the deputies. As it is understood that the New York, New Haven & Hartford Railroad has withdrawn from the export grain business, it is expected that the present help will be adequate to handle the business unless there should be a considerable unexpected increase in volume."

BALTIMORE ELECTS OFFICERS.

The annual meeting of the members of the Baltimore Chamber of Commerce was held on January 29, with the retiring president, Douglas M. Wylie, in the chair. Mr. Wylie, in his annual report, spoke of the apathetic condition of the grain trade during the past year and said it was difficult to account for in the face of record-breaking crops. He believed that most excellent results would be brought about by the establishment of the government grain-testing laboratory at Baltimore, with which the grain committees and inspection department were co-operating. Referring to terminal facilities, he said:

"Your committee on terminals has assurances from the Pennsylvania Railroad that it is about to build a series of concrete bins, of a capacity of 1,000,000 bushels, in connection with one of its Canton elevators; and the Baltimore & Ohio Railroad has now in course of construction a large, new conveyor which should greatly facilitate the handling of grain on the Locust Point side of the harbor.

"The proposed arrangements whereby the Wabash Railroad is to become part of a great transcontinental line, together with the recent linking of the Baltimore & Ohio Railroad and Illinois Central with the Union Pacific Railroad, promise vast tonnage, which must find its way to our city along the line of least resistance, we being nearer primary points than the more northern or southern ports.

"There is a legitimate demand for an elevator at the tidewater terminals of the Western Maryland Railroad. Regardless of its contemplated extension, that railroad already reaches grain-producing sections naturally our territory, but business cannot be successfully contended for without means for its proper handling here. In addition to this, there is much water-borne grain suitable for handling in connection with the rail grain that will be a source of considerable revenue to a favorably located and modernly equipped elevator."

Five new directors were elected, as follows: A. F. Sidebotham, Henry A. Lederer, Thomas C. Craft Jr., Harry C. Jones and William G. Scarlett. When the full board met for organization, on January 30, the following officers were elected: Blanchard Randall, president; Charles P. Blackburn, vice-president; Henry A. Wroth, secretary; James B. Hessong, assistant secretary and treasurer. The members of the executive committee are John H. Gildea Jr. (chairman), Charles S. Schermerhorn (vice-chairman), Edgar F. Richards, A. F. Sidebotham and Thomas C. Craft Jr.

COMMISSION

Goffe & Carkener Co. of St. Louis, Mo., have remembered their friends by the gift of a very attractive calendar.

E. W. Elmore, 617 Postal Telegraph Building, Chicago, has leased and is operating the Interior Elevator at South Bend, Ind.

Frank G. Coe, with the grain department of the Corn Products Co., Chicago, returned home the middle of February from a visit to Roswell, N. M.

Young & Nichols of Chicago reported the sale February 11 of a car of Choice Wisconsin Barley at 61 cents F. O. B. Chicago. It was the highest price of the season up to that date.

The Alabama Grain Company of Birmingham, Ala., has been incorporated with a capital stock of $8,000. The incorporators are B. A. Lee, R. S. Corry, J. U. McBride, C. E. Hamilton.

The Reingas-Wolff Grain Company of Milwaukee, Wis., has been incorporated with a capital stock of $10,000. The incorporators are John C. Reingas, Louis R. Wolff, August E. Wolff.

The Pittsburg Grain Company of Camden, N. J., has been incorporated with a capital stock of $100,000 to deal in grain. The incorporators are C. W. Stone, L. J. McChie and E. H. Huff.

The W. R. Hall Grain Company has been organized at St. Louis, Mo., to deal in hay and grain. The capital stock is $50,000, fully paid. Incorporators are W. R. Hall, W. H. White, J. V. Botto.

Hankinson, Ireys & Co. have succeeded Hankinson-Ireys Co. in the grain business at Minneapolis, Minn. The change is a nominal one only, and business is continued along the same lines as formerly.

John Dickinson & Co. of Chicago have removed their general offices from 171 La Salle Street to the first floor of the Board of Trade Building. In addition to grain they are also now handling cotton, coffee and stocks.

The Terminal Elevator Co. has been organized at Minneapolis, Minn., with a capital stock of $100,000. The incorporators are W. W. Cargill, La Crosse, Wis.; J. H. McMillan and D. D. McMillan, Minneapolis, Minn.

The H. J. Hasenwinkle Company has opened an office in Memphis, Tenn., for conducting a general grain commission business. It is under the personal management of H. J. Hasenwinkle, of the Hasenwinkle Grain Co. of Bloomington, Ill.

Gerstenberg & Co. of Chicago, Ill., have secured the services of Frank O'Heron to represent them in Minnesota and the two Dakotas. Mr. O'Heron was until recently in the grain business at Luverne, Minn., and has very many friends in the Northwest.

E. M. Higgins retired from the vice-presidency of the Armour Grain Co. February 1 and was succeeded by Ed James. Mr. James has been with the firm for 27 years, starting in as a boy, and has filled many important positions with the firm. Mr. Higgins expects shortly to go abroad with his family.

The Northern Grain Co., with head offices at Manitowoc, Wis., has moved its office at Cedar Rapids, Iowa, to Minneapolis, Minn. J. J. Donahue is manager of the Minneapolis branch and the elevators, and business that has been heretofore handled through Cedar Rapids will be done from Minneapolis. The company operates upward of 106 elevators in Iowa and Wisconsin and has 3,500,000 bushels' capacity at Manitowoc.

W. W. Alder, well-known grain dealer of Lafayette, Ind., and head of the firm of Alder & Stofer at Buffalo, N. Y., has sold his Lafayette business to Fred G. Heinmiller. Mr. Heinmiller has been with Mr. Alder for the past four years and will continue the track grain business and buying and selling of car lots without change. Mr. Alder will devote what time he has for the grain business to the Buffalo house. He has three farms, and these will receive a part of his attention.

Horace L. Wing has formed a connection with W. H. Lake & Co. of Chicago and will handle his trades through that house.

SEEDS

It is reported the F. B. Mills Seed Co. of Rose Hill, N. Y., is negotiating for a location at Atlantic, Iowr.

Incorporation papers have been granted the Enterprise Seed Co. at Oklahoma City, Okla. It is capitalized at $5,000.

Dan Pascal, of DeWitt County, Illinois, paid $150 for a prize ear of corn shown at the Iowa Corn Growers' Association.

O. H. Will & Co. at Bismarck, N. D., have shipped some Northwestern Dent seed corn to the government of Colombia, where it will be planted as an experiment in the interior.

F. Knorr, secretary of the Colorado Grain and Seed Growers' Association, has sent out from his offices at Fort Collins, Colo., a circular showing the purpose of the organization and describing a movement to promote good seed grain in the high altitude of that state.

Alfred Olson, a farmer of Deuel County, South Dakota, has just figured up what the timothy seed from a 400-acre tract has brought him. The crop averaged eight bushels per acre and the price $1.57½ per bushel, or a total of $5,040. This didn't include the money he received for the straw.

On January 30 the Illinois Corn Growers' Association, in session at Urbana, elected the following officers: President, E. E. Chester, Champaign; first vice-president, Charles A. Rowe, Jacksonville; second vice-president, C. W. Farr, Chicago; third vice-president, Dwight Dalbey, Jerseyville; fourth vice-president, H. G. Easterly, Carbondale; fifth vice-president, W. C. Griffith, McNabb; sixth vice-president, A. A. Hill, Casner; secretary, Leigh F. Maxey, Curen; treasurer, H. A. Winter, Wenona.

F. E. Winans, the Chicago seed broker at 6 and 8 Sherman Street, on February 5 closed the largest sale of timothy grass seed ever made, when he sold 50,000 bags for the Armour Grain Co. The purchaser's name is withheld, as is the price. Some of the seed has been held for more than two years, it having been taken on by the Armour Grain Co. when supplies were excessive, prices low and buyers hard to find. The lot weighs 7,000,000 pounds and sold at an advance of $1.50 per 100 pounds over the original purchase price.

The London "Corn Circular" of January 14 says: Clover seed continues in abundant supply, but, the low prices proving attractive, a good trade passes. The continent appears to be taking away large quantities of best grade, and lucky it is for the English farmer that this unusual demand exists, for otherwise an overwhelming glut would doubtless work havoc. Really fine seed is to be had for 50s to 53s and 54s, and above these prices it is unnecessary to go unless something superb is wanted. Useful lots, very fair 46s to 48s and 49s, and common down to as low as 35s per hundredweight. On the Herts and Essex exchanges plenty of red clover seed has sold, choice purple at 37s 6d, very fine 35s, very good 32s, useful brown 25s per bushel of 70 pounds.

Representative Mann of Illinois delivered a speech before the House of Representatives at Washington on January 26, upon the subject of "Seed Adulteration." Mr. Mann stated that the Canadian government permitted the exportation of two of the best-known adulterants, dodder and catchfly, and dilated at length upon their characteristics. Of 352 samples of alfalfa seed purchased in the open market, 160, or nearly one-half, were found to contain dodder seed. Of 521 samples of red clover seed obtained in the same way, 116, or over 22 per cent, contained seed of dodder. Mr. Mann said that two samples of red clover seed, representing about 10,000 pounds recently imported from Canada, were all practically the seed of catchfly, one of the commonest and worst clover weeds in the country to the north. He made the direct charge that a large proportion of the low-grade seed containing weed seeds and dead seed offered for sale in the United States is imported from Europe and Canada. "Canada," he said, "has a very strict seed inspection law, preventing the sale in that country of seed containing any of a long list of prohibited seeds. If a law could be framed which will prohibit the importation of and interstate commerce in seed containing weed seeds and dead seed much good can be done."

In a recent pamphlet C. A. King & Co. of Toledo, Ohio, say: "Bureau of Chemistry of the Department of Agriculture says the pure food law does not affect the importations of foreign seeds which are not used for food purposes. They thought the Bureau of Plant Industry had a special importation seed law covering it. The Bureau of Plant Industry says there is no national legislation covering it. It says: 'We quite agree with you that the low-grade clover and alfalfa seed which is now being imported is of very great detriment to this country, and that any steps which may be taken to prevent this being imported would be of value to the country at large.' The only specified authority the Bureau of Plant Industry has in connection with the adulteration of seeds is in the following order which has been observed: 'The Secretary of Agriculture is hereby directed to obtain in the open market samples of seeds of grass, clover or alfalfa, test the same, and if any such seeds are found to be adulterated or misbranded, or any seeds of Canada blue grass (Poa compressa) are obtained under any other name than Canada blue grass or Poa compressa, to publish the results of the tests, together with the names of the persons by whom the seeds were offered for sale.' It published the names and yellow trefoil seemed to be the chief adulterant used, varying from three to forty-seven per cent. Ten firms were named as flirting with it.

FEDERAL INSPECTION OF GRAIN.

Among embryonic laws now being fostered in the minds of legislators there is one of supreme importance to the grain trade the country over, namely, federal inspection of grain. The measure, if adopted, will practically revolutionize the system; and while it admits of wide possibilities, yet first thought does not suggest that any system whereby the interior grain inspection as supervised by the federal authorities can be any improvement over the present well organized inspection departments maintained by Minnesota, Illinois and other states.

At present the grain is well handled by these departments and there has been no complaint of any serious nature. There has been an effort made lately by these departments to get together and make the grading at the different markets more uniform and if this is accomplished there will be little to be asked for. Of course, the divergence of rules and regulations is necessary in some instances, as local conditions and the geographical position of the different localities wherein the grain is raised must enter into the question. For instance, a car of corn shipped to Chicago or Minneapolis would arrive in good condition and grade No. 3 yellow. The same car shipped to St. Louis would encounter different climatic conditions and arriving at that market would, in some cases, go no grade.

In the case of wheat there is little reason why the rules should not be the same as to weight and quality. Winter wheat arriving at this market could easily be graded the same as in Chicago, as well as spring and durum wheat. If the government intends going into the business along the usual governmental lines, one might expect to see an inspector of grain stationed any old place where they use or raise a car of wheat. The expense would be enormous and the results, perhaps, not as satisfactory as they are at present. The different state inspection organizations are self-supporting and are able to give good satisfaction for a very nominal fee. It remains to be seen just what ground the proposed legislation will cover, but a governmental set of rules to go by in inspecting grain, just as they have for weights and measures, would fit the case perfectly and allow things to run along smoothly without any unnecessary ripples.

A good inspection system covering shipping ports for the benefit of the foreign buyers would not be amiss where the cargo is broken in transit, but the interior system is running along nicely and it is hoped will not be disturbed.—Minneapolis Market Record.

Loewen Bros. of St. Louis are endeavoring to organize a broomcorn brokers' association among the dealers as a sort of protection against losses when their goods are refused.

A railroad man who has spent three weeks in the Dakotas says millions of bushels of wheat are stacked upon the ground, covered with snow, and is slowly rotting. He believes 50 per cent of this will be unmarketable.

CROP REPORTS

Correspondents in Ohio report wheat as well rooted, on the whole, and able to stand the rigors of a severe winter.

A report from Phœnix, Ariz., says a rain which fell late in December placed a fine edge on the soil and an immense grain crop should be secured.

Wheat was reported to be unusually green around Booneville, Ind., where a light snow had fallen February 1, and saved thousands of acres of the cereal.

Snow fell at an opportune time in the vicinity of Newton, Peabody and Marysville, Kan., on January 26, making the prospects for a fine wheat crop much better.

The Iowa Grain Dealers' Association reports 72 per cent of the marketable portion of the last oat crop and 41 per cent of the marketable portion of the last corn crop has left the hands of the farmers.

Two thousand acres of fall wheat and rye in the dry farming district around Nunn, Colo., is said to be thriving heartily and the farmers are assured of a good harvest, as is all the wheat in that section.

Green bugs are reported to be making disastrous inroads on the young wheat and oats in Dallas County and other sections of north Texas. The Dallas County Farm lost 100 acres of oats and wheat through the ravages of the bugs and other losses are reported from various parts of the county.

A late bulletin from the weather bureau shows the ground over much of the winter wheat belt to be well covered with snow. Moderate snows were indicated in portions of the Middle Mississippi and Lower Ohio valleys and heavier snowfalls in the Northern districts. On February 4, the area covered was greater than at any previous date this winter, the southern limit extending from the middle Rocky Mountain region southeastward to Northern Arkansas and thence through Tennessee and North Carolina to the Virginia coast. Only slight depths of snow were reported on Monday from the Central Mississippi and Ohio valleys and the lower lake region. But in the interior of the Middle Atlantic States there were depths ranging from three to twelve inches.

GRAIN STORAGE NOT INCREASING.

Grain storage has not expanded with the crops, say King & Co., Toledo. The total grain storage of the fourteen principal markets has not increased any during the past five years. It now equals 226,000,000 bushels. Of this 181,000,000 is old style wooden construction with high rates of insurance, while 45,000,000 is modern iron, steel or concrete with very low insurance. New York shows a big decrease. Seaboard capacity is very limited, partially causing the car famines every winter. Chicago has the greatest capacity, almost a quarter of all, but a trifle less of iron than either Duluth or Minneapolis. Kansas City and Minneapolis both have increased four millions. Toledo and St. Louis show no material change; both have about 9,000,000 bushels. There has been some increase in the capacity of interior mills and country elevators.

Storage capacity compares as follows:

	Total Grain Storage Capacity. Bushels.	Wooden. Bushels.	Iron. Bushels.	Change Past 5 Years. Increase. Bushels.
Toledo	9,000,000	6,000,000	3,000,000	*
Chicago	59,620,000	51,770,000	7,850,000	2,000,000
Milwaukee	14,160,000	14,160,000	0	2,000,000
Duluth	34,550,000	26,550,000	8,000,000	100,000
Minneapolis	38,000,000	27,850,000	10,150,000	4,000,000
St. Louis	9,500,000	9,500,000	0	*
Kansas City	10,500,000	5,500,000	5,000,000	4,000,000
Galveston	3,900,000	3,900,000	0	1,000,000
Newport News	2,750,000	2,750,000	0	0
Baltimore	5,300,000	5,300,000	0	0
New York	13,230,000	10,955,000	2,275,000	†16,250,000
Boston	3,000,000	2,000,000	1,000,000	0
Detroit	2,900,000	2,900,000	....	0
Buffalo	20,350,000	11,850,000	8,500,000	0
Total	226,760,000	180,985,000	45,775,000	11,100,000
Total net decrease				5,150,000

*No change. †Decrease.

Indianapolis grain shippers are endeavoring to secure one of the new government laboratories for the inspection of grain.

Michigan seems to be the banner bean state this year. The crop averages 20 bushels per acre and nets the grower $1 a bushel.

BARLEY AND MALT

The Bosch-Ryan Co. will soon resume the construction of its malting house at Cedar Rapids, Iowa.

Peter Van Vooren, a teamster formerly employed by the Duluth Brewing & Malting Co., is suing that company for $3,275 damages, claiming his back was seriously injured when a bag of grain fell on him.

Work on the new $250,000 malting plant, to be constructed by the Electric Malting Co. at Minneapolis, Minn., will begin in the early spring. The Electric Steel Elevator Co. in behind the enterprise, and C. E. Thayer, the grain man, announces the structure will be modern and fireproof throughout. It will be located near the Archer-Daniels Mill in Southeast Minneapolis and will have a capacity of 2,000 bushels per day.

A loss of $15,000 was suffered recently by Strauss, Kuhn & Co. when their malt house on the Viga Canal, Mexico City, was gutted. The large supply of malt was damaged the heaviest, the walls of the building being of stone. It is believed defective wires caused the fire. The company has been producing a carload of malt a day from barley grown in the United States, Canada, Germany and Switzerland. The firm is experimenting with the plant in various parts of Mexico.

Following are the stated imports and exports of barley malt for the month of December, 1906, and for the fiscal year ending with December, 1906, compared with the same period of 1905:

Imports—	1906	1905
Barley—December, bushels.	73,622	10,414
Value	$13,064	$5,570
Fiscal year, bushels.......	86,647	31,973
Value	$20,061	$16,624
Exports—	1906	1905
Barley—December, bushels.	1,194,478	1,946,508
Value	$631,512	$972,407
Fiscal year, bushels.......	14,528,245	13,769,219
Value	$7,363,805	$6,920,248
Malt—December, bushels...	35,118	115,829
Value	$23,884	$77,471
Fiscal year, bushels.......	633,504	701,726
Value	$432,223	$477,123

[For the U. S. Brewmasters' Association.]

PEDIGREE CULTURE OF BARLEY IN THE UNITED STATES.*

BY DR. R. WAHL,
Director at the Wahl-Henius Institute of Fermentology.

[Concluded from January number, p. 377.]

Although the idea of pedigree culture has been received with enthusiasm in the United States for a few years, the scientific means of controlling the outcome of such culture, at least as far as the cultivation of barley is concerned, have not received that attention which a personal visit to Sweden by one who, like Nilson, is familiar with the language would have brought.

Shortly after Nilson's return from Sweden our Institute, considering the importance of obtaining in the shortest possible time such pure races of barley as would at once be satisfactory to the farmers and to the brewers, concluded that the best way to reach this desirable goal would be to solicit the co-operation of the agricultural colleges. Consequently Nilson visited during July and August the agricultural colleges of Wisconsin, Minnesota and Iowa, and was most cordially received by the respective professors, who all declared themselves willing and anxious to co-operate with us. At all three colleges (especially so, perhaps, in Madison) Nilson found a great interest in barley culture, all three colleges having experimental plots and larger areas set apart for pedigree culture of barleys. The two favored varieties were the Manchury and Oderbrucher barleys. The farmers of the three states do not willingly take to two-rowed barley, as in nearly all localities it will lodge badly and yield less per acre than the six-rowed barey. . . .

When applying the Swedish method of analyzing these different samples of six-rowed barley, Nilson soon found that the two ordinary barleys, the Manchury and Oderbrucher, were composed in very much the same way, as far, at least, as indicated by the hairiness of the basal bristles and the conditions of the side veins. Both showed about 88 per cent of heads of the short-haired basal bristles and 12 per cent with long-haired bristles, both varieties having dentated veins. In other words, the Oderbrucher and the Manchury barleys were mixtures containing 88 per cent (about) of one type and 12 per cent of another type. Now as to the pure cultures of Manchury and Oderbrucher, both in Madison and St. Paul, they were, as far as observation of a limited number of heads of each goes, actually pure pedigree cultures, consisting in both places of the short-haired type, which might be expected, seeing that the single heads from which they were raised had been taken at random from a mixture containing only a small number of the long-haired type.

So much the greater was Nilson's astonishment when he examined the two six-rowed pedigree cultures known as the Golden Queen and Silver King, to find that Golden Queen actually was a pedigree culture of the long-haired type, whereas the Silver King was made up of the short-haired type. The originator of these two last types is unknown. Evidently someone happened to pick from an Oderbrucher or Manchury barley one head of each of the two types.

"I am aware of the fact," says Nilson, "that doubt has been thrown upon the constancy of these botanical marks, and that consequently it might not be well to rely too much upon such characteristics. Though not a botanist, I may be allowed to say that, as far as my experience goes with these six-rowed barleys, I have not once felt any doubt to what type a kernel belonged, and that within the thousands of heads I have examined I never saw any variation in the kernels of one and the same head, except as to size of the basal bristle. As far as the hairiness goes, it is as easy to distinguish between the two types as it is to distinguish between the hair of an Indian and a negro. This goes to show that we have not so far here in the United States, with this cereal, at any rate, been working according to strictly scientific principles in pedigree culture, and that in the future an exact botanical study must go hand in hand with the practical experiments in the field, if our pedigree cultures are to be of any reliability and certainty."

The question now naturally arises, which races of barley should be preferred. The first condition is that such a barley must be satisfactory to the farmer, as he is not likely to raise a barley unless it pays him to do so. That condition limits, as far as I know, the choice to six-rowed barley, at least in the three states of Wisconsin, Minnesota and Iowa. Taking, then, this for granted, we have already two barleys, the Manchury and the Oderbrucher, of which the first has been grown successfully for a long period, and is therefore thoroughly acclimatized. The Oderbrucher seed was obtained by Professor Moore, of the Wisconsin Agricultural Experiment Station, from Germany about six years ago, and this barley seems to do equally well, which is not to be wondered at, if the two varieties really are one and the same. That both of these barleys are excellent brewing barleys has been found by experiments carried out on a large scale at our Institute. The question would then limit itself to a decision in favor of one or the other type represented in the two barleys. Is it the short-haired type which is superiod, or does the prize belong to the long-haired type? Incidentally, it may be mentioned that one of the best of the Swedish six-rowed varieties, the so-called six-rowed Giant barley, really is derived from Manchury barley, and is a pure race of the long-haired type.

Well, these questions must be decided by our agricultural colleges. Possibly the long-haired type may possess the stiffer straw and therefore be the most suitable for a heavy soil, and it may also be that it runs higher in nitrogen. Such would, in fact, be the case if further experiments verify the analyses of two heads of the two types selected from the ordinary Manchury barley. Further examinations will decide whether this is a rule or not.

Again, in looking over the material to be collected in other states, we might find varieties better adapted to the climate and soil of those states, and to the requirements of both farmer and brewer, than the mixed barleys there grown at present, or better adapted than the pedigree barleys to be separated from the Manchury or Oderbrucher seeds of the Wisconsin, Minnesota or Iowa areas. We may find that for certain localities certain other varieties of barleys are best suited. We intend to take in hand the Bay Brewing six-rowed and Chevalier two-rowed barleys, extensively grown in the western and northwestern states, and resolve them into their component varieties. Not until that time will the question of systematic barley valuation find a final solution. That the six-rowed barley deserves preference at least for American conditions is indicated by a number of circumstances.

Six-rowed barley is cultivated above the arctic circle; is content with a soil where the two-rowed would prove a failure; has a thicker skin and a stiffer straw; and is enzymatically stronger, its diastatic strength being greater than that of the two-rowed European barley. The six-rowed barley is, therefore, capable of giving a beer of more stable qualities, a beer which will stand high and low temperatures better. And it is according to this enzymatic energy that the value of a brewing barley should be estimated also and not alone according to whether it yields a few per cent more or less of starch. The quality, not the quantity, of the beer should be of first importance.

Nilson reports that the use of six-rowed barley is increasing in the Swedish breweries, thanks to the efforts of the Svalöf Institute, and the Danish breweries do not seem to consider it entirely unsuitable. He says: "When in Copenhagen I visited the famous Carlsberg breweries, and in a conversation with the head inspector, Mr. Paulsen, I asked whether any six-rowed barley was used. To my great astonishment Mr. Paulsen answered: 'Yes, indeed, whenever we make a beer for export to hot countries, we always use a large percentage of six-rowed barley to make the beer more stable.'" Now, it is just such a stable beer that the American public demands. And when the farmers of this country are able to deliver pure race, six-rowed barleys for brewing purposes, then there is hope that the question of higher or lower nitrogen content may find a satisfactory solution. Then we can take up with some hope of success the investigations of the role played by the different nitrogenous compounds in the barley grain, which investigations so far have been almost useless in a barley consisting of an unknown number of varieties with different properties.

For years the attention of the students of our Institute has been drawn to the fact that the albumen of barley possesses very different properties in the various parts of the grain. So, for instance, has it been shown that the so-called aleurone layer, which is very rich in albumen, is notat all changed during the malting and brewing operations. In fact, it is only during the last stages of its growth in the soil when the barley kernel is permitted to grow as far as it can by its own resources, and after the starch body is almost entirely consumed, that the solid cells in the aleurone layer begin to show some partly empty cells. It is, therefore, clear that these cells cannot be affected by the short period of germination of the barley during the malting process, and still less by the mashing operation. Now, when it is considered that a barley grain possesses more or less of such albumen, some barleys showing two, others three, rows of cells in their aleurone layer, it is evident that two barleys may differ in total amount of albumen contents, and still give the same amount of albumen to the beer, and vice versa. The way in which the nitrogenous bodies of a barley are going to influence a beer is decided not alone by the total quantity of nitrogenous substances in the barley, but also by the quality of such bodies, as is here instanced by the different behavior of the aleurone albumen, compared with the endosperm and germ albumen.

The work of the agricultural colleges for the next three or four years would, then, be to separate and cultivate as pure pedigree races the two varieties in the Oderbrucher as well as in the Manchury barley, and to test thoroughly which of these is the most promising from the farmer's standpoint, while the brewer's standpoint should be looked after by experts in that line. But if these experiments are to be of real value, they must be carried out with the greatest care. No seeds should be used for these experiments which are not taken from heads carefully examined as to type, in order to insure a pure race barley from the start. And the experiment plots should be well separated from each other, so as to prevent one plant or head of one variety from getting in among the plants of another plot, and thus vitiating the result from the very beginning. The experiments should be carried out in the same exact and painstaking manner in which they are carried out at the Swedish Institute.—American Brewers' Review.

*Address delivered at the Brewmasters' Convention at St. Paul-Minneapolis, September 10-13, 1906.

OUR CALLERS

[We have received calls from the following gentlemen prominently connected with the grain and elevator interests during the month.]

Theo. Kipp, Peoria, Ill.
C. H. Seybt, St. Louis, Mo.
F. Kohl, Jr., Centralia, Ill.
Louis Kunda, Oshkosh, Wis.
Jas. McGrew, Kankakee, Ill.
G. I. Toevs, Lindsborg, Kan.
W. G. Palmer, Middletown, Ohio.
Frank E. C. Hawkes, Goshen, Ind.
Edwin Kilburn, Spring Valley, Minn.
J. D. Shanahan, Bureau of Plant Industry, Department of Agriculture, Washington, D. C.

TRANSPORTATION

It is proposed to haul grain into Omaha on the interurban railways.

Announcement is expected soon of the building of a railway direct from Winnipeg to Hudson Bay.

It is generally believed that the Soo will build a line from Glenwood to Duluth, Minn., which will enable the company to handle its own traffic to Duluth.

G. A. Tomlinson of Duluth, Minn., said on February 1 that but four cars of grain were arriving daily and believes there will be no improvement for sixty days.

An order of the Kansas railroad commissioners reducing the rates on grain and coal will be put into effect March 15, by the Union Pacific, Leavenworth & Kansas, Burlington, Chicago Rock Island, Chicago Great Western, Santa Fe and Missouri Pacific railroads.

Commissioner C. A. Prouty of the Interstate Commerce Commission has been at Oklahoma City, Okla., investigating alleged excessive freight rates between Oklahoma and Texas points. The Rock Island, Santa Fe and Missouri, Kansas and Texas companies are the defendants.

No protest to the order of Judge Niles of Jackson, Miss., putting in force and effect the interstate order on grain shipped over the Mobile and Ohio from St. Louis to points in the Aberdeen group has been made. A saving of some $75,000 will be made by the Aberdeen towns on rates.

A $2 reconsignment charge on grain has been established by the Santa Fe at Omaha and it is reported other roads are about to take similar action. The Frisco has placed a reconsignment charge on hay, while the C. G. W. has removed its charge on grain because it acted as a direct discrimination against the Kansas City market.

Grain men at Fort Worth have been notified by the Rock Island that, effective March 15, the Chicago, Rock Island and Gulf Railway Company will absolutely discontinue recognizing track grain where it involves the change of billing and the protection of the through rate from originating point to new destination. This will not interfere with the present practice of handling grain through elevators and accepting reconsignment from elevators and change in billing in order to protect through rate.

The North Dakota Elevator Association and the Independent Grain Shippers' Association consolidated under the name of the North Dakota Shippers' Association, at a recent meeting held in Grand Forks. It was voted that a national clearing house for the interchanging of cars belonging to different companies be favored, and that the reciprocal demurrage law, if enacted as now proposed at Bismarck, would prove detrimental to the small shippers; and that in the distribution of cars it was resolved the blocked houses should be given the preference.

The Illinois Central Railroad has asked the Illinois state railroad commission to amend rule 23, which applies to switching service within the limits of Illinois, and Chicago in particular. It also wants the term "switching service" defined to be the initial or final auxiliary movement between elevators, warehouses and factories to junctions with other railroads and eliminating the clause defining switching as the transfer charge ordinarily made for moving loaded cars for short distances, for which no regular waybill is made, and which do not move between two regularly established stations on the same road. This application is being fought by the Illinois Manufacturers' Association.

[For the New England Grain Dealers' Association.]

ON RECIPROCAL DEMURRAGE.

BY HENRY L. GOEMANN.

I have given this subject considerable thought, not only because of the agitation it has been receiving in the public press, at the meetings of the various associations, in discussions by the Interstate Commerce Commission and also because of the attention given it by President Roosevelt, but because of the fact that I have been directly interested, being a large shipper.

The general prosperity of the country has been such that it has been impossible for the railroad companies to provide facilities to take care of the business properly; and although they have made every effort to increase their supply of cars and locomotives, the producing capacity of the country in that line is such that they have been unable to take care of the demands of the railroads in this respect. My firm has probably suffered as much as any shipping firm, and I know that the inability of the roads to furnish equipment promptly at interior points where we have had grain bought has cost us a great many thousands of dollars; but with all this I cannot believe that reciprocal demurrage, as outlined by its advocates, is the correct thing.

I notice that the Madden bill, which is known as House Bill No. 23558, states that a carrier, on failure to supply cars to a shipper, shall pay to the shipper the sum of one dollar per day for every car ordered that is not furnished within three days, provided such application shall be for less than twenty-five cars, and if application is for twenty-five cars or more, the carrier shall have ten days in which to supply the cars before the penalty of one dollar a day goes into effect. Also, that if the property given for transport is not forwarded at the average rate of not less than sixty miles per twenty-four hours, the carrier issuing the receipt, or bill of lading, for the shipment shall pay to the owner or consignee or to the parties whose interest may appear the sum of one dollar per day or fraction of a day on all carload freight, and one cent per hundred pounds per day or fraction of a day on freight in less than car-lots, for all time consumed in transportation in excess of that named.

Now it seems to me that this would open up a way for discrimination and give the railroad companies an opportunity to pay in a new manner rebates to the freight shippers. Naturally, with a law of this kind in effect, the distribution of the cars on a certain road would be concentrated in the hands of one official, and he no doubt would have to distribute his cars pro rata to all the interests at all the points on his line. A large shipper, say, for instance, a grain elevator carrying a stock of a million bushels or more, having facilities, we will say, for handling one or two hundred cars per day and probably needing for their ordinary shipping wants fifty or a hundred cars a day, could very easily put in orders to a railroad company for the full handling capacity of his plant; and it could also be very easily understood that he was to get only just what cars he needed, which in periods of car scarcity would of itself be a big advantage, and that the balance of the cars ordered each day in excess of his requirements would draw a dollar a day demurrage. You can readily figure up what a refund there would be at the end of thirty days to a concern of that kind. When this refund had reached a sufficient amount, it would be very easy to say that the market opportunity for moving this grain was past, the cars, therefore, not needed, and the order cancelled. Under circumstances of this kind, I do not think that anyone could prove that any rebating was being done, because the volume of business would be such that it would be impossible to prove anything.

On the other hand, the small shipper would put in his order for the cars. He might get them on time and he might not. In the latter case, he would present his bill to the railroad company and they would say, "The law is not constitutional and we will not pay this bill." Will the small shipper sue for the few dollars that are at stake, or will he simply take the loss?

Then, again, when it comes to collecting from the shipper who has ordered cars in excess of his wants, unless a law is passed compelling a shipper to deposit a certain sum of money with each order for cars, the railroad company would have no way of enforcing payment of the penalty that would accrue on the empty cars which the shipper had ordered in excess of his wants.

In this matter of reciprocal demurrage the state of Texas had a similar law, which was tested by the case of John A. Mayes vs. the Houston & Texas Central Railroad. This case was begun by Mayes to recover a penalty of $475 by reason of defendants' failure to furnish seventeen stock cars which had been applied for in writing by the plaintiff, in accordance with the law in the state of Texas; and the provisions of this law were that when the applicant for cars furnished his order in writing for the number of cars he required, and deposited with the agent of such company one-fourth of the amount of freight charged for the use of such cars, and the railroad company (where the application was for ten cars or less) did not furnish the cars in three days, they were compelled to pay to such applicant the sum of $25 per day for each car that they failed to furnish. On the other hand, if such applicant did not within forty-eight hours after such car or cars had been delivered and properly placed, load same, that he should forfeit and pay to the railroad company the sum of $25 for each car not fully loaded. In this case the Supreme Court held that while the railroad companies may be bound to furnish sufficient cars for their usual and ordinary traffic, cases will inevitably arise when by reason of an unexpected turn in the market pressure upon the road for transportation facilities, which good management and a desire to fulfill all its legal requirements cannot provide for, and against which the statute in question makes no allowance, may occur. Although it may be admitted that the statute is not far from the line of proper police regulation, "we think that sufficient allowance is not made for the practical difficulties in the administration of the law, and that, as applied to interstate commerce, it transcends the legitimate powers of the legislature."

You will see from this that in putting into effect any law, we have got to take into consideration the fact that at certain seasons of the year there is a larger demand on the railroads than they can under any condition take care of. Furthermore, it would seem to me to be a great hardship to the railroad companies to expect them to furnish a car in Kansas or Nebraska on an order for shipment to New York, Massachusetts or Georgia, and be compelled to deliver same within three days' time. If they can only be compelled to furnish the car as far as their own line goes, then the car will get to the transfer point, and if there are a large number of cars at that point at the same time, they will simply be delayed pending the ability of the parties in interest to transfer the car. The great trouble to-day, to my mind, is the fact that at such large markets as Chicago, St. Louis and Milwaukee, the Western cars are held for transfer to Eastern cars, which quite often, owing to scarcity of Eastern cars, means the tying up of the Western cars from one to six weeks, thus depriving the Western road of the use of these cars.

The states of Virginia, Texas and Kansas have reciprocal laws, and I believe that bills covering same have also been introduced in the legislatures of Illinois and Michigan. These are all in addition to the one introduced in Congress at Washington, D. C., by Mr. Madden of Illinois.

I am told that in Virginia, which state leads in reciprocal demurrage, as well as in other states where it is such a law, it is not enforced, and that large numbers of shippers do not know that such a law is in force.

It would seem to me that something different from the reciprocal demurrage law will have to be approved in order to overcome the conditions existing at present, either a large car pool, such as I understand some of the roads are talking of forming, with headquarters in Chicago, which will allow cars to run through from point of origin to final destination, or a high rate of rental per day for each car, which will more than cover the interest on the investment and also fully cover all charges for repairs and maintenance. This latter would no doubt bring the cars back to the original line more quickly than the present fifty cents per diem charge which is in effect between the different roads.

If this rental charge for the use of equipment were put up higher, say at $1.50 or $2 per car per day, it would mean that every road would hurry these cars back home at the best possible speed, and it would also be an incentive to all the roads to build cars freely, which they no doubt would do, or buy them as fast as the manufacturers could turn them out.

In addition to the above, if transfer elevators of large capacity and warehouses for merchandise were built at junction points of the various roads, away from the center of large cities, so that all cars could be emptied quickly and the carrying of the property be done in warehouses instead of in railroad cars, and switching services and train movements by all the roads perfected, the situation would be vastly improved.

I also have a legal opinion from Mr. John B. Dafsh, attorney-at-law, Washington, D. C., regarding the legal side of a reciprocal demurrage law. This opinion is quite lengthy and I will therefore just read to you the conclusion, which is as follows:

"(a) The Congress has no constitutional right to provide for a reciprocal demurrage law, in so far as it relates to the furnishing of transportation facilities or the movement thereof in interstate traffic, such being exclusively within the powers of the several states.

"(b) That the Congress has a right to provide for a reciprocal demurrage law in so far as it shall relate to withholding of cars and facilities and instrumentalities of carriage, upon the ground that it can regulate (prescribe rules by which they shall be governed) such facilities.

"(c) That the Congress has a right to provide for reciprocal demurrage in so far as it shall relate to the movement of cars and other facilities and instrumentalities of carriage in interstate commerce, being a proper regulation of interstate commerce, upon either or both of two grounds—the power of the Congress to regulate the goods after they begin their transportation, or its power to regulate the vehicles containing them.

"(d) That the Congress has a right to provide for reciprocal demurrage in so far as it shall relate to the prompt placing of cars, notification of arrival by the carrier and the discharge of the cars upon either or both of the grounds just mentioned.

"(e) That such a law must, however, in my judgment, except from its operation unusual and unprecedented demands, unavoidable accidents and acts of God."

Now, do not misunderstand me. I want relief from this car shortage as badly as anyone; for if I cannot do business freely and supply my customers when they want grain, I am losing money, for there are fixed expense charges that must be earned; but I do not want a law which will permit discrimination by rebating, such as this reciprocal demurrage law would open up. I do not want government ownership of railroads; but I do want to champion something that will be fair and just to both shippers and railroads, for anything that is one-sided cannot last or work along satisfactorily.

I believe that the real solution of the car situation lies in the hands of the railroads themselves. A car pool would give interchangeability of cars; would result in fewer empty cars; place cars where most needed; cause less congestion at terminals or junctions awaiting transfers, or initial roads awaiting connecting line cars so that their own cars would not be loaded for points off their own lines.

I believe that reciprocal demurrage is not fully understood by the public at large, and that they simply have an idea that it means the refunding of money and in that way equalizing the payment of car service, which they have to pay when they do not load or unload cars within the 48-hour period. I presume that the receiver of car-lot freight is more interested in the cancellation of the car service charge than he is in reciprocal demurrage; and I therefore believe that you want something on the order of the average plan of settlement which has been in effect in quite a number of places in the West, and which I understand is still in effect in the state of Michigan.

I will now read you the rules covering this average plan, which were in effect in eastern Ohio some time ago, but which have been cancelled:

"Rule 4. Any person so desiring may enter into a special written limited average agreement through the manager of the association for settlement of car service charges on basis of 30 hours, adjustment to be made monthly, this agreement to be made with each railroad company separately and only with railroad companies delivering directly to or receiving directly from party accepting the agreement.

"The handling of material of party accepting the agreement by any railroad company not delivering directly to or receiving directly from said party will come under regular rules of the Cleveland Car Service Association. Settlement for charges which accrue under average agreements will be made at end of each month with each railroad company with whom party has agreement, regardless of what the average working with any other railroad company may be."

The limit is that any car held over 15 days by party accepting agreement shall be taken out of agreement for the period elapsing after the 15 days and shall be paid for at the rate of one dollar for each day that it is held after the 15 days regardless of what average may be.

To illustrate the working of the 30-hour average: "A" loads or unloads 100 cars during month, detaining them 110 days and 20 hours, or 2,660 hours—average would be 26.6 hours, which would be within the limit.

"A" loads or unloads 100 cars during month, detaining them 125 days, or 3,000 hours, average would be 30 hours, which is the even time.

"A" loads or unloads 100 cars during month, detaining them 160 days, or 3,840 hours, average would be 38.4 hours, and overtime on the 100 cars would be 840 hours, or 35 days, and "A" would pay the railroad company on whose tracks the cars were handled, for detention in month referred to, $35.

Sundays and legal holidays are not included in computing detention. The party accepting agreement agrees to pay to the railroad company and charge to the account of the shipper any car service charges that accrue by reason of cars being detained awaiting bills of lading, or otherwise detained on shippers' account. Such cars will be eliminated from the average account. Detention shall be computed from actual hours cars are placed for loading or unloading, except that in case cars cannot be placed on account of consignee's tracks being filled, then such cars will be considered as having been placed when the railroad company offering the cars would have delivered them had the condition of such tracks permitted. The time of release of a car fixes the month in which detention is computed. To illustrate: For a car received January 1, and released January 5, the total detention is computed in month of January. For a car received January 30 and released February 2, the total detention is computed in month of February. If either the railroad company or the party accepting the agreement desires to cancel the same, this can be done at the end of any month by giving 10 days' previous notice in writing.

I also note from a recent issue of a Buffalo paper that the Buffalo shippers have evidently been able through the Niagara Frontier Shippers' Traffic Association to get the Western New York Car Service Association to give large shippers full credit for average promptness in loading and unloading cars. Thus, if a shipper received several cars a day for a month of 26 working days, and the average excess detention was but a few hours on a car each day, he would be charged a day's detention when the number of excess hours amounted to 24, and not charged a day's detention in each case of holding a car a few hours over the free time. Under the average contract rule of the Western New York Car Service Association, shippers have from 29 to 47 hours' free time for loading or unloading a car from the time the car is placed.

OBITUARY

Ezra Martin, manager of the Eagle Milling Co.'s elevator at Northville, S. D., is dead.

Mrs. Mary Drew Peavey, mother of the late Frank Peavey, millionaire grain merchant, died at Sioux City, Iowa, on January 20.

William H. Adair, who conducted a grain business in Somerset County, N. J., before the Civil War, died at Raritan, N. J., in his eighty-fifth year.

James Conway, proprietor of a hay and grain business at Brooklyn, N. Y., for many years, is dead. He was born in Ireland and was 64 years of age. A widow and three daughters survive him.

Gustave Strekewald, 80 years old, and one of the oldest members of the Chamber of Commerce of Milwaukee, having joined in 1865, died at Geneva, Switzerland. He was long engaged in the seed business.

Milton Eugene Mirick, 69 years old, who for more than twenty years operated a large malting house at Lyons, N. Y., died at his home there one day recently. Some time ago his failing health forced him to retire from active business.

John Rastmus, 35 years old, was hurled to death on a shafting in the boiler room of the Calumet Grain Elevator Co. on the Calumet River, Chicago, on February 6. He was oiling the machinery when his clothes caught in the shafting.

Wallace L. Rice, 49 years of age, died at Quincy, Mass. He was formerly in the grain and hay business at Boston. Mr. Rice was a lodge member of prominence. Besides his parents, who reside in Hartford, he leaves a wife and two children.

Reid M. Duvall, a grain broker of Columbus, Ohio, collapsed in view of a carful of passengers and died a few moments later from the effects of carbolic acid. The son of Mr. Duvall declares the poison was taken by accident and was not intentional.

Loyal C. Kellogg, the first man to pay $1.00 a bushel for Michigan wheat and who took all offerings for three days during the Civil War at $3.90, died January 31 at Battle Creek, Mich., in extreme poverty. Once he cornered the flour market and stood to win a fortune. The fates were against him and instead he lost several fortunes.

Michael Whalen, 55 years old, was smothered to death in a bin containing several hundred bushels of flax at the American Linseed Co.'s warehouse, Chicago, on February 5. He was at work cleaning the grain with a companion and accidentally fell in. Several workmen assisted in digging the body out from the center of the bin.

Ex-Governor John W. Davis of Pawtucket, R. I., died January 25, after an illness of a year. Mr. Davis will be remembered as conducting a grain business at Providence from the early fifties until he entered upon his second term as governor in 1890. Besides that office "Honest John Davis" held that of state senator, mayor of Pawtucket, and president of the board of councilmen. Mr. Davis was born at Rehoboth, Mass., on March 7, 1820, and while a youth learned the stone cutter's trade. Subsequently he became a contractor at Charlestown, N. C., and after a trip to New Orleans settled in Rhode Island and entered the grain business, in which he has always been very successful.

James Trotter, once prominent as a grain merchant of Bloomington, Ill., died at his home there suddenly the morning of January 16, from paralysis. He was born at Duleek, County Meath, Ireland, on March 20, 1824, coming to this country in '49. With his brother and sister a grain business was conducted at Bloomington before and after the Civil War, deceased acting as buyer.

W. W. Miller, a former grain merchant at Kansas City, Mo., died January 22 at Roswell, N. M., of heart disease. He had lived to enjoy the biblical allotment of time of three score years and ten. Charles E. Miller, a son, lives at South Haven, Kan., where the deceased made his home for a number of years, and W. A. Miller, another son, resides at Anthony, the headquarters of the Miller Grain Co.

J. A. Culbertson, a grain dealer at Glidden, Iowa, blew out his brains while his family was at breakfast, the morning of February 6. The tragedy occurred in the bathroom just as he was being called to the table. When the shot was heard the members of the household rushed to the room and found him standing, but lifeless. His affairs were in good condition and his home life was happy. He is estimated as being worth $100,000.

Labannah Sylvester McKallip, for several years president of the Pittsburg Grain Exchange, died at his home in Pittsburg, Pa., the night of February 5, after a lingering illness. He was born May 1, 1842, in Westmoreland County and in 1870 entered business in the city of Pittsburg. As a bank director and investor in other successful enterprises he amassed a comfortable fortune. The widow, two sons and a daughter survive.

Moses Dorr, senior member of the grain and flour firm of Moses Dorr & Co. in the Chamber of Commerce, Boston, Mass., died at his home in Cambridge early in January. He was born at Westmoreland, N. H., in August, 1823, and for the past 25 years has been engaged in the grain business, his associate being his son-in-law. Mr. Dorr has befriended and started many a young man upon the road to success and his will be a figure sadly missed in Boston.

Francis H. Crane, prominent as a grain man at Quincy, Mass., died January 13, after a lingering illness. Mr. Crane went to Quincy in 1892, and, with his sons, Frank W. Crane and H. Everett Crane, bought out the hay and grain business of the late Edward Russell, with stores at Quincy Center and South Quincy. In 1898 he enlarged his business at South Quincy and built a large grain elevator. He was married Nov. 19, 1863, and his wife, with his two sons, survives him.

William H. Osborne, a grain dealer of Toledo, Ohio, for many years, died at the home of his son in Detroit, Mich., on January 15. Some twenty years ago he was associated in the grain business with the late Vincent Hamilton and J. D. Cook. Mr. Osborne was born in New York state 84 years ago, and went to Michigan 65 years ago. He located at Sturgis, where he opened a general store, and later came to Toledo, where he was prominent in the business life for many years. A son and daughter survive.

John Kammer, a scientific farmer at Half Day, Ill., received a call from secret service men recently, who were under the impression his grain sprouting plant was an illicit still. He entertained his visitors by describing a new scheme for fattening stock on sprouted grain.

The Grain Dealers' Mutual Fire Insurance Co. was organized at Boston, Mass., on February 6, and from the 200 firms identified with the organization applications for more than half a million dollars of insurance have already been received. Officers of the corporation are: President, Dean K. Webster of Lawrence; vice-president, Milton L. Cushing of Fitchburg; treasurer, C. P. Washburn; secretary, H. A. Crossman.

Owing to lack of cars large quantities of grain are spoiling in Kansas, as elsewhere in the West. One Kansas town, Valeda, is rather more serious a sufferer than most of its class, but its story is interesting. Here are stored some 15,000 bushels waiting for shipment. The corn has been there for a long time. A rough board shelter has been built around it and an attempt made to place a roof over it to protect it from the elements, but the corn has been soaked with water and exposed to the elements for months. One can smell the fermentation all over the town. Meantime with no grain moving the merchants also are in distress, their goods out on credit or on their shelves for want of cash buyers.

IN THE COURTS

Fuller R. Dale, formerly a grain dealer at Gardner, Ill., is in the bankruptcy court.

Thomas H. Wheeler, a grain dealer at Cayuga, Ill., has declared himself a bankrupt, with liabilities of $6,729.02 and assets of $550.69.

G. B. Gordon of Fairbury, Ill., has been appointed trustee for the creditors of the bankrupt Weston Grain Co. of Weston. Claims to the amount of $3,819.92 were presented.

John M. Root, agent for the Northwestern Grain Elevator Co. at Clontarf, Minn., is a voluntary bankruptcy, with liabilities of $5,386.28 and assets, including an insurance policy, of $3,000.

Creditors of James Kitchin, owner of an elevator at Mattoon, Ill., who failed recently with liabilities of $5,000 and assets of $3,252, have appointed Joseph A. Williams of Danville, trustee.

H. S. Yarrow, formerly manager for the Cummings Commission Co. at Fergus Falls, Minn., has taken up the claims of three of his patrons and has sued the company, which recently discontinued operations, for $113.32.

An appeal to the Common Pleas Court has been taken in the case of the Bucyrus Hay and Grain Co. of Bucyrus, Ohio, against Agnes Vantilberg and M. A. Hamwett of Shelby, from whom the plaintiff seeks $150 damages for 30 tons of hay which were not delivered as per agreement.

Norton & Co., millers of Chicago, Ill., with mills at Lockport and a grain elevator at Romeo, Ill., filed an involuntary petition in bankruptcy on February 9, because of pressing claims amounting to $595.47. The attorneys say the assets are $600,000 and the liabilities $250,000. Secured claims amount to $350,000, mostly held by banks which advanced money.

Albert Engle, Ludwig Dreyer and J. A. Timmerman of the Hydraulic Milling Co. of Buffalo, N. Y., have petitioned the bankruptcy court to recover debts owed by Gottlieb Hessenthaler, a grain merchant. He has debts of $3,000 and assets of $2,500. Engle claims $890.78 as due him for grain which he sold Hessenthaler. Timmerman, for the Hydraulic Milling Co., claims $243 for grain, and Dreyer wishes to collect on a loan of $250 due him from Hessenthaler.

Suit for $47,671, alleged to be the value of grain, which, it is claimed, was destroyed by the collapse of the Ontario Elevator on October 30, 1904, was begun in the Supreme Court at Buffalo, N. Y., on January 24, by the Buffalo Grain Co. The defendants are George F. Sowerby, president of the Western Elevating Association and the company bearing his name, Albert J. Wheeler, Mary J. Wheeler and Mabel Wheeler. Justice Marcus on February 2 refused to non-suit the plaintiff.

The Corn Exchange Bank of Chicago has instituted suit against James Hodge, F. O. Paddock, A. L. Mills, Samuel Beaumont, L. S. Churchill and Milton Churchill of Toledo, Ohio, for judgment to the amount of $40,000. The plaintiff alleges that the defendants guaranteed indebtedness of the United Company to the extent of $200,000 and became surety on four promissory notes to the bank of $10,000 each. The bank alleges that the Company has not paid any of the principal or interest of the loan since September 30, 1906.

The Railroad Commission of Wisconsin recently heard complaint from the Board of Trade at Superior, Wis., against the Great Northern, Omaha and Northern Pacific railroads for making excessive charges for switching grain, for failing to supply proper facilities for handling grain and for discriminating in leasing their elevators at Superior. The complaint involves the questions that have been in controversy so long between the Superior and Duluth Boards of trade over the handling of grain at the head of the lakes.

F. P. Hannifin of Coweta, I. T., who was recently arrested on the charge of smuggling wheat across the Canadian border, is the owner of a line of elevators running out of Coweta and bears a good reputation. He tells the following story: "I was at the time cashier of the Hansboro State Bank, Hansboro, N. D., three miles from the Canadian boundary. There was a car of wheat of 1,200 bushels loaded by a farmer two weeks after I got there, and they came, after getting the bill of lading from the depot agent, and drew $500 on the car. I, in turn, billed the car out in the name of the bank to secure me against loss until I got returns on the car. I got nothing out of the transaction at all, and did not know that the wheat was smuggled over the line, being a stranger in that locality myself. The depot agent and I were indicted for aiding and abetting smugglers. I did not leave there until one year after this transaction."

Because service was illegally secured against C. Hoffman the case which the Farmers' Co-operative Shipping Association brought against him in the Shawnee County (Kan.) District Court, has been thrown out of court by Judge Dana. The plaintiffs aver they will take the case to Dickinson County.

St. Louis courts have been asked to appoint a receiver and secure an accounting against the Union Grain Co. for C. A. Dayton. The plaintiff with A. J. Brunswig, C. G. Benton and Harry Lichtig owned the Union Grain Co. at St. Louis, the C. A. Dayton Grain Co. at Kansas City, Mo., and the South Park Grain Co. at St. Joseph, Mo. The plant at St. Louis was burned with considerable stock, and while Dayton was at Kansas City, in charge of the establishment, his partners moved to St. Joseph and since then, the plaintiff asserts, they have failed to settle with him for his share of the St. Louis company. The amount involved is $20,250.

Suit for $45,000 has been filed in the Circuit Court at St. Louis, Mo., against the estate of Corwin H. Spencer, by Harry Troll, public administrator. The suit was brought for Mrs. Bessie Taylor, widow of William J. Taylor, who formerly lived near Chicago. The petition alleges that the firm of Spencer and Denniston, commission merchants, bought 500,000 bushels of wheat for Taylor during the latter part of the summer of 1903, which was sold in December of the same year for $45,000 profit. Mrs. Taylor, as executrix of her husband's will, alleges that she was misinformed as to the number of bushels purchased for her husband and that she sold her claim against the firm of Spencer & Denniston to them for $13,910. She was then discharged as executrix, and John F. Wright was appointed in her stead. According to the petition, Wright discovered that the wheat deal involved 500,000 bushels, instead of 200,000.

ARBITRATION DECISIONS.

Following are several decisions by the arbitration committee of the Kansas Grain Dealers' Association, as reported to the annual meeting at Wichita: Ferguson-Dorman Grain Co., Winfield, Kan., vs. J. F. Cheatum, Cleveland, Kan.—In the above entitled cause the evidence shows that the plaintiffs (the F.-D. G. Co.) purchased from the defendant, Cheatum, by telephone, three cars 2 hard wheat, with the understanding and agreement that No. 3, and even good, sweet No. 4, might apply on contract at 1 cent per pound scale of discount, and that defendant might have "ten or fifteen days" in which to ship; that such a contract was actually made by and with said broker; that when said broker reported such purchase to his principals (the plaintiff) he did not specify any particular details; that plaintiffs' confirmation of purchase by such broker was for "prompt" shipment and did not provide any specific basis of discount for lower grades; that on receipt of this incomplete confirmation, defendant by letter positively refused to fulfill his contract; that immediately on receipt of said letter plaintiffs telegraphed a correction of their confirmation and told defendant to ship as per his verbal contract with their broker; that defendant by mail still refused to fulfill his agreement with such broker; wherefore plaintiff asks judgment for 1 cent per bushel damages, which defendant has refused to pay.

This committee cannot and does not attempt to overlook plaintiffs' error in confirmation; but defendant does not deny, on the contrary, he admits, having made a verbal contract with the plaintiffs' duly authorized agent, and yet he refuses to fulfill that contract, even under the terms and conditions which he, himself, specifically states such contract provided. We cannot see where or how a subsequent error as to details should invalidate a contract previously made and admitted by both parties thereto: and we therefore award judgment in favor of plaintiffs and against defendant for the amount claimed under and upon the terms of such verbal contract, and assesses against said defendant the costs of this action, which costs amount to $5.

Witness our hands this 21st day of January, 1907.

E. R. & D. C. Kolp, Wichita, Kan., vs. B. F. Kelsey, Oxford, Kan.—In the above-entitled case, the plaintiff (Kolp) purchased from the defendant (Kelsey) during the month of July, 1906, several cars of wheat at an agreed price, basis a No. 2 grade. In the confirmation by plaintiff, covering these purchases, a portion of them provided that No. 3 hard 58 pounds should apply at 1 cent discount, while a portion of them made no reference thereto. Defendant made no confirmation at all. Two cars (1,751 bushels) graded No. 3 hard 59-pound test, and were applied by the plaintiff at 1 cent per bushel discount; and he asks judgment for $13.88 alleged overdraft.

Defendant claims that it was his intention and expectation to have 59-pound without any discount; also that he is entitled to a refund on a third car, which was weighed at a different point than agreed upon and at an additional expense of $1.45, for which he asks judgment against the plaintiff.

The evidence introduced shows that at the time the contract was in effect it was the general custom of the trade in this state to discount all No. 3 wheat at least 1 cent per bushel, regardless of whether it tested 5 or more pounds; that it was the intention of the seller to have his 59-pound No. 3 wheat applied on contract without discount, but that this intention was not sufficiently expressed so that the buyer had any such understanding; that the buyer supposed and understood that his purchase was based on the usual customs then in effect; that had he understood defendant's desire to have 59-pound No. 3 wheat applied without discount, no trade would have resulted; that the grain was shipped to one of the regular markets, where the customary application and discount governed; that this discount was made against the buyer, and while the wheat tested 59 pounds, yet it graded No. 3 because it was of inferior quality; that the quality and not the test weight prevented this wheat from grading No. 2; hence, while the clause "3 hard 58 1c off" prescribes the limit of discount down to 58-pound test, it must also be construed as prescribing the minimum of discount, because no lesser discount was provided for nor customary, and it could not properly be construed that wheat testing 59 pounds should suffer no discount, for if this were to be the interpretation, No. 4, or even rejected wheat, if it tested 59 pounds, would be entitled to the same basis of application, and the injury and injustice which such interpretations would inflict upon purchasers is too apparent to admit of consideration, without a full and complete understanding and agreement between both parties upon this point.

It is therefore held by this committee that defendant was not sufficiently explicit in regard to the desired application of 59-pound 3 hard wheat, and that said plaintiff was justly entitled to make such discount; and he is therefore awarded judgment against the defendant as prayed for, less the clerical error of $1.45, leaving a net award of $12.43 in favor of the plaintiff and against the defendant, together with the $5 costs of this action.

Witness our hands this 22d day of January, 1907.

C. L. Moss Dallas, Texas, vs. Antle-Linley Grain Co., Atchison, Kan.—In the above-entitled action, the plaintiff (Moss) telegraphed the defendants (Antle-Linley Grain Co.), requesting them to quote prices on certain kinds of grain, and asking defendants to answer by telegraph. In doing this, the plaintiff constituted and appointed the telegraph company his agent, not only to transmit and deliver his request for quotations, but also to receive and deliver defendant's reply.

This agent, the telegraph company, rendered proper and efficient service in the transmission and delivery of the request and quotation, which quotation was evidently satisfactory, because plaintiff at once, and through the same agency, requested defendants to ship two thousand bushels, using the cipher word "Absconded" to represent the quantity desired; but in this message, sent by plaintiff, the said agent of the plaintiff made an error in its transmission, and misspelled the cipher word representing the quantity desired, so that it read "Absconed," which the defendants supposed was intended for the word "Abscond" (meaning 1,000 bushels); and said defendants promptly booked, confirmed and shipped the said 1,000 bushels, while plaintiff entered and confirmed the transaction at 2,000 bushels, as per telegram which he had written and delivered to his transmitting agent, the telegraph company. When defendants received plaintiff's confirmation for 2,000 bushels, said defendants disregarded it, nor did they communicate with plaintiff about it.

When plaintiff received the defendants' confirmation, he, too, disregarded the 1,000 bushels difference between these confirmations, and made no reference to it until nineteen days afterward, at which time the market had advanced two cents per bushel; which plaintiff now asks defendants to make good.

It is a rule of law that the minds of both parties must meet before any contract can take place. It is also a rule of law that a party who constitutes another individual, corporation or firm as his agent is liable for the errors and actions of such agent (see Supreme Court decisions from many states); and while this committee cannot uphold the negligence and carelessness of either plaintiff or defendant in failing to call the other's attention to an apparent error in the confirmations, even as a matter of business courtesy, the error occurred in plaintiff's telegram, and inasmuch as he was equally negligent in making any correction of this error and made no subsequent demand for the extra 1,000 bushels until fourteen days after the time of shipment prescribed in his telegram had expired, it is the opinion of this committee that through this negligence plaintiff forfeited all rights which he originally may have had under the contract, and that the defendants are not, therefore, liable to the plaintiff in this case, the opinion of the secretary of the Texas Association to the contrary notwithstanding. Award is therefore made in favor of the defendants and against the plaintiff, and all costs are assessed against said plaintiff.

Witness our hands this 22d day of January, 1907.

H. F. Probst, Arkansas City, Kan., vs. E. R. & D. C. Kolp, Ft. Worth, Texas.—In the above-entitled cause, the plaintiff (Probst) sold to defendant (Kolp) one car of No. 2 Soft Wheat, with the understanding that the No. 3 testing 58 pounds should apply at 1 cent discount and No. 3 testing 57 pounds, 2 cent discount; also subject to destination grades and destination rates.

Defendants instructed plaintiff to bill the same to Ft. Worth, Texas, which he did. On arrival at Ft. Worth, the wheat graded No. 4, testing 57 pounds; and the defendants, from their office in Ft. Worth, informed the plaintiff that unless he would consent to their deducting 5 cents per bushel, they would refuse that shipment entirely and require him to furnish another in its stead, to which demand said plaintiff, on account of distance, condition of the market, etc., reluctantly consented, supposing that Ft. Worth was the final destination, as indicated by billing instructions, and that the shipment would be unloaded there. Instead, however, the defendants, of their own choice and pleasure, and without consulting with plaintiff in any manner, elected to change the destination entirely, and set the car forward to a mill. On arrival at the mill, the wheat was found to be satisfactory and was unloaded and an affidavit furnished, showing that the shipment contained "1,078 bushels of 58-pound wheat."

Defendants sent plaintiff returns based on mill weights, but Fort Worth inspection, and discounted the same 5 cents per bushel; to which plaintiff objected, claiming that inasmuch as defendants had elected to give him mill weights, he was, under the expressed terms of the contract, entitled to mill grades as well, and asked judgment for 4 cents per bushel, less a clerical error in returns.

It is the opinion of this committee, backed by the judgment of legal counsel, that if defendant desired to hold plaintiff to the Ft. Worth inspection, he must also furnish Ft. Worth weights; that the contract, which provided destination grades and destination weights, will not permit of grading at one point and weighing at another; that when defendant, without consulting plaintiff, elected to change the destination which he at first had designated, and had made his settlement of weights taken at the final destination, he must also make settlement of grades at the same place, and that in his election to change the destination and basis of settlement, so far as weights were concerned, ignoring the terms of the contract in regard to weights, he must also ignore the Ft. Worth inspection and allow settlement as to grades at the same place where he elected to base his settlement of weights.

The committee therefore awards judgment in favor of the plaintiff, and against the defendant, in the sum of $26.88, as claimed, and assesses the costs, amounting to $5, against said defendant.

Witness our hands this 22d day of January, 1907.

A. H. BENNETT,
PERRY N. ALLEN,
L. NOEL,
Committee.

J. F. Zahm of J. F. Zahm & Co., Toledo, Ohio, has accompanied Mrs. Zahm to France, where they will remain until the middle of the coming summer. It is hoped the health of Mrs. Zahm will be benefited by the change.

Edward Phelps Allis Jr., a son of the late Edward P. Allis of Milwaukee, has had conferred upon him the knighthood of the Legion of Honor, a distinction of great importance in France. The honor was bestowed in recognition of Mr. Allis' researches in science.

FIRES--CASUALTIES

There was a small fire at the Eagle Elevator in Boyd, Minn., a short time since.

A new elevator in the course of erection was destroyed by fire at Mansonville, Iowa, on January 14.

A storehouse belonging to the Chenoweth Grain Co. was burned at Dallas, Texas. The loss will reach $9,000.

Gale Bros.' elevator, on the banks of the Miami Canal at Cincinnati, Ohio, was flooded with water when the stream overflowed on January 17.

A loss of $700 was suffered by the Richmond Elevator and Milling Company of Richmond, Ind., when fire attacked its elevator on January 18.

The Hunting Elevator at Lyle, Minn., was damaged by fire one day in January, but the efficient work of the fire department prevented a serious loss.

The Fouke-Shepherd Grain Co. was burned out of its building at Texarkana, Ark., on January 15, at a loss of $7,000. All but $1,000 was covered by insurance.

A fire destroyed the Hildebrandt & Blair Elevator at Edison, Ohio, and a large quantity of grain, the night of January 31. A loss of several thousand dollars was suffered.

A stove is held as the cause of a fire which, in January, destroyed the Baltimore & Ohio Elevator at Alida, Ind., together with its contents. The loss will reach several thousand dollars.

Of an unknown origin, a fire destroyed the elevator of the Toledo Grain and Milling Co. at Bailey Station, Ohio, the morning of February 6. D. W. Camp says the loss will be about $2,000.

The frame elevator built two years ago at Lakeview, Ohio, and occupied by Joseph Timmons of Kenton, fell the night of February 3, and 15,000 bushels of corn were poured out onto the ground.

A fire of unknown origin swept away the Phoenix Roller Mills and Elevator at Edgerton, Kan., on January 26, at a loss of $40,000. The plant was owned by W. H. and M. J. Kelly and was partly insured.

Larkins & Thompson's Elevator at Lily, S. D., burned down on February 5, at a loss of $5,000 on the building; 5,000 bushels of wheat, 3,000 bushels of oats, 1,000 bushels of flax and as much barley were consumed.

The Cannon & Haase Elevator at Granville, Iowa, burned to the ground on January 8, together with 10,000 bushels of grain. The loss will reach $15,000. Metcalf & Cannon will build a 100,000-bushel elevator on the site.

An elevator at Boissevain, Man., belonging to R. Hurt, burned down on January 15, together with 20,000 bushels of wheat. It is thought the stove in the office was responsible. The contents were fully insured and the building partially.

The elevator owned by the Keel Grain Co. of Gainesville at Krum, Texas, burned down the night of January 12. About 8,000 bushels of wheat and 500 bushels of oats were in storage, but half of this will be saved as salvage. Some insurance was carried.

A spittoon consisting of a soap box filled with sawdust came near causing J. P. Larson & Co. of Baldwin, Wis., a severe fire loss, on January 24. A lighted match left to burn out in the box "started things," but a bucket brigade stopped the blaze from spreading.

It is thought an incendiary was responsible for the fire which destroyed the two-story iron-clad warehouse at Jonesboro, Ark., belonging to the Crescent Commission Company, on the morning of January 26. The house was valued at $5,000 and was insured for $2,000.

Two negroes were seen running away from the elevator owned by the Andrew & Spellman Co. at Providence, R. I., just as fire broke out in the hay and grain store in the back of the building. The loss will approximate $9,000, there being $3,500 worth of hay alone in the building. Three firemen were injured while at work on the fire.

Following a hot air explosion in the head house at the top of the 100-foot tower a spectacular fire gutted the elevator at Fitchburg, Mass., belonging to the J. Cushing estate, about noon of January 30. The fire at first was confined to a 70-foot leg and a dozen firemen were at work in the head house when the explosion occurred. All were more or less shaken, but luckily escaped serious injury. It is believed the blaze found origin in the leg, where a friction was created by the belt striking the wooden boxing. Manager Milton L. Cushing places the loss at $3,000.

During a storm fire of unknown origin destroyed the Miller Elevator Co.'s elevator at Christine, N. D., on the afternoon of January 24. About 9,000 bushels of wheat and 1,500 bushels of flax burned. An estimate of $20,000 is made as the loss, which is covered by insurance.

Recently the Cain Elevator at Newman, Cal., collapsed, the foundations having been decayed and weakened by the continuous rains. A large quantity of grain was spilled, but this was all secured and the loss will be confined to the building, where the damage is estimated at $1,000.

The Cleveland Grain Co.'s elevator at Harris, Ill., burned on January 17, there being no means of fighting the blaze. A passing locomotive is believed to have been to blame for the blaze. About 18,500 bushels of grain was consumed. The loss was $13,500, with $9,400 insurance. The plant will be rebuilt.

Thousands of sacks of wheat were wasted in a train wreck near Mabton, Wash., on January 20, when the track of the Northern Pacific Railway Co. was washed out by a snowslide. The freight train loaded with grain and hay was running at a fast speed when the stretch was reached and the entire train was smashed up.

On the evening of January 13, the Farmers' Elevator at Toronto, S. D., was completely destroyed by fire. The building was built but a year ago and the loss will aggregate $9,000, with $4,000 insurance. About 7,000 bushels of grain were burned, as well as 10,000 pounds of timothy. The building will be rebuilt in the spring.

Fire destroyed the elevator at Volga, S. D., owned by G. W. Van Dusen & Co., early on the morning of January 15. It is believed the fire caught from a chimney. About 20,000 bushels of grain was held in storage, but part of this will be saved as salvage. The building has been in service since '79 and W. H. Smith, the company's auditor, states it will probably be rebuilt at once.

A Chicago Great Western fast express train ran through a switch at German Valley, Ill., early the morning of February 7 and crashed into the east elevator belonging to the H. A. Hilmer Co. Three lives were lost, several persons were injured and the major portion of the train with its passengers was buried beneath several tons of oats and the wreckage of the elevator. Regarding the accident the owners write: "We have two elevators at this point, about forty feet apart, and the east elevator was totally destroyed. There is practically no salvage on the building, though we naturally expect to save some of the grain. We had assurance from the Great Western claim agent that the company would assume responsibility for the loss of the grain, but later the company wired that they would not do so. Both of our elevators were on railroad ground. We valued the building destroyed at $5,000, and we had between 9,000 and 10,000 bushels of grain in the house, mostly oats."

A peculiar accident happened last month in Meech & Stoddard's grain elevator at Middletown, Conn., which, equipped with a new 100-horsepower steam engine, new grinding machinery and new belting and shafting, had just started up. Owing to the complexity of the situation extra long hangers had to be used for the shafting, and it is thought the speed of the jack shaft, coupled with the lightness of the shaft and the large size of the driving pulley, which was 72 inches, was the reason the shafting commenced to wabble, snapping the hangers, the large 20-inch belt catching in the broken shafting, and throwing it in every direction. The large 72-inch pulley with a 24-inch face, and weighing several hundred pounds, went all to pieces and one of the spokes went through the side of the engine room, tearing out the window and knocking out a portion of the brick wall. The flying piece of iron continued across the street. A portion of the heavy pulley struck the roof, breaking it away and also cutting off a four by eight beam and knocking down a brick pier that supported the roof over the boiler room. Several of the employes narrowly escaped injury. The damage will approximate $1,000, according to Superintendent Samuel Stevens.

Prof. W. T. Foster of Washington predicts that the drouth of 1906 in the corn belt was only a forerunner of one in 1907, which will be far more serious. The 1907 drouth will not be general, but it will seriously affect the corn crop and farmers are therefore advised to hold as much of their old corn as they possibly can.

THE CO-OPERATIVES

The Odell Farmers' Elevator Co., Odell, Neb., on a business of $82,568.87 in 1906, paid a 6 per cent dividend.

The Ludlow Elevator Co. of Ludlow, Ill., in 1906 handled 330,844 bushels of grain and made a profit of $999.67.

The Farmers' Elevator Co. of Waupun, Wis., in 1906 handled 101,743 bushels of barley and 22,613 bushels of oats. No dividend was paid.

The Fullerton Elevator Co., Fullerton, Neb., handled 198,689 bushels of grain and 437 cars of coal, and made a total profit of $1,564.12.

On a business of 213,960 bushels the Dennison Farmers' Mercantile and Elevator Co. of Dennison, Minn., earned a profit of $1,010.57 in 1906.

The Kenyon Farmers' Mercantile and Elevator Co. of Kenyon, Minn., in 1906, handled 408,821 bushels of grain, but was able to pay no dividend.

The Hutchinson Co-operative Elevator Co. of Hutchinson, Minn., handled about 85,000 bushels of grain, besides flour, feed, etc., and made $399.96.

The Farmers' Mill and Elevator Association of Devils Lake, N. D., reports resources of $70,958.07 and liabilities of $65,323.67, and hopes to pay a dividend in July next.

FARMERS' INDEPENDENT GRAIN DEALERS' ASSOCIATION OF KANSAS.

The Farmers' Independent Grain Dealers' Association of Kansas met at Salina on January 22. Its most important piece of work was the adoption of the following most extraordinary resolution:

Whereas, There has come to the notice of the farmers, especially of Kansas, through the efforts of Mr. John H. Marble and Mr. Ralph M. McKenzie of the Interstate Commerce Commission, very convincing evidence of the existence to-day of one of the most diabolical and monopolistic grain trusts, operating in this territory; and,

Whereas, It was developed at a hearing of the Interstate Commerce Commission in Kansas City that the Kansas City Board of Trade absolutely controls the grain market of that city by operating a boycott against independent concerns, particularly the National Grain and Elevator Company, which company was organized for the benefit of the farmers; therefore, be it

Resolved, That this meeting extend a vote of thanks to Mr. John H. Marble and Mr. Ralph M. McKenzie for their good work in the development of these trust methods and practices, and that a copy of these resolutions be sent to the Interstate Commerce Commission at Washington.

ELEVATOR MEN OF NORTH DAKOTA.

In connection with the Tri-State Grain Growers' Association meeting at Fargo in January, representatives of the independent elevator interests of North Dakota held two sessions, the result of which was the amalgamation of all the independent grain-buying interests of the state into one organization known as the Independent Shippers' Association of North Dakota, with a view to getting control of a terminal elevator at the Head of the Lakes, probably at Superior, Wis.

The North Dakota independent elevator men and the independent buyers, who have not been co-operating, are now together. The new officers are: President, A. J. Killdahl, Maxa; vice-president, O. G. Major, Hope; secretary and treasurer, E. E. Beitah, Brinsmade.

There were a number of addresses, one by H. B. Sherman, national organizer of the American Society of Equity; another by H. A. Johnson of Superior, a member of the Wisconsin Grain Commission, in which North Dakota has membership, and several North Dakotans spoke. The gist of the remarks was an appeal to get all the farmers' elevators and independent buyers in the state together to insure enough wheat to operate a terminal elevator, then the North Dakota Bankers' Association would finance the plan and a terminal house, probably the Great Northern Elevator at Superior, will be secured. Committees were appointed to work out these plans.

Duluth Board of Trade men were represented at the meetings but did not participate in the discussions.

The resolutions adopted included the following:

"Resolved, That it is the sense of this Association, that our representativees, both state and national, use their honest endeavor to bring about legislation to relieve the present deplorable conditions; that we are in favor of national inspection, and of a national car clearing house or the interchanging of cars between the different railroad systems; that we believe the so-called reciprocal demurrage laws as advocated at present by the press would be a detriment to the small shipper; that in the distribution of cars the blocked houses should be given the preference; that we favor a national law making the standard weight of all cereals 100 pounds; and that we sincerely appreciate the assistance of the North Dakota State Bankers' Association to better the grain interests of North Dakota."

The Association adjourned to meet again at Valley City on June 7.

CO-OPERATIVE GRAIN ASSOCIATION OF NEBRASKA.

The Co-operative Grain Association of Nebraska in session at Lincoln appointed the following legislative committee: O. G. Smith of Kearney, Fred Brown of Funk, J. S. Canaday of Minden, J. C. Brunke of Campbell, Milo May of Sutton and E. Gailey of Elgin.

The Association took steps intended to place before the Commerce Commission the matter of railway discrimination against the Omaha grain markets. It was claimed at the meeting that grain shipped to the other markets was graded higher than that which went to the Omaha elevators, thus enticing the trade away from the Nebraska metropolis.

A committee was appointed to investigate the new co-operative creamery recently established at Omaha.

The following board of directors of the Association was elected: First congressional district, F. M. Stump of Falls City; second district, Hans Selck of Elgin; fourth district, D. W. Baker of Benedict; fifth district, J. S. Canaday of Minden; sixth district, L. S. Deets of Kearney; at large, O. G. Smith of Kearney.

The officers of the Association were chosen by the directors, as follows: O. G. Smith of Kearney, president; T. W. Langdon of Gretna, vice-president; J. S. Canaday of Minden, secretary.

FARMERS' GRAIN DEALERS ASSOCIATION OF IOWA.

The annual meeting of the Farmers' Grain Dealers' Association of Iowa was held at Fort Dodge on January 30 and 31. The local papers name 106 delegates present.

There was much talk by Secretary C. G. Messerole, W. M. Stickney and E. G. Dunn of Chicago, rival claimants of the loaves and fishes, and a Mr. Burkholder of Minneapolis, who talked lumber.

The secretary's report showed receipts, including the amount on hand last year, of $1,606.89. The disbursements have been $1,210.45. This leaves $396.84 in the hands of the secretary. With the amount left over in the hands of the treasurer, the whole balance in the treasury amounts to about $525.

The legislative committee reported that a state reciprocal demurrage bill has been drafted, but that it could not be put through the legislature.

The remainder of the time was given to talk—three sessions of it, in which Mr. Stickney talked anachronisms and Prof. B. H. Hibbard of Iowa College on "The Spirit of Co-operation."

The following officers were elected: J. H. Brown, Rockwell, president; B. Hathaway of Pearsons, first vice-president; J. H. Hagan of Barnum, second vice-president; C. G. Messerole of Gowrie, secretary; Peter Gorman of Dougherty, treasurer; board of directors, L. F. Barringer of Ruthven, H. C. Stoughton of Dayton in place of G. C. White of Nevada, Thomas McManus of Dougherty, W. S. Foley of Melvin, William McCandles of Sloan, J. J. Gaffney of Lohrville, and James L. Wiley of Gilman.

Resolutions were adopted reciting that the over-capitalization of railroads, favoritism and unjust rates has been, and is now, a menace to free institutions; that state and national laws are still inadequate to protect the shipper, producer and consumer and insure a square deal; calling on Senators Allison and Dolliver and members of the House to secure national reciprocal demurrage laws, penalizing railroads for wantonly neglecting to perform their duties, by supporting the bill of Martin B. Madden of Illinois recently introduced; declaring in favor of a 2-cent mileage bill on steam roads, the state reciprocal demurrage measure, and the restriction of lobbying and drastic anti-pass laws; favoring the erection of a state twine factory at Anamosa prison and the revision of the law creating a railroad commission to enlarge powers to enforce its decisions; endorsing the election of United States senators by direct vote of the people in order to clean out corporation boodlers; asking Governor Cummins to support measures to drive out corporation lobby at the state capitol, bag and baggage; and congratulating President Roosevelt on the great work he has performed.

HAY AND STRAW

James Burbridge of Pittsfield, Ill., recently sold 600 tons of baled hay to one customer.

Hay growers around Ellensburg, Wash., have been receiving $21 a ton for their timothy hay.

The Purdue University Experiment station pronounces clover hay and ear corn as the best cattle feed.

E. L. Reiman of Terre Haute, Ind., has purchased the interests of the Standard Hay Co. (not incorporated).

An optimistic view of the hay situation is observed at Peoria, Ill., where the price is around $16. It is not thought there will be a noticeable increase.

W. J. Davis of Eau Claire has opened a hay market at Menomonie, Wis., with Edgar Johnson as manager. He will erect warehouses and pay good prices.

Late in January a hay famine was reported to be imminent in Yakima, Wash. It was difficult to secure alfalfa even at $16, a price twice what it has ever been before.

Recently the Oklahoma Board of Agriculture sent to the legislature a resolution indorsing the adoption of the alfalfa plant as the official floral emblem of the new state.

The Colorado Alfalfa Milling Co. has been incorporated at Denver, Colo., by Harry Cassady, Gilbert A. Callahan and H. B. Kooser of Boulder. It is capitalized at $1,000,000.

A report from Owensboro, Ky., says hay is higher than has been known in the lifetime of most of the dealers. Best timothy and best clover sell equally well at $25 per ton.

W. H. Enos has disposed of his interests in the firm of Ford B. Strough & Co. of New York, N. Y., to Mr. Strough. Harry H. Taylor also leaves the firm after several years in the company's employ.

Because of the success which has attended the Wise Elevator Co.'s alfalfa feed mill at Canfield, Colo., there is now being erected a $30,000 mill at Minot by Boulder capital. Manager Thomas Wise, of the Wise Elevator Co., is offering to build meal plants wherever the farmers will sign up for 3,000 acres of alfalfa and to pay $5.50 per ton for the hay. Alfalfa feed mills are reported to be starting at various points near Lafayette, Colo., where they can secure cheap electric power from the great power plant at that place.

Arguments were heard January 30 in the Circuit Court of Appeals at Toledo, Ohio, in the famous hay case brought against the railroads by the National Hay Association many years ago. The hay raisers convinced the Interstate Commerce Commission that the rates were too high for the middle West to eastern points, were discriminative, and were such as permitted the Canadian hay raisers to monopolize the markets in the East. The Commission ruled that the rates should be reduced and the railroads refused to obey the ruling. Then an appeal was taken to the courts for an enforcement of the commission's orders.

The receipts and shipments are about equal for the present, with not quite enough moving to call the market active. Timothy hay has arrived in quite sufficient volume to well supply the demand this week. Clover and clover mixed of good quality are readily placed and quite a few cars of the right kind can be sold at quotations. Shippers will do well to turn the cars they are loading now to this market. The weather creates a demand at this time and that will make the market broader shortly. Prairie hay is still active and in demand. The future price will depend entirely on the supply. The invoices and billings at this writing show a slight falling off.—Pittsburg Grain & Hay Reporter, February 5.

On February 1, the Fruit and Produce News of New York said: "Hay dealers pronounce the market 'rotten.' There is a great accumulation of trashy, undergrade stuff and the Erie terminal shows more of this than any other one of the roads. For the first time for months the embargo on hay on the Central road has been lifted, so far as its own cars are concerned. This road will not load outside cars now. The Erie and D. W. & L. both have embargoes at their terminals. The trouble with the market is there is too much very poor hay. There is a call for good hay in a limited way, but the trade seems to have stocked up well recently. Present conditions will probably continue for a couple of weeks, which will cause the shipping to drop off and the trash will clean up. It will not pay the country shippers to send stock to the market at present prices."

On February 7 the Interstate Commerce Commission commenced an investigation of alleged extortionate rates on the reconsignment of hay and grain in St. Louis. The complaints are the St. Louis Hay and Grain Co., the Bartlett Commission Co. and Lucas & Ensley Co. The grain and hay dealers buy the product to be shipped to East St. Louis. The cars are then placed on the warehouse tracks of the company, assorted and reconsigned. to some point in the Southeast. The railroads charge 4 cents per hundred pounds above the Ohio River rate on hay and grain on all reconsigned shipments. If the shipment is a through one, only 2 cents a hundred pounds, is charged. The dealers contend that they should not pay the extra 2 cents for reconsignment.

T. D. Randall & Co., Chicago, report February 11—Timothy hay markets continue very firm. Arrivals as well as offerings are very light. Choice Timothy selling readily $18.00 to $19.00 per ton. No. 1, $16.50 to $17.50. No. 2 Timothy and Good No. 1 Mixed Hay, $15.00 to $16.00. Lower grades, $12.00 to $14.50. Rye Straw, $9.00 to $9.50. Oat Straw, $7.00 to $7.50. Wheat Straw, $6.50 to $7.00. Ill., Ind. and Wis. Feeding Prairie Hay, $10.00 to $11.00. Packing Hay, $8.50 to $9.50. Iowa, Minn. and Nebr. Prairie in liberal supply, not quotable lower, choice selling $13.00 to $13.50. No. 1, $11.50 to $12.50. Lower grades, $9.00 to $11.00. Kansas and Ind. Ter. Prairie steady. Choice, $14.50 to $15.50 per ton. No. 1, $13.00 to $14.00. No. 2, $11.50 to $12.50. Lower grades, $9.00 to $11.00.

F. W. Eva, chief inspector of hay and grain for Minnesota, has compiled a report covering the 14 months ending August 31, 1906, in which he speaks of the lack of weighing facilities and reiterates his opinion that the weighing of hay and straw should be discontinued. It will be remembered that it was at Mr. Eva's suggestion the department went out of existence for two weeks last August, but was reorganized at the instance of the dealers. Mr. Eva's report shows a gain in cash of $882.50 for the department outside of the $500 advanced by the legislature. The inspectors affixed their seals to 2,353 carloads of hay and straw at St. Paul, 2,053 carloads at Minneapolis and 2,145 carloads at Duluth. They weighed 1,488 carloads at St. Paul, 2,493 at Minneapolis and 2,039 at Duluth. It is shown that out of a total of 7,150 carloads of hay and straw inspected 1,221 carloads were No. 2 Timothy hay, while 1,143 were No. 1 Prairie hay and 1,143 No. 2 Prairie hay. But 551 carloads of straw were inspected. There were 243 reinspections and 2 appeals. One of the appeals was sustained.

There seems to be a growing belief even among farmers that hay prices have about reached their zenith, judging from the fact that they are beginning to show more inclination to sell at current rates. Country dealers, however, are not as keen buyers as they were a short time ago, owing to prices being above an export basis for the British markets. No sooner did the resumption of shipments of Canadian hay to Liverpool take place than prices declined 5s. per ton. When it is considered that farmers to-day are receiving about double the price ruling a year ago those who have been holding their hay for higher prices may well begin to think it's time to realize. It is stated that one of the farmers in the Ottawa section, referred to by us some weeks ago as holding between 400 and 500 tons, but who refused to sell while hay was being imported into his section, is now asking for firm offers. Reports are to the effect that he was holding for $30 per ton on track at point of shipment. Experience teaches us that when values reach a certain altitude consumption falls off. It is true the New York market has kept firm, at pretty high figures, but as those at country points in Canada are correspondingly high there is not much inducement for American buyers to purchase on any extended scale. A few lots, however, are going forward to the Eastern states, where cars are obtainable. Growers of hay in Quebec and Ontario have reaped splendid profits on that portion of their last crop which has been marketed.—Montreal Trade Bulletin, January 29.

CONDITIONS OF HAY.

Secretary P. E. Goodrich of the National Hay Association has just issued a report on the conditions of hay as gathered from 300 correspondents. It is pleasing to note that the quality of hay where it is produced is good, save in Connecticut and Arkansas, where it is poor, and Colorado, where it was fair. A low grade of hay is reported in Missouri, while it is mostly alfalfa in Kansas. Ohio boasts of good and excellent hay. The questions asked by Mr. Goodrich in his letter of January 12 follow:

1. What per cent of an average crop was harvested last year?
2. What was the quality?
3. What per cent yet in the farmers' hands?
4. Will the shipments from your station for the year be more or less than usual, and how much?
5. What per cent held in store by shippers and dealers?
6. If located at terminal markets, are dealers holding more or less hay than usual?
7. Are you placing written orders for cars? If not, why not?
8. In your opinion, would a national reciprocal demurrage law be of benefit to the hay trade?

In response to the last question it was agreed by all correspondents save those in Kansas that the demurrage law would be beneficial. No opinion was formed on this question by the writers from Connecticut, Missouri and West Virginia.

The following table will give a more comprehensive idea of the replies:

Question No.	1	2	3	4	5	6	No. Re-plies 7 plies
Alabama......	Does not produce any but Johnson grass. Demand for hay not as good as usual. Pastures still good, winter very mild.						
Arkansas......	25%	50%	Average	little	Less	Yes	3
	Produces little						
Connecticut....	hay	85%	None	33%	Less	No	4
Colorado........	10%	30%	10%	more	Ave.	Less	Yes 1
Florida.........	Produces very little hay, depends on surplus hay states for supply.........						2
Georgia.........	Produces no hay, depends on North for supply. Stock in dealers' hands small						3
Iowa...........	90%	35%	15% more	None	Ave.	x	5
					Same as		
Indian Territory..	65%	10%	last year	35%	Less	Yes 2	
Illinois.........	17%	11%	30%	less	30%	No 13	
Indiana.........	63%	35%	35%	less	41%	Ave.	Yes 30
					60%		
Kansas.........	100%	50%	55% more	75%	more	No	3
Louisiana.......	Raises very little hay, not enough for local consumption. Demand less than usual on account corn winter and good pastures						
Maryland.......	65%	85%	35% less	5%	Less	No	5
Michigan.......	75%	31%	14% less	39%	Less	x	25
Minnesota......	85%	43%	30%	more	None	Yes	3
Missouri.......	90%	10%	Average	35%	Ave.	No	3
New York......	90%	35%	6% less	37%	30% less	No	36
New Jersey.....	Produces very little hay for marketing, depending on hay surplus states for supply. Dealers carrying small stock at present account high prices.						
Ohio...........	65%	37%	35%	less	10%	5% less	Yes 40
Pennsylvania....	63%	35%	10%	less	15%	10% less	Yes 15
Tennessee......	Does not produce very much hay, mostly fed on farms. Hay being shipped in is very fast and accumulating account being in excess of demand.						
Virginia........	65%	94%	25%	less	30%	more	Yes 7
West Virginia...	75%	50%	Average	30%	more	x	2
Wisconsin......	89%	99%	6%	less	5%	10% less	Yes 3
Total..........							310

YEAR'S RECEIPTS AND SHIPMENTS.

Completing the statement of receipts and shipments of grain at the principal markets of this country for 1906 compared with 1905, found on page 372, January number, we append the following:

Duluth—Reported by H. H. Moore, secretary of the Board of Trade.

Articles	Receipts 1906.	Receipts 1905.
Wheat, bu....	41,558,161	31,198,735
Corn, bu....	162,122	242,982
Oats, bu....	7,953,388	9,470,038
Barley, bu....	9,705,792	9,866,887
Rye, bu....	589,413	549,188
Flaxseed, bu.	21,784,628	10,751,790
Flour, bbls.	6,551,566	6,135,445

Articles	Shipments 1906.	Shipments 1905.
Wheat, bu....	39,152,541	28,196,628
Corn, bu....	184,480	241,625
Oats, bu....	11,541,584	8,861,808
Barley, bu....	10,096,776	9,598,948
Rye, bu....	608,401	584,965
Flaxseed, bu.	31,949,110	15,807,352
Flour, bbls.	6,653,835	5,138,446

Kansas City—Reported by E. D. Bigelow, secretary of the Board of Trade.

Articles	Receipts 1906.	Receipts 1905.
Wheat, bu....	37,422,000	40,058,000
Corn, bu....	15,882,000	21,508,000
Oats, bu....	6,483,500	6,874,500
Barley, bu....	562,000	556,000
Rye, bu....	312,000	232,000
Flaxseed, bu.	98,300	12,860
Bran, tons..	11,430	5,985
Hay, tons..	123,890	153,170

Articles	Shipments 1906.	Shipments 1905.
Wheat, bu....	25,656,000	29,265,000
Corn, bu....	11,882,000	17,034,000
Oats, bu....	5,485,000	5,136,500
Barley, bu....	141,000	588,000
Rye, bu....	186,000	150,000
Flaxseed, bu.	14,400	10,400
Bran, tons..	45,345	49,365
Hay, tons..	84,890	37,220

Flour, bbls.	Receipts	Receipts
bbl.	1,886,090	1,516,400

Philadelphia—Reported by L. J. Logan, secretary of the Commercial Exchange.

Articles	Receipts 1906.	Receipts 1905.
Wheat, bu....	8,775,059	8,500,372
Corn, bu....	9,709,153	9,741,268
Barley, bu....	9,526,077	10,336,947
Rye, bu....	292,100	382,000
Timothy seed,		
bags	6,857	6,395
Clover a e e d,		
bags	5,422	4,139
Flaxseed, bu.	1,215,500	600,000
Hay, tons	85,939	94,230
Flour, bbls.	4,304,897	2,445,264

Articles	Shipments 1906.	Shipments 1905.
Wheat, bu....	5,887,886	1,122,293
Corn, bu....	9,308,198	7,839,200
Barley, bu....	4,975,830	6,416,296
Rye, bu....	....	....
Flaxseed, bu.	773,147	....
Hay, tons	....	....
Flour, bbls.	193,139	1,264,577

The Chicago Great Western Ry. has removed its reconsignment charge at all terminals.

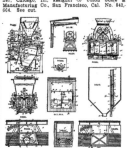

On February 6 a large purchase of wheat was made in the stock markets of the United States, for shipment to Russia. These are the only ones of their sort recorded in the memory of the oldest dealers. The Russian government in December appropriated $50,000,000 to relieve the distress in seven provinces where the crops were practically total failures. About 20,000,000 people will need assistance.

PERSONAL

Charles Page is managing the Farmers' Elevator at Burr, Neb.

E. Mitchell is manager of the Cber-Johnson Elevator at Rockford, Iowa.

T. S. Baird is in charge of the Cooper & Linn Elevator at Elk Creek, Neb.

H. W. Lowder is now in charge of the Harrison-Beggs Elevator at Lowder, Ill.

William Zierfuss, proprietor of the elevator at Randolph, Ill., has been quite ill.

Frank Baker is the new manager of the McFadden Elevator at Kilbourne, Ill.

T. S. Hoare is now manager of the Omaha Elevator Co.'s plant at Silver Creek, Neb.

John Puetz will take charge of the Sheffield Mill & Elevator Co.'s plant at Pratt, Minn.

George Robinson is the new grain buyer at Sprague's Elevator at Caledonia, Minn.

I. N. Jones, a prominent grain dealer at Aurora, Neb., is mourning the death of his wife.

Ole Dahl of Buchanan, N. D., is at Horace in charge of an elevator for the Monarch Elevator Co.

Bruce H. McFadden, a grain man of Havana, Ill., recently was made a widower by the death of his wife.

William Kagel of Buffalo Lake has accepted a position as grain buyer in the elevator at Hutchinson, Minn.

Ralph L. Briggs of Alpha, Minn., will take charge of an elevator at Madison, S. D., for the Rippe Grain Co.

Clyde Campbell, manager of the Atlantic Mill and Elevator Co. of Atlantic, Iowa, is at Colfax Springs for his health.

George B. Arnold has succeeded H. M. Hastings as buyer at the Cooksville Grain Co.'s elevator in Cooksville, Ill.

Frank Lindsay, who has been in charge of the Neola Elevator at Mt. Morris, Ill., has been transferred to Grand Ridge, Ill.

Frank I. King of C. A. King & Co., Toledo, Ohio, was recently honored by being appointed trustee of the city sinking fund.

Ed. Summers has resigned his position as grain buyer for the Great Western Elevator Co. at Stratford, S. D., because of poor health.

Charles Brown, for many years in charge of the Taylor Elevator at St. Paul, Neb., has resigned to take a similar office at Bradshaw.

Oscar A. Pink, a salesman for a hay and grain house in New York City, is a juror in the sensational Harry Thaw murder trial at New York.

J. O. Lafgreen will continue as manager at the Westbrook Elevator in East Lynn, Ill., which Peter Peterson and a Mr. Olson have acquired.

W. J. Frantz, who has been in charge of an elevator at Childs, Minn., now closed, has been sent to Rugby, N. D., by the Imperial Elevator Co.

James Corbet, formerly grain buyer at the North Side Elevator in Ormsby, Minn., has gone to Worthington, Minn. J. F. Hayes is his successor.

F. W. Werdin, who has been with the Freemire, Remund Co. at Glenwood, Minn., is now representing C. C. Wyman & Co. of Minneapolis and Duluth.

W. B. Heaton of McKenzie, N. D., who has been at Grand Mound, Iowa, in charge of the Northern Grain Co.'s Elevator, will return to North Dakota for the company.

Charles H. Quackenbush, formerly with the Cargill Elevator Co. at Green Bay, Wis., is now managing one of the terminal elevators for the company at Minneapolis.

John Hornick, president of the Sioux City Terminal Elevator Co., has been quite ill at his home in Sioux City, Iowa, and plans of the new company were at a standstill for some days.

Oliver Klinger of Manseld, Ill., whose limb was broken early in November while working in an elevator, is at the Decatur Hospital, where an operation was recently performed upon the limb.

John Peters has resigned as superintendent of Marshall & Hammel's grain elevator at Little Chute, Wis., and is succeeded by Michael Molitor. Mr. Peters has purchased the Zeeland Flour Mills.

E. M. Higgins, vice-president of the Armour Grain Co. of Chicago, Ill., retired from active business on the first of February and left for an extended sojourn on the continent. He is succeeded by E. A. James, who has been connected with the company for 27 years.

Linus Harris, 21 years old, of Frankfort, S. D., fell a distance of 50 feet from a scaffold on the Great Western Elevator at Brentford, S. D., where he was doing carpenter work. Mr. Harris received internal injuries and severe bruises but did not lose consciousness. He is convalescing rapidly.

MILL OWNERS' MUTUAL FIRE INSURANCE COMPANY OF IOWA.

The thirty-second annual statement of the Mill Owners' Mutual Fire Insurance Company of Des Moines, Iowa, by J. G. Sharp, secretary, for the year 1906 is as follows:

Insurance in force	$8,484,930.00	
Deposit notes		$282,762.89
RECEIPTS.		
Assessments	$ 122,373.76	
Guaranty deposits	41,954.03	
Interest, etc.	9,674.21	$174,002.00
Mortgage loans repaid		39,300.00
Cash in hands treas. Jan 1, 1906		29,536.31
		$242,838.31
DISBURSEMENTS.		
Losses	$91,503.10	
Expenses	26,932.03	
Guaranty dep. returned	20,566.58	
		$139,001.71
Mortgage loans made		56,210.00
Cash in hands treas. Dec. 31, 1906		47,626.60
		$242,838.31
Losses adjusted and paid since January 1, 1906		$ 91,503.10
Losses adjusted, not due		None
Losses resisted		None
ASSETS.		
Deposit notes subject to assessments		$282,762.89
Real estate loans, first mortgage	$179,557.10	
Interest accrued on loans, not due	4,866.46	
Cash in hands treas. Dec. 31, 1906	47,626.60	232,050.16
		$514,813.05
LIABILITIES.		
Losses adjusted, not due		None
Losses resisted		None
Surplus over all liabilities		$514,813.05

Statement showing the total receipts and disbursements since the organization of the company, April, 1875:

RECEIPTS.		
From all sources		$1,878,602.15
DISBURSEMENTS.		
Losses	$1,245,041.20	
Expenses	300,977.22	
Guaranty dep. ret'd	105,325.08	
Entrance fees ret'd	75.00	
Real estate loans	179,557.10	
In hands treas. Dec. 31, 1906	47,626.60	$1,878,602.15

The amount at risk in 1906 was $8,484,930; the amount of premium notes, $282,762.89; losses and expenses, $118,485.13; net saving, $164,327.75.

The amount at risk, 1876 to 1906 inclusive, $75,222,550; deposit notes, $3,122,079.42; losses and expenses, $1,546,018.42; net savings, $1,576,061.

The deposit notes of this company represent the amount of but one annual premium.

MICHIGAN MILLERS' MUTUAL FIRE INSURANCE COMPANY.

President C. G. A. Voigt and Secretary A. D. Baker of the Michigan Millers' Mutual Fire Insurance Company of Lansing, Mich., in submitting their twenty-sixth annual report of the company, under date January 1, 1907, say the company in 1906 made substantial gains in the three directions which are of most vital importance to our members, viz.: Increased dividends, increased net cash surplus and increased volume of business. Summarized, the items in our statements of most interest are:

Total assets	$2,211,030.03
Total cash assets	680,151.62
Net cash assets	367,268.93
Losses paid during year	259,251.99
Losses paid since organization	1,766,407.89

The increase in net cash surplus has been accompanied this year, as it has in years past, by a decrease in the cost of insurance, so that at the present time your insurance with us is costing you less than ever before, and our net cash surplus is larger. We are glad to state that it is the expectation of your board of directors that our present rate of 55 per cent dividends will be continued during the coming year, thus keeping your insurance at the low cost which obtained during 1906.

The steady reduction in the ratio of our losses from year to year is, we believe, due to our continually improving system of inspection, and we are glad to report that our facilities for inspection are now on a more efficient and at the same time a more economical basis than at any time in the past.

The financial statement is as follows:

ASSETS.		
First mortgage bonds		$ 59,425.00
U. S. government bonds, market value		4,326.00
Municipal and county bonds, market value		397,652.98
Home office building		6,000.00
Cash in banks and office		164,785.84
Interest due and accrued		10,178.18
Premiums due (net)		37,789.22
Cash assets		$ 680,151.62
Premium notes (net value)		1,530,878.41
Total assets		$2,211,030.03
LIABILITIES.		
Losses in process of adjustment	$ 19,328.90	
Reinsurance reserve	293,563.79	
Total liabilities		$ 312,887.69
Net assets		$1,898,142.34
Net cash assets		367,263.93

There were 629 losses under $1,000 and 52 in excess thereof, the greatest loss of the year being $10,000 on the Beaumont Rice Mills.

The total of losses paid to January 1, 1907, by the company was $1,766,407.89.

MILLERS' MUTUAL FIRE INSURANCE ASSOCIATION OF ILLINOIS.

The thirtieth annual statement of A. R. McKinney, secretary of the Millers' Mutual Fire Insurance Association of Illinois, dated at Alton, Ill., January 1, 1907, shows the following facts:

The assessments for 1906 were but 45 per cent of the bases rates, although the losses ($112,797.04) were $16,000 more than the Association has ever had in a single year.

The ratio of expense of management to income was but 16½ per cent. The financial statement (condensed) is as follows:

ASSETS.	
Municipal, county and other bonds, market value	$ 230,717.85
Mortgage loan	6,000.00
Real estate	3,000.00
Interest accrued	4,043.08
Premiums and assessments unpaid	5,797.85
Cash in office	247.90
Cash in bank	50,335.28
Deposit notes	1,100,341.25
Total gross assets	$1,400,482.21
LIABILITIES.	
Unadjusted losses	$ 4,077.16
Gross surplus to policyholders	1,396,405.05
Net value of notes (deducted)	1,100,341.25
Cash surplus	$ 296,063.80
Reinsurance reserve	81,977.84
Net cash surplus	$ 214,085.96
Losses incurred during the year	$ 112,797.04
Losses paid during the year	$ 110,724.10
Losses paid since organization	$ 1,093,101.13
Amount of insurance in force	$10,158,139.43
Face value of notes on which to levy assessments	$ 1,451,877.80

GRAIN DEALERS' NATIONAL MUTUAL FIRE INSURANCE COMPANY.

The fourth annual financial statement of the Grain Dealers' National Mutual Fire Insurance Co. of Indianapolis, under date of January 1, 1907, is as follows:

ASSETS.		
Cash in bank	$22,050.66	
Warren County, Ind., bridge bonds	11,497.10	
Terre Haute, Ind., school bonds	15,366.90	
City of Columbus, Ind., funding bonds	14,492.80	
Huntington Co., Ind., court house bonds	5,166.00	
First mortgage loans	37,700.72	
Available cash assets		$106,834.18
Accrued interest		713.04
Outstanding assessments		335.14
Outstanding premiums		1,580.26
Total casu assets		108,962.62
Premium notes (net value)		669,399.56
Total assets		$778,362.18
LIABILITIES.		
Losses reported (estimated)		$ 4,050.00
Losses adjusted	None	
Losses resisted	None	
Surplus to policyholders		$774,312.18

There were twenty-four losses during 1906, including eleven of sums under $500 and two unadjusted, the total being $40,438.87. The total amount paid during the four years was $114,384.30.

In submitting this report, Secretary McCotter says: "The record for the year has been one for congratulation. More business has been added than in any previous year, and there has been a large increase in amounts carried for old members. The total increase amounted to over $1,500,000. A larger saving than usual has been made on short term grain insurance. To better supply the needs of grain dealers for insurance at the actual cost that elevators should pay, and make capacity for short term grain insurance, the maximum amount taken, subject to loss by one fire, has been increased to $10,000.

There are now insured 1,701 separate risks, an increase for the year of 25 per cent. The increase resulted in a larger average amount of line on each risk, the average liability now being $3,053. As compared with the previous year there was a slight decrease in the expense ratio and a decrease of 26 per cent in the loss ratio.

For the year there was a reduction of 13½ per cent in the assessment or cost. This now means an annual saving of over $90,000 from the basis rate or charge of other companies under the same rate schedule.

At the annual meeting the directors were re-elected, as were all the officers except Mr. Golt as treasurer, who is succeeded by J. W. Sale.

For Sale

[Copy for notices under this head should reach us by the 12th of the month to insure insertion in the issue for that month.]

FOR SALE.

Or exchange for elevators in Northwest—store building and stock of general merchandise of about $18,000. Located in Wisconsin, about sixty miles east of St. Paul. A clean stock and paying business. Reason, manager wants to go West. Address

S. E. OSCARSON, White Rock, S. D.

FOR SALE 1,000-TON HAY BARN.

Indian Territory, 75 miles south of Kansas line; 27½-cent hay rate to Chicago, 13 to Kansas City. Barn equipped with patent elevators for hoisting and placing hay 35 feet high, almost anywhere it is wanted, and faster than a man can dump the bales. Scales and all kinds of hay tools and machinery. Reason for selling, dissolution of partnership. One member of firm going South on account of ill health, other member will continue the business here in Kansas City and can't look after hay barn so far away. This is a snap for a good hay and grain man. Will show books to prove profits. Write for particulars or call on

WOOLSEY-STAHL HAY CO., Kansas City, Kan.

ELEVATORS AND MILLS

FOR SALE, RENT OR EXCHANGE.

Good mill and elevator located in fine wheat country. Favorable terms. Address

F. S. R., Box 1, care "American Elevator and Grain Trade," Chicago, Ill.

FOR SALE.

One-hundred-thousand-bushel elevator, doing an annual business of 500,000 bushels, located in best grain district of western Indiana, on the Chicago & Eastern Illinois Railroad, about 100 miles from Chicago. The plant has first-class equipment and is in perfect order. Write for full description and particulars to

BOX 3, Freeland Park, Ind.

ELEVATORS FOR SALE.

We have a large list of extra good bargains in elevators, first-class locations, doing good business. Write for prices and descriptions, giving location you prefer. We furnish managers and buyers for elevators and secure positions for men who wish to change their location. If interested in an elevator or milling proposition be sure and write to us.

IOWA MILL AND ELEVATOR BROKERS, Independence, Iowa.

MACHINERY

ENGINES FOR SALE.

Gasoline engines for sale, 5, 7, 10 and 20 horsepower.

TEMPLE PUMP CO., 15th Place, Chicago, Ill.

FOR SALE.

One No. 37 Howes Oat Clipper, good as new. Address

THE ADY & CROWE MERCANTILE CO., Denver, Colo.

SPECIAL BARGAIN.

In No. 2 Nordyke & Marmon Cornmeal Dryers, capacity 50 bushels per hour. Good as new; write for prices.

A. S. GARMAN & CO., Akron, Ohio.

FOR SALE.

Gasoline engines; one 54-horse Fairbanks-Morse; one 28, one 16, one 12, 3, 5 and 25 horsepower Sterling Charter. All sizes and prices in small sizes.

A. H. McDONALD, 33 W. Randolph St., Chicago.

WANTED.

Three good, second-hand gasoline engines, 20 or 25 horsepower, and three 12 to 15 horsepower; prefer Fairbanks. Have quit the grain business and wish to sell my new Standard Adding Machine, or will trade on engines. Address

H. EVERSOLE, Newman, Ill.

FOR SALE.

One No. 6 Monitor Dustless Receiving Separator. Two No. 7 Eureka Warehouse Scourers. One No. 3½ Western Corn Sheller. One lot second-hand elevators and conveyors. One lot of second-hand buhr mills and grinders.

THE STRAUB MACHINERY CO., Cincinnati, Ohio.

FOR SALE.

One 50-horsepower Westinghouse Gas or Gasoline Engine, as good as new. Has not seen to exceed 9 months of actual wear.

One dynamo, Fairbanks-Morse, No. 1303 D, K. W. 10, A. M. P. 83, volts 120, R. P. M. 1,250.

One dynamo, Fairbanks-Morse, No. 1386 K, K. W. 60, A. M. P. 110, volts 525, R. P. M. 925.

S. M. ISBELL & CO., Jackson, Mich.

FOR SALE.

One 135-horsepower, left-hand Automatic Atlas Engine, heavy duty.

Two 80-horsepower return tubular boilers, full-flushed front.

One 200-horsepower Cochrane Heater.

Three Gardner Duplex Pumps.

One 60-inch x 7-foot ¼-inch steel tank, with all necessary piping, cut and threaded, to connect boiler and engine, 20-foot centers.

CAPITAL GRAIN AND ELEVATOR CO., Oklahoma City, Okla.

MACHINERY FOR SALE.

One second-hand 40-horsepower horizontal steam boiler, return flue.

One second-hand 15-horsepower horizontal Atlas Steam Engine.

One second-hand Cochrane Open Heater for 60-horsepower boiler.

One second-hand steam boiler feed pump for 60-horsepower boiler.

One second-hand Snyder Hughes Duplex Horizontal Steam Pump, having 12x12-inch steam cylinder and 10x12-inch water cylinder, a 6-inch suction and 6-inch outlet. Also pipes, pulleys and valves for connecting this machinery. All practically as good as new and are in the way and must be sold.

J. R. MARSH, Cedar Vale, Kan.

FOR SALE VERY CHEAP.

One Wheelock Automatic Engine, cylinder 20x48, diameter of shaft, 8 inches; length of shaft, 7 feet 10 inches. Engine right hand.

With engine goes full set of oil cups, one cylinder lubricator (Detroit Double Connection) and one receiver and separator, 5 feet by 10 inches by 15 inches. Engine and fittings in good condition. Reason for selling, plant requires larger engine. Address all inquiries to

HYGIENIC FOOD CO., Battle Creek, Mich.

VALUABLE MACHINERY FOR SALE CHEAP.

One double stand 9x24 Allis Roll, Style A.
One double stand 6x15 Noye Roll.
One 9x18 6-roll Noye Feed Mill.
One Robinson Corn and Cob Crusher.
One 18-inch Robinson Feed Mill.
One Buffalo Sieve Scalper—Noye make.
Two 22x36 Noye Reels.
One George Smith Reel.
One 28-inch Burnham Water Wheel.
One 1,000-bushel hopper scale.
One 36x9 Hill Friction Clutch Pulley.
One 32x9½ Hill Friction Clutch Pulley.
One pair core gears.
Seven rope pulleys—various grooves and sizes.
Iron pulleys—48-inch diameter down.
Quantity of 16x7 elevator buckets.
Elevator heads and boots complete.
Lot of 2 7-16 and 2 15-16 shafting and hangers.

Our stock is constantly changing and we probably have just what you require, although it may not appear here. Write us.

HONEOYE FALLS MANUFACTURING COMPANY, Practical Millwrights, Honeoye Falls, N. Y.

SCALES

SCALES FOR SALE.

Scales for elevators, mills, or for hay, grain or stock; new or second-hand at lowest prices. Lists free.

CHICAGO SCALE CO., 299 Jackson Boulevard, Chicago, Ill.

Miscellaneous Notices

[Copy for notices under this head should reach us by the 13th of the month to insure insertion in the issue for that month.]

GRAIN TABLES.

Quick method for reducing corn, wheat, oats, rye and barley from pounds to bushels. Shows at sight from 1,000 to 100,000 pounds. An indispensable book for the grain dealer. Published by STROMBERG, ALLEN & CO., 302 Clark Street, Chicago, Ill.

ELEVATORS WANTED

TO EXCHANGE.

Illinois corn and wheat farm to trade for good paying grain elevators. Address

J. M. MAGUIRE, Campus, Ill.

WANTED.

Elevator or mill and elevator for good improved Illinois or Iowa farm. Address

IOWA, Box 1, care "American Elevator and Grain Trade," Chicago, Ill.

LOCATIONS FOR ELEVATORS.

Good locations for elevators and other industries on the line of the Belt Railway of Chicago. Low switching rates and good car supply. For further information address

B. THOMAS, Pres., Room 11, Dearborn Station, Chicago, Ill.

GRAIN RECEIVERS

GRAIN RECEIVERS

GRAIN RECEIVERS

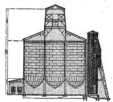

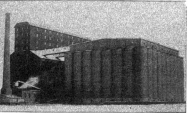

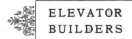

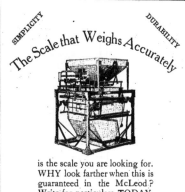

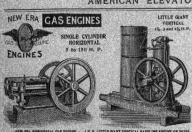

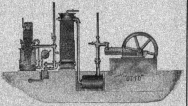
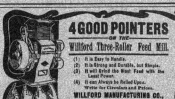